THE LAST DAYS OF THE BRITISH RAJ

The Last Days of
THE
BRITISH RAJ

(Oswald)

LEONARD MOSLEY

HARCOURT, BRACE & WORLD, INC.
NEW YORK

CONTENTS

LIST OF ILLUSTRATIONS

(between pages 104 *and* 105*)*

A victim of the Calcutta riots in August 1946. *Wide World Photo*

Pandit Nehru with Mahatma Gandhi at a committee meeting in Bombay, July 6, 1946. *Wide World Photo*

Field Marshal Lord Wavell talking to Lord Mountbatten in March 1947. *Photo: New York* Times

Lord Mountbatten being greeted by Pandit Nehru and Liaquat Ali Khan on his arrival in New Delhi to take up his post as Viceroy. *Photo: United Press International*

The Nizam of Hyderabad. *Photo: Paul Popper*

Princes and representatives of Indian states discussing plans for independence with Lord Mountbatten and Lord Ismay. *Photo: Paul Popper*

Pandit Nehru, Lord Ismay, Lord Mountbatten, and Mohammed Ali Jinnah at the conference in New Delhi on June 7, 1947 when the British plan for partition was accepted. *Photo: Keystone*

Lord Radcliffe. *World Wide Photo*

Lord Mountbatten with Sardar Patel. *Photo: United Press International*

Pandit Nehru being sworn in as first Prime Minister of India, August 15, 1947. *Photo: United Press International*

Mohammed Ali Jinnah making his first speech as President of Pakistan. *Wide World Photo*

Muslim refugees crowding a train leaving for Pakistan. *Wide World Photo*

Victims of the riots in New Delhi. *Photo: Keystone*

MAPS

AUTHOR'S PREFACE

IN HIS RECENTLY published book, *The British in India*, the distinguished Indian scholar, R. P. Masani, writes:

'The histories of [the] last phase of British rule in India which have been published leave several questions unanswered. What efforts were made by Lord Wavell, one of the most conscientious and liberal-minded viceroys of India, to bring together the two warring political parties? What were the circumstances which impelled Attlee as Prime Minister of Britain to change horses midstream and send out Lord Mountbatten to expedite the withdrawal? What endeavours were made to evolve a friendly policy between the Dominions of India and Pakistan? Why did they prove abortive? Why were adequate precautions not taken to avoid the holocaust? The reasons remain to be told dispassionately.'

This book is an attempt to give the reasons, without passion and without partiality.

It is the fruit of three years' research in India, Pakistan and Britain, during which a wealth of material which has not previously been available to the historian was put at my disposal. I have endeavoured, to the best of my ability, to make use of it with no other idea in mind than to fill the gaps in a moving and fantastic story which has, until now, been full of gaping holes. Official documents dealing with the transfer of power in India will not be officially released until 1999, but in the interim period between that date and the present moment, I hope this book will shed some light upon events which have hitherto been obscured.

In addition to the privilege of studying or ginal documents and letters, I have also been fortunate enough to be able to talk to most of those who played a prominent part in the relinquishing of British power in India and the achievement of Indian and Pakistan independence. Those who were kind enough to talk to me and answer my questions include:

Pandit Nehru, Prime Minister of India; President Ayub Khan

of Pakistan; Admiral of the Fleet Earl Mountbatten of Burma; Lord Ismay; Sir Conrad Corfield; Sir George Abell; Sir Evan Jenkins; Mr Chaudri Mohhamed Ali; Shri V. P. Menon; Lord Radcliffe; Begum Liaquat Ali Khan; Shri K. M. Munshi; General K. S. Thimayya; Lieut.-Gen. Sir Francis Tuker; Master Tara Singh; Mr Alan Campbell-Johnson; Admiral (S) Ronald Brockman; Rajagopalachari; Mr D. F. Karaka; Mr S. C. Sutton, the Librarian at the India Office Library and many others, Indians and Britons, civilians and soldiers.

I hasten to emphasize that unless they are specifically quoted, none of the opinions expressed in this book is to be attributed to them. But I am most grateful for their help.

CHAPTER ONE

AIDE MEMOIRE

YOU DO NOT need to be a chemist, nor do you need to be in India for very long, before you realize that its widely disparate peoples have one thing in common: a remarkably low boiling point so far as political temper is concerned. Nowhere in the world does a mob respond so quickly or so savagely to a fire-brand's call for action; and in the unlovely city of Calcutta the cauldron, if so lighted, bubbles faster and more sulphurously than in any other city in the sub-Continent.

Between dawn on the morning of 16 August 1946 and dusk three days later, the people of Calcutta hacked, battered, burned, stabbed or shot 6,000 of each other to death, and raped and maimed another 20,000. This may not seem to be a considerable figure to students of India's recent history. Three million people died of starvation during the great famine of 1943 in Bengal alone. Close to three-quarters of a million Punjabis massacred each other during the first days of Indian independence in 1947.

But the filthy and dreadful slaughter which turned Calcutta into a charnel house for seventy-two hours in August 1946 is important because it did more than murder innocent people. It murdered hopes too. It changed the shape of India and the course of history. The corpses of men, women and children lay stinking in the gutters of Chowringhee Square until the only reliable garbage collectors of India, the vultures, picked them clean; and with every mouthful, they picked away the fabric of a unitary India, which Britain had painstakingly built up over more than a century and a half, and finally tore it in two.

The tragedy of the Calcutta massacre is not simply that it was unnecessary (that could probably be said of most bloody riots in India's history), but that it disfigured a summer which had hitherto seemed full of hope and optimism. Both in India and Pakistan today you will discover, in the higher circles of government, that 1946 is remembered as a black and abysmal year in which their struggle for independence seemed far, far away and no gleam of light showed anywhere.

Yet, in fact, that summer they came nearer to the goal of most Indians than ever before—the goal of a united, independent India—and then they missed it by a series of monumental blunders, underhand tricks and political manœuvres which culminated in appalling bloodshed. As a preamble to the story of the last days of the British as overlords in India, an aide memoire is necessary to remind everyone (the protagonists and participants, perhaps, especially) of what they were doing, how they were fixed, and who was negotiating with whom in those last days before the situation began to quicken.

One thing should be said at the start to make the situation clear: from the moment, in 1945, when the war was over and the post-war world began to reshape itself, no one of clear mind had any doubt that the Indian peoples would achieve the independence from British rule for which they had been fighting, from a practical point of view, since 1917 (when Gandhi took over Congress) and, from a neo-Indian point of view, since the days of the Mutiny. Even the government of Winston Churchill had grumblingly and reluctantly conceded—not, it is true, without some goading from the United States—the need to accord to India the same hopes of freedom as those which British and Indian soldiers fought to achieve in Europe and Asia. With the advent in Britain in 1945 of a Socialist Government under Clement Attlee, the question of India's freedom was never in doubt. To prise the Indian jewel from the British crown and hand it back to the Indians had always been one of the main objectives of Socialist policy; it was a policy, moreover, with which the bulk of the electorate at the time agreed; and, from a purely practical point of view, even the diehards at home and the imperialist British in India could do little to stop it. The processes of Indianization of government had begun before the war and were now reaching their culmination; by 1948 only three hundred civil servants of British nationality, even if independence did not come, would still remain. The British troops, which might hold the country against rebellion and insurrection, were clamouring, after years of fighting, to go home. And, above all, British power and prestige, in spite of victory, had been diminished by the war. The campaigns in Asia had shown up Britain's weaknesses. After Singapore, Burma and the sinking of her finest ships by the Japanese, Britain would never again be able to demonstrate in Asia the background of strength and influence—the *macht-politik*—which had for so long enabled her to rule a million people with one-man-on-the-spot.

The men on the spot in India after 1945 were still men of great influence, but it was an influence which depended more upon their skill than their strength, their goodwill than their nationality, their personal prestige rather than the might of the once all-powerful British raj. And, waiting to step into their shoes, all over India, were Indians.

Yet such was the spirit of goodwill among the British people—a remarkable reaction to the pangs, pains and restrictions which they themselves had suffered during the war—that the question of giving freedom to India was never viewed by them simply as a hard-headed acceptance of facts, but was rather a spontaneous desire to set people free, as they were free. It was as simple as the action of a child who sees a bird in a cage and wants to open the door and let it fly away. In no sense was the Government ahead of the people in 1945, when it announced that independence for India was a principal part of its programme, to be fulfilled as rapidly as possible; even though it may have been ahead of some members of the Opposition.

But independence for whom? And in what circumstances?

India at the end of the war was a country divided not into two parts but into two factions. Its 350,000,000 people, approximately one-fifth of the population of the world, spoke many languages and subscribed to every kind of religion, principally Hinduism and Mohammedanism, but also everything from Christianity to animism; but so far as politics were concerned, the country was run (always under the control of the British, of course) by two main parties. The most powerful was the Congress Party, which claimed to be a secular party speaking for the whole of the people no matter what their religion or class; presided over by a Muslim, but dominated by Hindus. The Opposition was the Muslim League, which made no bones about representing the interests of none but those of Mohammedan belief. To attempt to equate Congress and the Muslim League with, say, the Tory and Labour Parties in Britain or the Democrats and Republicans in the United States is, the way things were after the war, impossible. The situation between the two factions was not that of two parties fighting each other for political supremacy at the polls. Since the Muslims were a minority in India—90,000,000 against some 250,000,000 Hindus—the British had given them a separate electoral roll. This meant that Congress, its members and supporters being overwhelmingly Hindu, always carried those provinces which contained a majority of Hindus, which meant most of India. They also put up pro-Congress Muslims to fight the Muslim League in the Muslim sector, thus proving—with some success until 1946—that they were genuinely non-sectarian and represented all Indians no matter of what race or religion.

But by 1946 it could be said that something over ninety per cent of India's Muslims supported the Muslim League and its all-powerful leader, Mohammed Ali Jinnah. In the North West Frontier Province a pro-Congress Muslim Government was in power, but precariously, by the skin of its teeth. As I have said, the President of Congress at the time was himself a Muslim, Maulana Abul Kalam Azad. But by a combination of driving, dominating personality and coercion, both physical and psychological, Mohammed Ali Jinnah was rapidly bringing most hesitant Muslims under his banner.

Like the Congress Party, the Muslim League under Jinnah wanted independence from the British. But unlike Congress, whose battle cry hurled at the British was simply 'Quit India', the League cried 'Divide and Quit'. In other words, they wanted not only freedom from the British but also freedom from the Hindus, who, they claimed, had dominated and exploited them for too long. The main plank in the League's platform was the partition of India and the achievement of a separate state— Pakistan—comprising those parts of India where there was a majority of Muslims: in Bengal, the Punjab, Sind and the North West Frontier Province.

It was a policy which no leader of the Congress Party, right until the last, would take seriously. To accept Jinnah's aim of Pakistan would be to admit that the Muslims in India were not only members of a different religion but also members of a different race. And, as every Congress leader—Azad, Gandhi, Nehru, Patel—constantly pointed out, they were not. The majority of Indian Muslims had been converted to Islam either by Moghul invaders or because, as Untouchables or members of the lower classes, they had found greater freedom of opportunity under Mohammedan law than within the strangling circles of the Hindu caste system. Nehru drew attention to the fact that Jinnah was himself only a second-generation Muslim whose grandfather had been a Hindu. The battle cry for Pakistan, maintained the

Congress leaders, was synthetic and artificial; it had been raised by Jinnah simply out of greed for power and a desire to revenge himself on Congress. (Jinnah had once been a member of the Congress Party, but had resigned after failing to gain ascendancy among the leaders.)

But whether the Muslim League's claim to their own Pakistan was ethnically invalid or not, the British, whose task it was after the war to give India her independence, certainly accepted it as a reality. Congress maintained that they did so because it was 'convenient' politically. So long as India was embroiled in the Hindu-Muslim battle, so long could the British say: 'How can we give India her freedom, when the Indians themselves cannot decide in which form freedom shall come? If we accept the Congress viewpoint and hand over the whole of India, the Muslims will revolt and there will be civil war. If we accept Pakistan, the Congress will rally their forces and fight against partition.' And Congress accused the British in India of artificially stimulating and helping the Muslim League in order to prolong the conflict and thus preserve their own hold on the sub-Continent.

Now it is certainly true that there were many British officials in India, some very high officials, who did not wish to see the end of the British raj and were prepared to use every stratagem possible to preserve British hegemony, and their own jobs, as long as possible. One British governor of an important Indian province successfully wrecked a conference at Simla at which the Hindus and Muslims had come together, first by advising Jinnah on tactics and then using his influence on the Viceroy to make sure that the tactics worked.

It is also true that, emotionally, the majority of British civil servants in India were pro-Muslim. He was easier to get on with. He was less arrogant (the Hindus would say he was more subservient) and more gregarious. A British official could visit a Muslim in his home and take a meal without feeling, as in the case of a Hindu, that afterwards a whole ritual of 'purification' would have to be gone through because the house had been sullied by the presence of a foreigner. The British suspected (wrongly, in the case of the Congress leaders who abhorred the caste system) that their meetings with the Hindus were superficial contacts with men who despised them. They suspected that most Hindus considered them inferior, and they knew that many Hindus considered them unclean. (It occurred to only a few of them that most Hindus resented them not because they were British, or unclean, but because they were overlords.)

Above all else, however, pro-Muslim feeling among most British in India was encouraged by the events which had taken place during the war. When war came, the Congress Party refused to co-operate whereas the Muslim League responded at once. Congress had good solid reasons for their attitude, for India was pitchforked into war in 1939 by a simple declaration from the Viceroy without any consultation with the people or the Party, and they could, with good reason, point out that Britain had no right to use them in a struggle for freedom in faraway Europe when they were denied freedom for themselves at home. But later on, in 1942, when Japan was knocking at the gates of India itself and the safety of India's own people was threatened, Congress still refused to join in the war effort. The idea that the Hindus would be prepared to accept Japanese occupation out of sheer resentment of the British was more than most British officials could stomach. They shuddered at the idea of the Indian sub-Continent in the hands of men like Gandhi, the Congress leader, who, in 1942, calmly contemplated a Japanese victory and sent a message to the British people expressing his abhorrence of German Nazism and Italian Fascism but hoping that they would submit without fighting to both. Not unnaturally, they were inclined to embrace the Muslim League which not only supported the war effort enthusiastically but encouraged its members to join the armed forces and fight. In fact, sixty-five per cent of the soldiers of the Indian Army who fought in North Africa, Italy, Malaya and Burma were Muslims—which means that there were thirteen Muslims to every seven Hindus in the fighting forces, though there were only nine Muslims to every twenty-four Hindus in India.

So most British officials, especially after 1942, were pro-Muslim. But were they pro-Pakistan?

Pakistan was something else again. As I have said, there may well have been substance in the Congress charge that certain among the British wished to stoke the fires of Hindu-Muslim animosity in order to justify the status quo. But the bulk of the Britons who ran the machinery of government in India were men not only of great and dedicated skill but also of goodwill. It is true to say that they loved India. They may well have had fears for India's future once they no longer guided its destiny, for all men are human in thinking that their successors will not be prepared to give so much and will probably not do so well. All of them were, however, resigned to the fact that India was one day, very soon now, about to pass from British control. It was a very rare official indeed—and one, certainly, not steeped in the traditions of his service—who could contemplate without distress the prospect of the partition of the country into what would obviously be artificial divisions, economically, geographically, and even sociologically. By much sweat, blood and brain-work the British in India had worked to achieve unity; to the enormous benefit of the coffers at home, it is true. They had taken warring tribes, diverse religions, disputatious people and arrogant princes and welded them into a viable nation larger than any other in the world, with the exception of China.

That their work should end in the division of the country into two separate nations was not something which any sincere British official in India could contemplate without abhorrence. Liking the Muslims or not, he could not swallow their desire for this vivisection; and such was the British reluctance to face up to the possibility that, in March 1946, there was not a single paper in the official archives in Delhi preparing the ground for what would have to be done if partition should come. In that month, on his own initiative, one was written and submitted by Lieut.-General Sir Francis Tuker, at the time General Officer Commanding the Eastern Command in India. His viewpoint was purely that of a soldier, but he did make the point that if Indian independence was rushed, partition would inevitably follow; and that, therefore, certain measures should be taken in advance to prepare for such an eventuality. He got a note back (dated 9 April 1946) from Mr Ambrose Dundas, Secretary to the War Department in Delhi, saying: 'I find your note on "Defence—Hindustan and Pakistan" most interesting. It is also extremely practical . . . Unfortunately, it is out of your hands and mine to decide how much weight is to be given to practical conditions and how much they are to be ignored to suit sentiment or appearances. Well, we shall know soon, of course!' But no action was taken on the note though Dundas had, of course, forwarded it to his superiors; and, as we shall see, if it had been 600,000 lives might have been saved eighteen months later.

The Viceroy in 1946 was Field Marshal Lord Wavell.

To him, the prospect of an India torn artificially in two by a misguided (sincere, perhaps, but still misguided) clash of religious beliefs and political ambitions was particularly distressing. As a student of history, he believed that the division of India into Hindustan and Pakistan would inevitably be followed by a gradual Balkanization if not fragmentation of the sub-Continent; that once religion had been accepted as a basis for partition, the Sikhs would one day follow the Muslims into separation; and that then India would start to break up into a series of linguistic states. As a student of war, he believed partition would dangerously weaken India's defences and lay her open to attack from Russia in the north and China in the east. And as a soldier, he realized that partition would mean the break-up of that magnificent instrument of war and defence, the Indian Army.

At first sight, the appointment of Field Marshal Lord Wavell as Viceroy of India had been a strange one indeed. His record as a commander in the field, brilliant, distinguished though he might be, had been one of disappointment and setback; he had seen the armies under his command driven back in both Africa and Asia, and though no soldier could possibly have done better with the resources at his disposal, he had inevitably been saddled with the responsibility for defeat.

Wavell had always maintained that he was nothing but a simple soldier (who wrote a little, studied a little, considered a little), and if the quality of a statesman is to be supple of mind, visionary in concept and bold in execution, he was far from being a statesman. Moreover, he had one quality which in India might well have been considered a fundamental fault for one who would be engaged in continuous discussion, argument, and negotiation. He did not know how to talk.

In a land filled with politicians, who often did not know when to keep their mouths shut, he found it almost impossible to open his. The Indian leaders, Hindu and Muslim alike, were loquacious. Words fell like drops of saliva from their tongues. They spoke like poets at their best and like Welsh Baptists at their worst; but one thing was certain, they were never at a loss for words or quotations. One by one, they would troop in to see him, Gandhi, Jinnah, Nehru, Azad and Liaquat and they would spray him with jets of eloquent argument.

It so happened that every single one of the Indian leaders, of both sides, was a lawyer. As a soldier, Wavell had been trained to suspect all lawyers. His particular *bête noire* was Gandhi. To India (as to many beyond India) Mahatma Gandhi was a saint, but to the Viceroy he was an irksome obscurantist. Wavell was too intelligent a man to be contemptuous of Gandhi; he had no doubt of his great power and influence for good, and he admired his indefatigable work for the betterment of his people. But he found personal contact with him both disturbing and irritating, and he complained that he could never pin him down to a straightforward statement of fact or intention. At the end of one interview with him, he said: 'He spoke to me for half an hour, and I am still not sure what he meant to tell me. Every sentence he spoke could be interpreted in at least two different ways. I would be happier were I convinced that he knew what he was saying himself, but I cannot even be sure of that.'

There came a time when the prospect of another talk with Gandhi filled him with so much mental discomfort that he could not sleep the night before. 'He would sit there,' recalled one of his secretaries, 'while the little man prattled on, and the expression on his face was one of sheer misery. He would fiddle with his pencil and I could see his single eye gradually beginning to glaze, and at the end of it, all he could think of to say would be: "I see. Thank you." '[1]

Yet despite the catalogue of faults which could be filed against Wavell—his tongue-tied manner, his lack of political suppleness, his shyness, his awkwardness in argument and discussion—he had one great virtue which was badly needed in India in the years after the war. Of all the actors in the drama of Indian independence, he was the only one who always spoke the truth. I am not suggesting that the others were liars; but they were politicians and lawyers, and for them truth had many sides. Gandhi was once asked to describe his policy. 'I will write it down for you in five sentences,' he replied. The reporter took the message away with him and discovered that each sentence contradicted the one before it. Nehru had a way of speaking and writing with forthright sincerity, but (as we shall see) he always left himself a way out. And Jinnah, when given something for which he had asked, went away apparently satisfied, but shortly afterwards returned to ask for more.

When Wavell said he wanted to see an independent India, he not only meant it; he sincerely tried to achieve it. His methods may have lacked the subtlety which those on the Indian side

[1] In a conversation with the author.

expected in a negotiator; he may never have descended to the
market place and haggled; he may have been slow to exploit a
situation; but he was always aware of the goal ahead, and right
until the last he was determined to achieve it.

In the summer of 1946, he came so close that subsequent events
are tragic indeed. On 15 March 1946 Mr Clement (now Earl)
Attlee announced in the House of Commons that the Labour
Government was sending a Cabinet Mission to India with the
intention of making a supreme effort to break the deadlock
between Britain and the Indians on the one hand, and Congress
and the Muslim League on the other. In a private telegram to
Lord Wavell, Mr Attlee made it clear that his government was
not trying to bypass the Viceroy but felt that a delegation from
home, armed with the power to make decisions on the spot—as
the Cripps Mission of 1942, sent by Churchill, for instance, had
not been armed—would give the negotiations a shot in the arm
and convince the Indians, suspicious as they still were of British
intentions, that this time we really meant business. He asked for
the Viceroy's fullest help and co-operation. Wavell's commentary
on that was: 'He didn't think I would withhold it, did he? What
does he think I have been working for?'

The Cabinet Mission consisted of Sir Stafford Cripps, Lord
Pethick Lawrence, Secretary of State for India, and Mr A. V.
Alexander. Cripps was a political theorist with a brilliant mind
who had studied the Indian problem from every standpoint
except the emotional one; this, in the opinion of some, meant
that he would never really be able to understand it. He was a
great expert at the preparation of plans. He took all factors into
consideration: religious antipathies, regional rivalries, political
standpoints, racial susceptibilities and suspicions. But there were
those who felt that he always forgot the importance of the human
element, and he was continually disappointed that his plans,
perfect on paper, never seemed to succeed in practice.

He had with him on this occasion, however, a man who
appealed to all Indians who met him, Hindu and Muslim alike.
Lord Pethick Lawrence was liked, even loved, by both sides
because he wore his heart on his sleeve; he loved India, he genuinely enjoyed being with Indians, and he was emotionally
anxious to help India's aims for freedom in any way
possible. The Cabinet Mission arrived in Delhi towards the end
of March, when the Indian summer begins to scorch the earth,

the skin and the mind. Though he was an old man, Pethick Lawrence never complained. He sweated through temperatures of
115 degrees and once, at an important conference, fainted from
heat prostration. He returned after a short rest and apologized
for his 'stupid weakness'.

In the discussions which began almost immediately after the
Cabinet Mission's arrival, Mr A. V. Alexander was not much more
than a passenger. He never had any really serious contribution
to make to the discussions. The two serious members of the
Mission were Cripps and Pethick Lawrence, and, in the event,
they proved to be a combination of great intelligence and
broad-mindedness. Mixed with the milk of human kindness which
Pethick Lawrence dispensed, Cripps's cold-water logic became
potable to Indian leaders, if not entirely pleasant.

The aim of the Cabinet Mission was to talk to the Indian leaders
and endeavour to persuade them to formulate their own scheme
for independence. It did not take more than a few days to convince
all three of them that this way led to hopeless deadlock. Jinnah
depressed them by his cold, arrogant, insistent demand for Pakistan or nothing. An encounter with Jinnah cast them down, for
he always appeared before them in immaculately cut clothes, his
sapling-thin figure always spry, his eyes clear and bright, his skin
dry even when they, in the heat of the day, were dripping with
sweat. 'He is the only man I know', Alexander commented,
'who walks around with a built-in air-cooler.' And never once
did he relax, no matter what friendly overture they made
to him.

They gained their greatest comfort from Maulana Abul Kalam
Azad, the President of Congress, and not simply because he felt
the heat as much as they did.[1]

He was a Muslim. He sympathized with the fears of India's
90,000,000 Muslims that, in the event of independence, they would
be swamped by the all-powerful Hindu majority; that they might
well become a persecuted minority in a Hindu raj. But he always
refused to believe that Jinnah's plan for Pakistan was a solution.
After consulting his Hindu colleagues in the Congress Party, he
drew up his own idea of how communal differences might be

[1] Maulana Azad was a great admirer of Lord Wavell, and almost the only
criticism he ever voiced of him was his insistence on carrying on the Cabinet Mission
negotiations in the furnace heat of Delhi instead of the coolness of Simla. 'My
comment was that Delhi presented no difficulty for him as the Viceregal Lodge was
air-conditioned and he never moved out of it.'

resolved and a unitary India preserved. He had several consultations with the Cabinet Mission, and, on 15 April 1946, he issued
a statement which is worthy of reproduction here, since it is
conveniently forgotten in India today.

'I have considered from every possible point of view', Maulana
Abul Kalam Azad wrote, 'the scheme of Pakistan as formulated
by the Muslim League. As an Indian, I have examined its implications for the future of India as a whole. As a Muslim, I have
examined its likely effect upon the fortunes of Muslims in India.
Considering the scheme in all its aspects, I have come to the conclusion that it is harmful not only for India as a whole but for
Muslims in particular. And in fact it creates more problems than
it solves.

'I must confess that the very term Pakistan goes against my
grain. It suggests that some portions of the world are pure while
others are impure. Such a division of territories into pure and
impure is un-Islamic and a repudiation of the very spirit of Islam.
Islam recognizes no such division and the Prophet says, "God
has made the whole world a mosque for me." Further, it seems
to me that the scheme for Pakistan is a symbol of defeatism and
has been built up on the analogy of the Jewish demand for a
national home. It is a confession that Indian Muslims cannot hold
their own in India as a whole and would be content to withdraw
to a corner specially reserved for them. One can sympathize with
the aspirations of the Jews for such a national home, as they are
scattered over the world and cannot in any region have any
effective voice in the administration. The condition of Indian
Muslims is quite otherwise. Over 90 millions in number they are
in quantity and quality a sufficiently important element in Indian
life to influence decisively all questions of administration and
policy. Nature has further helped them by concentrating them in
certain areas.

'In such context, the demand for Pakistan loses all force. As a
Muslim, I for one am not prepared for a moment to give up my
right to treat the whole of India as my domain and to share in
the shaping of its political and economic life. To me it seems a
sure sign of cowardice to give up what is my patrimony and content myself with a mere fragment of it.'

Azad proposed instead a formula which he had already persuaded the Working Committee of the Congress to accept, one
which secured whatever merit the Pakistan scheme contained,

while all its defects—displacement of population, particularly— were avoided. Azad realized, as many of his Hindu colleagues did not, that a major fear of the Muslims was that if a unitary India came into existence the Hindu-controlled administration at the Centre would dominate, interfere, bully, economically oppress and politically smother the Muslim minority. His scheme was to meet this fear by proposing that both sides should accept a solution which 'ensures that Muslim majority provinces are internally free to develop as they will, but can at the same time influence the Centre on all issues which affect India as a whole.

'The situation in India', Azad went on, 'is such that all attempts to establish a centralized and unitary government are bound to fail. Equally doomed to failure is the attempt to divide India into two States. After considering all aspects of the questions, I have come to the conclusion that the only solution can be on the lines embodied in the Congress formula which allows room for development both to the provinces and to India as a whole . . . I am one of those who consider the present chapter of communal bitterness and differences as a transient phase in Indian life. I firmly hold that they will disappear when India assumes the responsibility of her own destiny. I am reminded of a saying of Gladstone that the best cure for a man's fear of water is to throw him into it. Similarly, India must assume responsibility and administer her own affairs before fears and suspicions can be fully allayed. When India attains her destiny, she will forget the present chapter of communal suspicion and conflict and face the problems of modern life from a modern point of view. Differences will no doubt persist but they will be economic, not communal. Opposition among political parties will continue, but they will be based not on religion but on economic and political issues. Class and not community will be the basis of future alignments and policies will be shaped accordingly. If it be argued that this is only a faith which events may not justify I would say that in any case the nine crores [90,000,000] of Muslims constitute a factor which nobody can ignore and whatever the circumstances, they are strong enough to safeguard their own destiny.'[1]

Here was a statement written from the heart. Such views coming from the President of Congress made a profound impression on both the Viceroy and the Cabinet Mission. When they discovered the impossibility of persuading the two opposing

[1] In a memorandum to the Viceroy and Congress.

sides to find a solution between them, the Mission produced a scheme of its own. Basically, it followed the lines of Azad's proposals. A unitary India would be formed, but the central government would be responsible for only three subjects—Defence, Foreign Affairs and Communications. For the rest, the country would be divided into three main administrative groups. Group A would comprise the great slab of India where the Hindus were in the majority. Group B would be composed of the Punjab, Sind, the North West Frontier Province and British Baluchistan, where the Muslims were in a majority. And Group C would consist of Bengal and Assam, where the Muslims would have a small majority. Thus the Muslim minority would have charge of their own domestic affairs and would be protected from Hindu domination.

To everyone's astonishment, and to the great joy of the Viceroy and the Cabinet Mission, both sides accepted the proposals. Both Congress and the Muslim League had certain reservations; but the working committees of the two organizations signified their willingness to go ahead with the Plan. Though Gandhi no longer had any official position in the Congress Party, his influence upon its members was still as powerful as ever. He described the Cabinet Mission proposals as 'the seed to convert this land of sorrow into one without sorrow or suffering . . . After four days of searching examination of the State paper issued by the Cabinet Mission and the Viceroy on behalf of the British Government, my conviction abides that it is the best document that the British Government could have produced in the circumstances.'

The air seemed bright with promise. Delegates of the Congress Party from all over India gathered for their annual conference, and there, after a moving speech from Azad, the opposition from the Left Wing of the party was mowed down and the Mission Plan's scheme for independence accepted. So far as the Muslim League was concerned, there was no need for a conference. The influence of Mr Jinnah was all-powerful. What he said was law with the members of his working committee; and he told them that the Mission Plan was the nearest to Pakistan that the Muslims could hope to get.

Peace at last? Independence for India, after 150 years of British rule? The end of communal differences and fratricidal strife? It looked like it.

At which point, the bull came lumbering into the china shop.

It should always be remembered that Mohammed Ali Jinnah, the Muslim leader, was intensely suspicious of Congress motives and intentions. His Hindu opponents called him a cold, arrogant, inflexible man, and so he could be; but he believed, not without reason, that Congress was flexible in quite a different way. He did not trust the party leaders. In the past, the Muslim League had made political agreements with Congress and—as in the United Provinces before the war—had fought elections on a joint platform, with the stipulation that when the elections were won the Muslim League would have its share of places in the Cabinet. But wherever Congress secured a majority of seats on its own, and therefore no longer needed Muslim League help, it had repudiated the agreements and offered the Muslims a single, unimportant seat—or none at all.

Now that he had made the gesture of accepting the Cabinet Mission Plan, Jinnah was as highly strung as a lean and hungry jockey who has conceded a couple of pounds in order to keep in the race. The use of racing parlance to describe his attitude would have shocked him, but it is not inapt in the context in which it is used. He suspected that certain members of Congress were out to 'nobble' the Muslim League, and that he was determined to prevent at all costs. To his way of thinking, his acceptance of the Cabinet Mission Plan had been a great concession; it meant, if carried through, the abandonment of his conception of a separate state of Pakistan. He and his fellow Muslims would have regional independence in their provinces, but they would still be part of a Hindu-dominated raj, and he was determined to keep every safeguard for the protection of his people which the Cabinet Mission Plan had suggested. This the Congress Party, at their conference, had seemed to have accepted by an overwhelming majority.

But would they keep their word?

The Cabinet Mission sailed back to England, convinced that they had done a good job and that there was hope for India in the future. Both Sir Stafford Cripps and Lord Pethick Lawrence were so sure that the way ahead would be smooth that they telegraphed their congratulations and good wishes to Azad for the way in which he had secured the acceptance of their Plan by Congress. They wrote too soon. At the same conference which approved the Plan, the presidency of the party changed. Right-wing elements in Congress were canvassing for the appointment of Sardar Vallabhbhai Patel, the party's strong-man, as Azad's successor as president. Azad himself (to his lasting sorrow) decided that Pandit Jawaharlal Nehru would be the better man, and circulated a memorandum urging all members of Congress to vote for Nehru and elect him new president by acclamation. This, in fact, is what happened.

Nehru had been one of the Congress high command who had voted to accept the Cabinet Mission Plan, but his subsequent actions would seem to indicate that he did so only because Gandhi was for it, and he felt he would be outvoted if he opposed it. Now he was President he showed his real feelings. The way his mind was working at this time would tend to suggest that, even this late in the day, he had no real conception of the power of Mr Jinnah and the enormous influence which he had built up as leader of the Muslim community. He decided on a show-down. His contempt for Jinnah was ill-concealed (the contempt was reciprocated) and his dislike of the aims and intentions of the Muslim League was such that he seriously underestimated its strength. Of the Muslim League he once said, in a conversation with the author: 'It was an organization which was both very strong and very weak. It could always bring its followers out on the streets, always cause trouble, always threaten violence. But it had no other *raison d'être* than a negative anti-Hindu feeling.' And of Jinnah he said: 'You know, the real reason why Jinnah left the Congress was because, about 1920, it suddenly broadened its base and began appealing to the masses. Jinnah did not like this. Congress was no longer a party for gentlemen. Jinnah always thought that membership should be confined to those Indians who had passed matriculation—a standard which would have been high for any country, but for India meant that the masses could never come in. He was a snob. When the peasants began to join Congress, he was annoyed. Why, many of them did not even speak English. They dressed in peasant clothes. It was no party for him.' And, of Jinnah's assumption of leadership of the Muslim League, he said: 'He had no real feelings about the Muslims. He wasn't really a Muslim at all. I know Muslims. I know the Koran. I have Muslim relatives and friends. Jinnah couldn't even recite a Muslim prayer and had certainly never read the Koran. But when he was offered the leadership of the Muslim League, he saw the opportunity and accepted it. He had been a comparative failure as a lawyer in England, and this was a way out. But his attitude could be summed up by a story I once heard about him when he first went to England and was asked if he was going into politics. He said he had thought of it. He was then asked whether he would be a Conservative or a Liberal. "I haven't made up my mind, yet," he said. Jinnah had no qualities, except that he succeeded.'

Now this summing up of Jinnah's character (and I will be dealing with some other facets of it later in this story) may well have contained some elements of truth. But it is one thing to despise your opponent in politics and quite another to underestimate him. Jinnah had faults, but he also had strength and implacable determination. And in the summer of 1946 (not for the last time) Jawaharlal Nehru seriously miscalculated his potential. He could not believe that Jinnah spoke for all the Muslims in India. He still believed that Congress, under his presidency, could unseat him.

And on 10 July, after he had been elected President, he called the Press together for a conference to discuss his policy as the new head of Congress. It was a moment in history when circumspection should have been the order of the day. There was much to be gained by silence. The fortunes of India were in the balance, and one false move could upset them. Nehru chose this moment to launch into what his biographer, Michael Brecher, has described as 'one of the most fiery and provocative statements in his forty years of public life'. He was asked by Press representatives whether the approval by Congress of the Cabinet Mission Plan meant that they had accepted it *in toto*. Nehru replied with some petulance that Congress was 'completely unfettered by agreements and free to meet all situations as they arise'. He was then asked if this meant that the Cabinet Mission Plan could be modified.

He made it clear in his next words that he, as President of Congress, had every intention of modifying the Plan. 'We shall, no doubt, succeed in solving it [the problem of the minorities],' he said, 'but we accept no interference in it; certainly not the British Government's interference.' As to the Cabinet Mission's Plan for the division of India into three groups (a plan which Congress a few days before had voted to accept) he said:

'The big probability is, from any approach to the question, there will be no grouping. Obviously, section A [the Hindus] will decide against grouping. Speaking in betting language, there is a four to one chance of the North West Frontier Province deciding against grouping.[1] That means Group B collapses. It is highly likely that Bengal and Assam will decide against grouping . . . Thus you will see that this grouping business approached from any point of view does not get us on at all.'

Did Nehru realize what he was saying? He was telling the world that once in power, Congress would use its strength at the Centre to alter the Cabinet Mission Plan as it thought fit. But the Muslim League (as had Congress) had accepted the Plan as a cut and dried scheme to meet objections from both sides. It was a compromise plan which obviously could not afterwards be altered in favour of one side or another. In the circumstances, Nehru's remarks were a direct act of sabotage. Whether he meant them to be so, in the mistaken belief that Jinnah and the Muslim League were not really a force to be reckoned with, or whether they were the ham-handed remarks of a politician who did not know when to keep his mouth shut will never be known. It is a subject upon which Nehru nowadays prefers to keep his own counsel. But certainly his speech, as Brecher, his biographer, describes it, was 'a serious tactical error. Jinnah was given an incomparable wedge to press more openly for Pakistan on the grounds of Congress "tyranny".'

Maulana Abul Kalam Azad went further and wrote:

'Jawaharlal is one of my dearest friends and his contribution to India's national life is second to none. He has worked and suffered for Indian freedom, and since attainment of independence he has become the symbol of our national unity and progress. I have nevertheless to say with regret that he is at times apt to be carried away by his feelings. Not only so, but sometimes he is so impressed by theoretical considerations that he is apt to underestimate the realities of a situation. The mistake of 1946 proved . . . costly.'[2]

It did indeed. Mr Jinnah reacted to Nehru's statement like an army leader who has come in for armistice discussions under a flag of truce and finds himself looking down the barrel of a cocked revolver. He dived for cover, screaming treachery as he did so. It did not take him long to convince himself and his followers

---

[1] A completely wrong reading of the odds, as it turned out. Though the North West Frontier Province still had a pro-Congress Muslim government at the time, its hold on the masses was loosening fast; it became ninety per cent pro-Muslim League and anti-Congress shortly afterwards, and would, therefore, have opted for Group B.

[2] M. Azad, *India Wins Freedom.*

that the whole thing had been a great mistake; that in accepting the Cabinet Mission Plan and compromising with his goal of an independent Pakistan he had made a fundamental error; that Congress was just as tricky and dangerous as ever.

The consequences of the Nehru speech were profound and tragic. On 27 July 1946 the Muslim League met and at Jinnah's behest withdrew its acceptance of the Cabinet Mission Plan. This was bad enough; it shattered India's hopes of independence within a reasonably distant future; it put Hindus and Muslims back in two fuming, suspicious camps. The Viceroy tried desperately to bring the two sides together again, and Congress itself, urged on by Wavell, passed a resolution reiterating its faith in the Cabinet Mission Plan and deprecating (it felt it could hardly condemn) Nehru's remarks.

But Jinnah had had enough. He was through with flirting with the Hindus once and for all, he said. And he drew up a resolution —which was, of course, passed without dissent—in which he called upon the Muslim League to renounce all the titles they held from the British Government and to set aside 16 August 1946 as 'Direct Action Day' when the Muslims of India would demonstrate their determination to achieve a partition of India and a Pakistan of their own.

'What we have done today', he declared, afterwards, 'is the most historic act in our history. Never have we in the whole history of the League done anything except by constitutional methods and by constitutionalism. But now we are obliged and forced into this position. This day we bid good-bye to constitutional methods . . . Today we have also forged a pistol and are in a position to use it.'

On the morning of 16 August 1946 Nehru drove to Jinnah's ugly, sumptuous house on Malabar Hill, in Bombay, for a talk with the Muslim League leader. He had come reluctantly in response to an urgent appeal from the Viceroy, who had asked him to make one last attempt to bridge the gulf between the two contending parties. In accordance with the provisions of the Cabinet Mission plan, an interim Government was in process of formation, and five places in the Cabinet had been reserved for the Muslim League. So long as the British still remained in India, the Viceroy, in an emergency, could exercise a power of veto; but otherwise the new Government would run the central administration, and Pandit Nehru would be its head. It was his task on this fateful morning to plead with Jinnah to forget 'Direct Action' and bring his League into the Government.

It is unlikely that anyone, at this juncture, could have persuaded Mr Jinnah to change his mind, but it is difficult to think of anyone less likely to succeed than Pandit Nehru. Here were two men who had no common meeting ground (not even the future of India) and no respect for each other. Nehru, the Harrow and Oxford-educated intellectual, lover of poetry, writer of books, despised Jinnah as a narrow-minded racialist. 'He had no real education,' he once said. 'He was not what you call an educated man. He had read law books and an occasional work of light fiction, but he never read any real book.' Jinnah, intensely proud, constantly on the look-out for snubs, was unlikely to unbend in the presence of a man he had once described as 'an arrogant Brahmin who covers his Hindu trickiness with a veneer of Western education. When he makes promises, he always leaves a loophole, and when he cannot find a loophole, he just lies.'

The encounter between the two leaders lasted for eighty minutes, but encounter was what it was and not a meeting of minds. It would be less than just to Nehru to say that he did not try; he may have had his own ideas of how an independent India should be run, but there is no doubt of his desperate eagerness to achieve it. He had spent most of his life (a considerable part of it in jail) campaigning to rid India of the British, and, suspicious though he still was of British intentions, he was now almost convinced that they were at last ready to go. To have to ask favours of the man whose stubbornness was blocking the road to freedom must have been hard to bear; to have to admit to himself that his own maladroitness was responsible for the present situation must have been even harder; but he made the effort, with all the eloquence at his command. The response was absolutely null. Jinnah was polite but unyielding. The interview was not only abortive; after it was over, the antipathy between the two men was greater than ever. Pandit Nehru departed more convinced than ever that only this man really stood in the way of India's freedom, more determined than ever to destroy him and the 'myth of Pakistan' which he had created; and yet still unaware of how strong Jinnah really was, how powerful was his hold on Muslim India.

As he drove away from Malabar Hill, the Congress president

could see the black flags of mourning—the banners proclaiming 'Direct Action Day'—flying from Muslim houses and outside shuttered Muslim shops. But Bombay was a Hindu majority area; the streets were quiet and there was no trouble. Karachi and the Punjab, two of the greatest Muslim areas of India, were also under control, the first because the Chief Secretary of the Sind Government had refused to allow the day to be proclaimed a public holiday, the second because the province was under the quietly efficient control of the British Governor, Sir Evan Jenkins, and a reasonably stable provincial government.

In India, however, there was one provincial government under control of the Muslims. This was Bengal, whose capital, Calcutta, is India's largest city (population, 1946: 2,500,000). The Muslims in Bengal not only outnumbered the Hindus and other minor religions (33,000,000 Muslims against 27,315,000 others) and were thus able to assure themselves a majority at the polls, but they were also given extra seats under the 'weightage' system introduced by the British to ensure fair representation for minorities. This meant that even when their supporters did not vote in overwhelming numbers, they could always be certain of controlling the provincial legislature.[1]

The British Governor of Bengal was Sir Frederick Burrows, an ex-railwayman and union official, who had been appointed by the Labour Government in February 1946 to succeed Mr R. G. Casey. He was an able and amiable administrator who got on well with Hindus and Muslims alike, and was popular with the local British Army Command; but he was not exactly a man of great strength or quickness of mind. As a personality he was certainly no match for the Chief Minister of Bengal, Mr Shaheed Suhrarwardy, an Oriental politician of considerable shrewdness, deviousness of mind, and great natural charm. Mr Suhrarwardy was a member of the Working Committee of the Muslim League, and therefore might have been expected to jump at the crack of Mr Jinnah's whip with the same alacrity as the other Muslim satraps. In fact, he exercised considerable independence and made it clear to Mr Jinnah that he would brook no interference in his administration. Mr Jinnah did not like him, particularly since he suspected that Suhrarwardy—though he was always careful to pay lip-service to the idea of Pakistan—secretly cherished an

---

[1] Under this same 'weightage', the 20,000 British residents of Bengal also had a representation in the legislature far beyond that justified by their numbers.

ambition of his own: to carve an independent Bengal out of free India and run it as a separate state, outside Jinnah's control.

Mr Suhrarwardy was a party 'boss' of the type who believes that no politician need ever be out of office once his strong-arm squads have gained control of the polling booths; that no minister should ever suffer financially by being in public life; that no relative or political cohort should ever go unrewarded. He loved money, champagne, Polish blondes and dancing the tango in nightclubs, and he was reputed to have made a fortune during the war.[1] He loved Calcutta, including its filthy, festering slums, and it was from the noisome alleyways of Howrah that he picked the *goondas* who accompanied him everywhere as a bodyguard.

To this outwardly affable but inwardly ruthless politico, the decision of Mr Jinnah to declare 16 August 1946 as 'Direct Action Day' seemed a golden opportunity to demonstrate his power over Bengal's Muslims and his enthusiasm for Pakistan. He announced that 16 August would be a general holiday in Calcutta for Muslims and Hindus alike; and when Hindu members of the provincial legislature protested that they had no wish to share in a Muslim political *hartal*, he ordered his party machine to vote them down. On 5 August, under the nom-de-plume of 'Shaheed', he wrote an article in the *Statesman*, Calcutta, in which he said, ominously as it turned out: 'Bloodshed and disorder are not necessarily evil in themselves, if resorted to for a noble cause. Among Muslims today, no cause is dearer or nobler than Pakistan.' In a speech in Delhi on 10 August, he threatened to turn Bengal into a separate government if Congress went ahead and formed an interim government on its own. 'We will see that no revenue is derived from Bengal for such a Central Government, and will consider ourselves as a separate government having no connection with the Centre,' he declared. And in a declaration on the eve of 'Direct Action Day', one of his aides called upon the Muslims to adopt the slogan of *Lar ke linge Pakistan!* which could be translated as 'Pakistan by force!'

The stage was set for the demonstration that was to split India in two.

---

[1] Before he left India for Pakistan, income tax officials in Delhi began an investigation into his wartime earnings. Subsequently, after he became Prime Minister of Pakistan, he planned a trip to East Pakistan but discovered that his plane would have to stop at Calcutta on the way. He wrote to the Indian premier, Mr Nehru, and asked for an Indian assurance that he would not be met by tax officials when he landed.

Chicago, Chicago may well be, as the song says, a wonderful town, but Calcutta definitely is not. It is a thriving port and a rich business centre; it has been both a black hole and a splendid provider of wealth for the British in India; and its inhabitants are among the most fluent, intelligent, poetic and most successfully acquisitive in the sub-Continent. But only a businessman or a political boss—or a Bengali—could really love Calcutta, for it is a city of poverty, drabness, disease and despair. I can think of no more squalid place in which to live, or a more terrifyingly ugly and lonely place in which to die. The city is built on the mud-flats along the banks of the Hooghly River, and to Western ears there could not be a more appropriate name. In the centre are the great buildings, the palaces, administrative headquarters, the broad squares, the fountains and the monuments, which the British built to give a heavily majestic look to the city whose natural resources they had exploited; but the central showground is surrounded by the most leprous slums in the world. Here live the underprivileged deluded human termites whom politicians love because they are poor, they are ignorant, they are fearful and superstitious, and they are pathetically easy to exploit.

It would be stupid to ignore Bengal's contribution to the cause of Indian freedom, or to India's intellectual and cultural life. Rabindranath Tagore, the great poet, was a Bengali, as was Michael Madhusudan Dutt, the father of modern Indian poetry, and Rammohun Roy, Swami Vivekananda, and Bankim Chandra Chatterji, the founders of Hindu nationalism. But the Bengalis who counted on 16 August were the mobs from the slums.

They crossed the Hooghly River from Howrah into Calcutta soon after dawn. They were armed with *lathis* (long sticks), knives, bottles and automobile cranks or other kinds of iron bars. Most of them at this time were Muslims. They waited in doorways and alleyways until it was time for shops to open, and then they watched to see which shops did open (in the circumstances, they were bound to be non-Muslim). The doorkeeper who opened the shop was swiftly clubbed down, or kicked, or stabbed; then the contents of the shop were smashed or looted.

It began quietly at first, and scarcely anyone realized what terrible things were happening. A Briton cycling across Chowringhee Square on his way to a hospital where he worked, saw a sweeper running towards him, pursued by a mob. At the moment he dismounted, one of the mob reached the sweeper and whacked him so hard across the legs that the crack of his broken bones could be clearly heard. The moment he touched the ground, another member of the mob leaned down and cut the man's throat and then sliced off his ear. Then the rest of the mob came up, nodded and smiled and touched their hearts and foreheads to the Englishman, saying: 'Good day to you, sir' before turning to make off across the square. It all happened so swiftly that the Englishman found it hard to believe that it had happened at all.

In the beginning there were isolated incidents. An old woman was stopped, taunted, tossed from hand to hand, and then suddenly, when she scratched or bit or kicked, cracked over the head with a *lathi*. There was sport to be had with legless and armless cripples, of whom there are plenty in Calcutta. They were tipped off their wheel-trays and left helpless in the road, or stuffed into a sand-bin and left to yelp. There were small girls and old men who were frog-marched to a place where a cow—one of Calcutta's wandering sacred cows—had been caught and they were forced to hold the knife that cut its throat; a terrible act of sacrilege for a Hindu. (Even in the Bengal famine, no Hindu deliberately killed and certainly never ate a cow.)

By noon, however, the small, evil spurts of violence had begun to develop into flames and fires. It was catching. At first, it had been only groups of *goondas* who killed and battered, while small scatterings of wary onlookers followed them and looted smashed shops or helped to overturn cars. But, gradually, the onlookers became participators in the killings. Now, from many parts of Calcutta, the noise of human voices began to be heard; voices raised in anger or in pain, a steadily increasing keening sound that rose and fell, like the voice of hell, for the next four days to come.

At two o'clock on the afternoon of 16 August 1946, Mr Shaheed Suhrarwardy addressed a mass meeting in the Maidan, Calcutta's main square. He was in an ebullient mood and thanked his listeners for their numbers, their enthusiasm and their active work for Pakistan. While he spoke, men were being killed a couple of streets away. The smoke from fires started by the mob (who had broken into petrol stations by now, and were spraying nearby shops with fuel) could be plainly seen from the square, but neither Mr Suhrarwardy nor his considerable police bodyguard seemed to be aware of them.

In truth, the Calcutta police were finding the job of putting down the riots an almost insuperable one. There was the psychological difficulty at first (when the acts of murder were being mostly committed by Muslims) that the killers and violators were of their own religion, for most of the Calcutta police were Muslims. But by afternoon, the bellows of artificial fury had done the work and the Hindus and Sikhs came out on to the streets too, red hot for revenge and reprisal. They came out not to meet the Muslim *goondas* in head-on clashes, nor even to protect their own people and put down the rioting. That is not the way Calcutta mobs work. While the Muslim gangs went on hunting isolated Hindus and looting Hindu shops, Hindus and Sikhs went out on a hunt for helpless Muslims. It was always the old men, the children and the women that they were after. The women lost their breasts. The old men had their legs snapped. The children had their hands or arms cut off. The only pitched battle which took place between Muslims and Hindus happened at Ripon College, when the Muslims hoisted a Muslim League flag on the pole. A Hindu shinned up and replaced it with the Congress banner, while below the mobs fought briefly—and then swiftly retired. They were not there to get hurt themselves, but to kill and maim the unarmed among their enemies. And though the police managed to clear the main streets by firing tear-gas on the gangs, they reappeared as soon as the patrols had passed; there is always an alleyway in Calcutta down which you can disappear until the police have gone through.

Mr Jinnah had called the 'Direct Action Day' a demonstration against the British for their refusal to recognize Pakistan, but of all the communities in Calcutta once the rioting began, the British were the only ones who were safe. A number of them were besieged in the Grand Hotel, in Chowringhee Square, by a large gang of *goondas*. Presently, the leaders of the gang approached the hotel and offered to let the British guests go but would guarantee no safe passage for the Indians. The British held a meeting and decided to stay. Late that afternoon, they watched through the windows and saw a group of shouting, laughing Sikhs slowly chopping a live Muslim to pieces with their knives. 'I have a stomach made strong by experiences of a war hospital, but war was never like this,' wrote Mr Kim Christen later. 'I made my way on a cycle, up Chittaranjan Avenue, to the Medical College.[1] There I hoped to use my wartime experience in hospitals

[1] There was no transport, of course. Tramcars and buses had stopped, since they are the first things that Calcutta mobs overturn and burn when angry.

to do whatever I could to help. There had been a mob killing two hundred yards south of the Medical College, and bodies lay about in the roads amid the wreckage of burning cars. I waited awhile until the mob moved towards a side street and then continued to the hospital, where I first realized the enormity of the situation. Ambulances, Friends' service units, police trucks emptied themselves of bleeding, shattered wounded, while open carts were piled with those who had not survived the journey back. I approached a Red Cross truck and joined a group of young medical students. They pinned a paper cross to my shirt and then drove to the Mirzepur area, dismounted when the bodies grew thick, and searched among them for any flicker of life in the pulse. They were few, and they were lifted on to stretchers, already red and sodden, to be taken to a hospital already overcrowded. This search for survivors continued throughout the day and night. We went North and East, over the canal, gathering broken heads and stricken bodies, and took them to whatever hospital was nearest. Weapons of every shape and size had been gathered by the mobs—heavy tools, iron bars, spikes tied to *lathis*, while barrel loads of bricks were wheeled to the edge of the encounters. One man whose back was streaming with blood, having been hurled through a plate glass window behind him, squatted on the kerb. I saw him, while still bleeding, tear strips of cloth from his shirt and tie a piece of glass to the split of a stick, so as to use it as an axe. All the hospitals had hung 'Full' notices outside. Doctors and nurses operated continuously, and medical students whose medical books were still clean were called upon to exercise their knowledge in the most practical of schools. The ambulances were told to refuse all pleas for refuge and confine their loads to those not yet dead.'

At the end of the first forty-eight hours, an air of death and desolation hung over Calcutta. It was muggily hot and raining slightly. The smoke from fires hung heavy on the air. Only an occasional cycle (usually ridden by an Englishman) or a military jeep, canopied in wire netting, rushed by. The city had come to a standstill. No more trains were coming into Howrah or Sealdah from the country. The sewers overflowed; and in the foetid gutters the bodies of dead men and women and dead cows lay side by side, being picked over by the vultures.

There were already 4,000 dead and countless numbers of

wounded, but it was not over yet. The military (that is, the Army under British command) had been called in by now, and more troops were being rushed in from up-country garrisons. The sight of British or Gurkha troops was always a signal for the mob to stop their depredations, and often they received a cheer; they moved about the city, calmly moving barricades, breaking up demonstrations, stopping to investigate and rescue whenever they heard a cry from a house. But they had been called in too late to have the great psychological impact which might have put down the rioting right from the start. From now on, they would be able to stop the big riots and keep the gangs off the main streets, but there was little they could do to prevent the knifings and batterings which still went on in the alleyways.

The first Army troops had not been called upon to deal with the situation until the second day of the great Calcutta killings. Sir Frederick Burrows had made his own tour of the riot area on the first day, but the mobs squeezed back into the woodwork whenever he passed, and the Chief Minister, Suhrarwardy, had been able to persuade him that all was under control. It was only when the Hindus and Sikhs had come out in retaliation that the Chief Minister had called for military aid, afraid for the first time of the enormity of the tragic events which had been set in train. It was a misfortune for Calcutta that the GOC of the British and Indian forces in this area of India, Lieut.-General Sir Francis Tuker, had been called back to Britain for a staff conference, and military decisions were in the hands of his subordinates. Tuker had no great admiration for many Indian leaders or for the fighting qualities of the Bengalis,[1] but he was not the man to sit back and wait for orders when men, women and children were being massacred on the streets. He made it quite clear upon his return that he would have telephoned Sir Frederick Burrows and insisted upon intervening the moment it became obvious, on the first day, that the riots were serious; and, as he proved a year later, he had a short, sharp and effective way of dealing with goondas. But this was a job his subordinates had to handle—and they were hesitant and uncertain.

Slowly, very slowly, the great city of Calcutta began to recover. The fever died down, though the place was still one great festering scab.

[1] Bengalis were never recruited as fighting men into the Indian Army.

'When we wrote two days ago,' said the British-owned *Statesman*, 'conditions in Calcutta were horrifying. They have gone beyond that since. Whatever the appropriate adjective is, they were nothing in comparison with what we have subsequently seen. The latest estimate of dead is 3,000, who have lain thick about the streets. The injured number many thousand and it is impossible to say how many business houses and private dwellings have been destroyed. This is not a riot. It needs a word found in mediaeval history, a fury. Yet fury sounds spontaneous, and there must have been some deliberation and organization to set this fury on its way. The horde who ran about battering and killing with lathis may have found them lying about or brought them out of their own pockets, but that is not to be believed. We have already commented on the bands who found it easy to get petrol and vehicles when no others were permitted on the streets. It is not mere supposition that men were brought into Calcutta to make an impression . . . Thousands have been brutally hurt, smashed eyes, smashed jaws, smashed limbs, of men, women and children—these are the kind of political argument the twentieth century does not expect.'

The *Amrita Bazar Patrika*, a pro-Hindu paper, said: 'Hindus and Muslims must hang down their heads in shame that exhibitions of such unmitigated beastliness should have been allowed to occur in our modern city. The tallest among us must look small in the eyes of the outside world.'

There was blame for the holocaust to be apportioned. The *Statesman*, whose Editor at the time was reputed to be pro-Muslim, wrote: 'What befell India's largest city last week was no mere communal riot, as we have hitherto understood the sanguinary term. For three days, the city concentrated on unrestrained civil war. Upon whom the main guilt for it rests is manifest. There has been criticism of the Governor [Sir Frederick Burrows]. We do not think he has emerged particularly well. But none except a very great man holding his traditionally constitutional office during such a swift crisis could have done so. Where the primary blame lies is where we have squarely put it—upon the Provincial Muslim League Cabinet which carries responsbility for law and order in Bengal, and particularly upon the one able man of large administrative experience there, the Chief Minister [Suhrarwardy]. That in the whole of India the only Province where carnage occurred, on the League's professed peaceful

Direct Action Day, should have been in Bengal, where a League Ministry holds office, astounds us.'

Suhrarwardy himself made no statement in reply. It seems certain, from the actions he took later, that even he was appalled by the great massacre. Both Mr Nehru and Mr Jinnah were quick to condemn it. The Muslim League leader issued a statement saying: 'I unreservedly condemn the acts of violence and deeply sympathise with those who have suffered. At present I do not know who are responsible for the resultant loss of life and property which has been reported in the Press. Those who are guilty of resorting to indefensible conduct must be dealt with according to the law, as their actions, as far as the Muslim League is concerned, are contrary to instructions. They play into the hands of the enemy. They may be the actions of agents provocateurs.'

But though he may have condemned the orgy of violence, Mr Jinnah cannot have been anything but satisfied by the lessons that were inevitably drawn from it. Could anything prove more ruthlessly the validity of his claim that, in an independent India, Hindus and Muslims could no longer live together; that civil war would be the result?

One might have thought that the Indian leaders, Nehru of Congress and Jinnah of the League, would have come to Calcutta immediately and possibly shown themselves together to demonstrate their common abhorrence of violence and bloodshed for political purposes. But both of them were too busy for that. Mr Jinnah was in conference with the working committee of the Muslim League, planning new tactics in his fight with Congress. Pandit Nehru was holding the first meetings to pick the Cabinet (minus the Muslims) of the new interim Government.[1]

Only the Viceroy, Lord Wavell, came to Calcutta to mourn with its citizens and grieve at what he saw. It was he who listened to stories of how, in the midst of the carnage, when Muslim was killing Hindu, and Hindu Muslim, there had still been a gleam of light in the midst of the gloom. All over the city, examples were becoming known of Hindus who had died to save Muslims, of Muslims who had sheltered Hindus at the risk of their own lives and of how, towards the end, bands of mixed Muslim-Hindu young people had marched through the streets, dispersing mobs, crying *Hindu-Muslim ek ho* (Hindus and Muslims unite), with the flags of the Congress and the League tied together.

[1] Both Congress and Muslim leaders did go later—when rioting spread to Bihar.

It had been a moving demonstration that there was still some civilization left in the ugly city of Calcutta, and that there were still some Indians who could work and fight together, despite their religious differences. For them the bodies in the gutter were symbols of hope rather than despair, for they might jolt some sense of civilization—some common humanity—into the muddle-headed Muslims, Hindus and Sikhs of India.

There were many lessons, hard, bitter, bloody and practical lessons, to be learned from the massacre of August 1946.

A few weeks later, however, you would have found it difficult to believe that anyone (with the possible exception of Mahatma Gandhi) had taken any notice of them at all.

Not the Hindus. Not the Muslims. Not the British.

CHAPTER TWO

'THEY'VE SACKED ME, GEORGE'

IF IT COMES to a question of pinning down the exact day the Congress Party decided that they must get rid of Lord Wavell as Viceroy of India, a serious student would probably choose 27 August 1946.

That evening, Wavell called Gandhi and Nehru in to see him, and had they not been so concerned with their own affairs, they would have noticed that he was labouring under a burden of considerable distress. It has been noted before that the Viceroy was a man who did not find it easy to talk. He had no gift for conversation, and when he spoke it was because he had something important to say.

At the meeting on 27 August, he spoke at what, for him, was considerable length. 'I have just come back from Calcutta,' he said, 'and I am appalled at what I have seen.' He described to the two Hindu leaders the enormity of the crime against humanity and civilization which had been committed by Muslims and Hindus alike in Calcutta during recent days, and stressed the guiltiness of both communities for it. He admitted that, as an Englishman, he had no right to judge the actions of the Indian political parties, even though he condemned and was cast down by the barbarities which had been committed in their name.

But so long as he was Viceroy of India, he went on, he felt it necessary to do all in his power to prevent any more massacres of this kind. Neither as an Englishman nor as a human being could he stomach such savagery and bestiality. He would be abdicating his responsibilities if he did not make a supreme effort to bring the two communities, Hindu and Muslim, together and persuade them that working together was the only sure way to freedom.

'This,' he said to Gandhi and Nehru, 'is an appeal to you to help me to bring it about.'

While in Calcutta, Wavell had spent some time in consultation with a Muslim League leader named Khwaja Nazimmudin, who was a member of the League Working Committee and had the ear of Mr Jinnah. Nazimmudin had come forward with a proposition. The Cabinet Mission's Plan for Indian independence had been based on the idea of a Federal India based on three Groups: A (Hindu dominated), B (Muslim dominated) and C (with a slight domination in favour of the Muslims). The most important element in India would, of course, be Group A, controlled by an overwhelming majority of Hindus, which would always be more powerful than Groups B and C.

This was an arrangement which the Muslim League had accepted until Nehru's maladroit repudiation of the grouping scheme. Nazimmudin now proposed that Congress should make a declaration. They should announce that they had accepted the Cabinet Mission Plan not as *they* interpreted it, but as the Cabinet Mission had intended it. They should also guarantee that no minorities in the Groups should be allowed to opt out of them before the ten-year period specified by the Cabinet Mission Plan. The scheme, in other words, should be given a chance to work.

In these circumstances, Nazimmudin told Wavell, the Muslim League might reconsider its rejection of the scheme and decide to come into the interim Government.

Wavell put the question frankly to Gandhi and Nehru: *Will you give me the guarantee the Muslim League is asking for?*

He was almost immediately plunged into the most difficult argument he had ever had with Gandhi, who chose this day to be at his most polemical and devious. Here was a saint who could, in his ashram, dispense great wisdom and counsel tolerance, understanding and the necessity to give rather than take. But on this evening he spoke purely and simply as a Congress politician.

'Give me a simple guarantee that you accept the Cabinet Mission Plan,' asked Wavell.

'We have already said that we accept it,' replied Gandhi, 'but we are not prepared to guarantee that we accept it in the way that the Cabinet Mission set it out. We have our own interpretations of what they propose.'

Said Wavell: 'Even if those interpretations differ from what the Cabinet Mission intended?'

Replied Gandhi: 'But of course. In any case, what the Cabinet Mission Plan really means is not what the Cabinet Mission thinks but what the interim Government thinks it means.'

Wavell pointed out that the interim Government's opinion, as things were at the moment, would almost inevitably be pro-

Congress and anti-Muslim League, since the League was boycotting the Government. How could it be unbiased?

Gandhi replied that he was not concerned with bias. He was simply concerned with the legal basis of the discussion. Legally, this was a matter for the interim Government to decide. Once the interim Government was in power, such matters as the Muslim League's ambitions and artificial anxieties could be voted upon; but not before.

'But don't you see,' exploded Wavell, in an unusual burst of temper, 'it will be a Congress Government! They are bound to be lacking in impartiality.'

Pandit Nehru interrupted at this point. 'You misunderstand the composition of the Congress Party, your Excellency, not, I may say, for the first time. The Congress is not pro-Hindu or anti-Muslim. It is for all the peoples of India. It will never legislate against the interests of the Muslims.'

Replied Wavell: 'But whose Muslims, Pandit Nehru? Yours, the Congress Muslims, the so-called stooges? Or those of the Muslim League? Can't you see that the necessity of this moment is to satisfy the Muslim League that you are not trying to do them down? It is a moment—possibly the last we have—to bring the League and the Congress together. And all I ask is a guarantee. Will the Congress commit itself to a declaration, a declaration which will satisfy the Muslim League and assure the continuation of a stable and unitary government?' He reached into his drawer and pulled out a paper. 'This is what I have in mind.'

The declaration ran thus: 'The Congress are prepared in the interests of communal harmony to accept the intention of the statement of 16 May [the Cabinet Mission statement] that provinces cannot exercise any option affecting their membership of the sections or of the groups if formed, until the decision contemplated in paragraph 19 (vii) of the Statement of 16 May is taken by the new legislature after the new constitutional arrangements have come into operation and the first general elections have been held.'[1]

Gandhi handed it over to Nehru, who read it through and said:

'To accept this is tantamount to asking Congress to put itself in fetters.'

Wavell replied:

'So far as the Cabinet Mission Plan is concerned, that is what I

[1] Government of India Records.

feel you should do. When Congress accepted the Cabinet Mission Plan in the first place, I cannot believe that you did so not knowing its implications. If so, why did you accept it at all? The plan for dividing the country into groups was implicit. You cannot now turn round and say that you did not realize that is what was intended.'

Gandhi: 'What the Cabinet Mission intended and the way we interpret what they intended may not necessarily be the same.'

'This is lawyer's talk,' said Wavell. 'Talk to me in plain English. I am a simple soldier and you confuse me with these legalistic arguments.'

Nehru: 'We cannot help it if we are lawyers.'

Wavell: 'No, but you can talk to me like honest men who are interested in India's future and welfare. Dammit, the Cabinet Mission made its intentions as clear as daylight. Surely we don't need to go to law about that or split legal hairs, either. As a plain man, the situation seems to me simple. If Congress will give me the guarantee for which I ask, I think I can persuade Mr Jinnah and the Muslim League to reconsider their refusal to join the interim Government. We need them in the Government; India needs them, and, if you are seriously concerned over the dangers of civil war—and you must know as well as I that the danger is great—then you need them too. In the circumstances, I feel that it would be unwise, even perilous, if I allowed Congress to form an interim Government on its own.'

Gandhi: 'But you have already announced that the Government will come into being. You cannot go back on your word now.'

Wavell: 'The situation has changed. As a result of the killings in Calcutta, India is on the verge of civil war. It is my duty to prevent it. I will not prevent it if I allow Congress to form a Government which excludes the Muslims: they will then decide that Direct Action is the only way, and we shall have the massacre of Bengal all over again.'

Nehru: 'In other words, you are willing to surrender to the Muslim League's blackmail.'

Wavell (with great heat): 'For God's sake, man, who are you to talk of blackmail?'

So far as Nehru and Gandhi were concerned, it was the end of Wavell as a Viceroy with whom they could deal. That night both of them sat down to write letters. Gandhi first penned a cable to Mr Attlee, the Labour Prime Minister, in which he expressed concern over the Viceroy's state of mind. He was, he said, 'unnerved owing to the Bengal tragedy'. He needed to be bolstered by 'an abler and legal mind'. He followed this with a letter to Wavell in which he said:

'Several times last evening you repeated that you were a "plain man and a soldier" and that you did not know the law. We are all plain men though we may not all be soldiers and even though some of us may know the law. It is our purpose, I take it, to devise methods to prevent a repetition of the recent terrible happenings in Calcutta. The question before us is how best to do it. Your language last evening was minatory. As representative of the King, you cannot afford to be a military man only, nor to ignore the law, much less the law of your own making. You should be assisted, if necessary, by a legal mind enjoying your full confidence. You threatened not to convene the Constituent Assembly, if the formula you placed before Pandit Nehru and me was not acted upon by Congress. If such be really the case then you should not have made the announcement you did on 12 August [asking Congress to form a government] . . .'[1]

Wavell had made the point that if Congress formed a government on its own, the Muslim League would reply with Direct Action. This would result in further massacres, and British troops would have to intervene to restore order; a possibility, at this juncture, which he was desperately anxious to avoid. Gandhi's reply to this was a typical example of Gandhian reasoning of the kind which made Wavell writhe. *If the Viceroy was really worried about having to use British forces to preserve order,* his argument ran, *the solution was simple. Withdraw them. Leave the matter of keeping the peace to the Congress.* It did not seem to occur to Gandhi that such a peace would be a Congress-imposed peace, and the Muslims might well get short shrift from it.

'If British arms are kept here for internal peace and order,' Gandhi wrote, 'your interim Government would be reduced to a farce. The Congress cannot afford to impose its will on warring elements in India through the use of British arms. Nor can the Congress be expected to bend itself and adopt what it considers a wrong course because of the brutal exhibition recently witnessed in Bengal. Such submission would itself lead to an encouragement and repetition of such tragedies. The vindictive spirit on either side would go deeper, biding for an opportunity to exhibit itself more fiercely and more disgracefully when occasion occurs. And

[1] Pyarelal, *Gandhi: The Last Phase.*

all this will be chiefly due to the continued presence in India of a foreign power strong in and proud of its arms.'[1]

Now this was nonsense, and Nehru and the other leaders of the Congress Party knew it, even if Gandhi did not. They had been vociferous in their complaints about the dilatoriness of British military intervention in Calcutta. The strong-man of the party, Sardar Patel, had been to see the Viceroy several times to request military help in restoring order in Bihar, where the Hindus had begun to rape, kill and mutilate in reprisal for their losses in Calcutta. And Congress knew only too well that peace in the Punjab, where there were 16,000,000 Muslims and 12,000,000 non-Muslims, was maintained only because of the tight control exercised by the Governor, Sir Evan Jenkins, and the weapon of British military intervention should trouble begin.

To suggest that the British should withdraw their armies at this moment, when Hindu-Muslim relations were wider apart than ever before, was a counsel no Viceroy could possibly have accepted. To Wavell it seemed more necessary than ever that the British, before departing, should somehow bring the two opposing sides together in some sort of government, so that they might fight out their differences in the debating chamber rather than the back alleys; that he would be abdicating his responsibility if he allowed Congress to form a government and impose its will, so long as there was a remote chance that the Muslim League could be persuaded to co-operate.

For this attitude he was publicly dubbed pro-Muslim by Gandhi (though he apologized and withdrew the charge later). Pandit Nehru made the same accusation, but he did so in private letters to a number of friends in Britain. Nehru was always a firm believer in negotiation by private correspondence. He had a large number of friends, most of them Liberal or Left Wing, and they had been of considerable help in adumbrating the policies of Congress even during the wartime Coalition Government. Now, with a Labour Government in power, they had the ear of the Cabinet and were influential in forming Government opinion. No one could possibly blame Nehru for the tactics he used; as a politician who believed that Congress was right, that Jinnah was a threat to Indian freedom, he was, of course, justified in using every shot in his locker to smash him. And if one of the shots brought down the Viceroy, so much the better, from his viewpoint. So with

[1] Pyarelal, Op. cit.

great eloquence and assiduity, he pointed out in letter after letter —sure that the purport would be conveyed to 10 Downing Street—that though Wavell was an honest man and a sincere man, he was a weak man, too. He had lost all flexibility of mind and, in his desire to appease Mr Jinnah and the Muslim League, was rapidly leading India to disaster. This, Nehru maintained, was mainly because his two principal advisers, the only two who had any real influence upon him, were enemies of the Congress Party and strongly pro-Muslim and sought every opportunity of manœuvring Wavell into situations where he favoured the Muslim League at the expense of Congress, and of India. He called these two the 'English mullahs' and named them as Sir Francis Mudie (then Governor of Bombay) and Mr (later Sir) George Abell, the Viceroy's private secretary. Between them, Nehru maintained, they had succeeded in persuading the Viceroy that an interim Government must under no circumstances be formed unless the Muslim League came into it; and their reason was, in the case of Mudie, to help his Muslim friends, and, in the case of Abell, because he believed that the British were justified in remaining in India and postponing their promise of Indian independence.

There was certainly some truth in the charge that Sir Francis Mudie was strongly anti-Congress and was a perfervid supporter of Jinnah and Pakistan. Abell's attitude could possibly be summed up as: 'A plague on both your houses.' He had less patience than Wavell and grew increasingly exasperated with the twists and turns, the conspiracies, the dialectics and the spate of exhortatory chatter in which both Hindus and Muslims indulged. But the idea that either had any important influence on Wavell's thinking is to under-estimate the mind of the man, and the independence of his judgement. The only thing which was influencing him at this time was the thought of bloodshed. Calcutta had impressed itself upon him like a stigma. He was appalled at what Indian could do to Indian. The disgust he felt was great; the stench of evil was never out of his nostrils; but as yet it was not great enough to persuade him that there was only one way out for Britain—to cut the cable and let India drift away to perdition on her own.

At home in Britain the propaganda was beginning to do its work. In official Labour Party circles the Viceroy now had few friends left. Mr Attlee had little confidence in him. 'If I could find a better man,' he confided to friends, who confided it to Congress, 'I would replace him.' He was so lacking in understanding of the communal position that Gandhi's suggestion that Wavell needed the aid of 'an abler and legal mind' provoked the remark: 'What's wrong with Nehru? He's a lawyer, isn't he?' He might just as well have suggested Jinnah, who was a lawyer too. Only the Secretary of State for India, Lord Pethick Lawrence, continued to sympathize with Wavell's viewpoint and never failed to write him letters of cogent advice and warm appreciation of his sincere attempts to bring about some sort of *rapprochement*. Pethick Lawrence was far from being pro-Muslim. Jinnah's intractability had sorely tried his patience when they had met earlier in the year. But he saw what Mr Attlee apparently could not see: that there could be no peace, and no future, unless Congress—as the strongest party—made some gesture that would show the Indian Muslims (if not Mr Jinnah and the League) that they genuinely wanted to co-operate and were sincere in their assertions that independent India would not become simply a Hindu raj.

It is not the intention of this book to deal play by play, blow by blow, with the events in India during Wavell's term as Viceroy. The background of events is given here merely to set the scene for the drama that was to follow. So much of the futile squabbling, the litigious argument, the divagations of Congress, the mulishness of Jinnah, the cloudy idealism of Gandhi had no more effect on the eventual outcome than the chatter of birds in a thunderstorm. India in 1946 was a cauldron steeped in every ingredient calculated to produce the worst kind of noxious brew—obstinacy, venom, malevolence, anger, violence, jealousy and resentment. Absent in all hearts was the milk of human kindness. No one —not even Gandhi—was being generous that year.

And perhaps greatest of all the impediments to a solution was mistrust. Jinnah and the Muslim League mistrusted Congress. Congress mistrusted the Viceroy. The Viceroy mistrusted the Government at home, particularly Mr Attlee. Mr Attlee did not necessarily mistrust the Viceroy, but he had certainly lost faith in him. Just before the end of August 1946, he showed it. In a private telegram, he told Lord Wavell that he was overruling him. Wavell still wished to postpone the swearing-in of the interim Government until the Muslim League could be persuaded to join it. He was convinced that dogged effort and determination— plus a little Congress generosity and increasing pressure upon

Jinnah—would get them in. Attlee said that further delay would only exacerbate the tempers of the Congress Party leaders and perhaps lead to a definite break between them and the British authorities, as a result of which civil disobedience and anti-British agitation might once more sweep the country. This was a profound misreading of the state of mind of the Congress leaders; for civil disobedience would mean that they would go to jail again, and, as Nehru pointed out to the author—'We were tired men. We were not prepared to go to jail again.' The British Prime Minister did not, however, realize this. He ordered Wavell to bring the interim Government into being, and on 2 September 1946 it was sworn in. Five stooges were sworn in as 'caretaker' ministers until such time as the Muslim League decided to enter the Government.

The defeat for the Viceroy was considerable. The British Government, by overruling him, had demonstrated to Congress that they no longer had any confidence in him. From this moment on, neither side in India—Hindus nor Muslims—needed to consider him as a vital figure in their negotiations. It is perhaps difficult to imagine Mr Attlee in the role of Delilah, but by his action of August 1946, he lopped Wavell of most of his strength and left him practically helpless in the face of the increasingly intransigent communal leaders with whom he had to deal. Wavell in this hour of personal humiliation showed remarkable lack of resentment. His instinct was to resign at once, but he was aware of the difficult problem which would confront the British Government if he took this action, and of the crisis it might well provoke in India. He stayed on. He went on with the wearisome round of interviews, with Nehru, Jinnah, Liaquat Ali Khan, though he rarely saw Gandhi after this. (The Mahatma had gone to Bihar and Bengal to start his great, saintly, and marvellously effective crusade against communal violence.) With Nehru, Jinnah, Liaquat, he flew to London for an abortive conference with Mr Attlee and Lord Pethick Lawrence. He was definitely the odd man out on this expedition: Nehru made a great impression with the inner circles of the Labour Government, who were inclined (with the possible exception of Mr Ernest Bevin) to accept the Congress point of view and had little or no sympathy for the rigid, frigid, intractable Jinnah. Jinnah, on the other hand, found considerable support among the members of the Tory Party, and he stayed on after the conference was over to make speeches about Pakistan which won quite a number of converts to his viewpoint. Wavell's position was rather like the guest at the family conference who has to be invited because he is the titular head of the clan but has long since been considered a bit of a bore and a nuisance. 'I felt like a poor relation,' he said when he got back to India.

The conference in London hardened the attitudes of both Congress and the Muslim League, rather than made them more flexible. The bloody riots which were now beginning to spread across India and the increasing tension between the two communities were doing Jinnah's work for him. He could now say: 'Even the Hindus need Pakistan—if only to save their own people from this continual slaughter and destruction.' There were those even in the Congress Party who were beginning to agree with him, but they did not include either Gandhi or Nehru, and these were the two who were still the most potent influences on Congress thinking.

As he wrestled with mounting problems of communal agitation, political stubbornness and the legal 'double talk' of the Hindu and Muslim leaders, Wavell became firmer than ever in one thing: that though the problem of India's political future now seemed insuperable, he himself would never be responsible for splitting the land, its people and its army in two. From his viewpoint, there seemed to be now only one way out: a gradual withdrawal of the British administration from India so that bloc by bloc, province by province, the Indians would be faced with the responsibility of settling their own future and making their own peace with each other.

With the help of Mr George Abell, his chief adviser, and a number of British members of the administration, he drew up a plan which might, from its nature, be called Operation Ebb-Tide. It was a plan which, admittedly, contained the fundamental admission that Britain's day in India was drawing to a close. It was, briefly, a scheme to withdraw British troops and British administration stage by stage from India; but it was by no means a policy of cut-and-run such as some of Wavell's critics have since described it. Winston Churchill, for instance, was furious when he heard about it. In India, such administrators as Sir Evan Jenkins in the Punjab and General Auchinleck, the Commander in Chief of the Indian Army, were strongly against it—in the case of Jenkins because he thought it would not work, and in the case of Auchinleck because he believed that Britain still had a solemn duty to perform in India, and in spite of the clamour and killings, must not be panicked into withdrawal.

Operation Ebb-Tide was, however, no panic move. As Wavell visualized it, the process of British retreat would never be precipitate. No province would be left until conditions of reasonable safety and security had been gained. But the Operation would make clear, to Indian leaders particularly, that the British were on their way out and they must make a supreme effort to learn to live together before they were left to their own devices.

Wavell despatched Operation Ebb-Tide to Mr Attlee for the consideration of the Cabinet early in 1947. In view of the decision which was taken later, their reaction to it was remarkable. They sheered away from it like frightened rabbits. As Wavell said later, in a letter to King George VI: 'their chief difficulty was their reluctance to face Parliament with any proposal which would make it clear that we were withdrawing our control very shortly.' They were afraid of the right-wing members of their own Party, they were afraid of the Tories, and they were particularly afraid of Winston Churchill. They dropped Wavell's plan like a hot potato (though very soon afterwards, they were to pick up an even hotter one). Of Operation Ebb-Tide, Earl Attlee (as he had then become) said:

'Wavell was pretty defeatist by then. He produced a plan worked out by his Indian Civil Service advisers for the evacuation of India, with everybody moving from where they were by stages right up through the Ganges valley till eventually, apparently, they would be collected at Karachi and Bombay, and sail away. Well, I thought that was what Winston would certainly quite properly describe as an ignoble and sordid scuffle and I wouldn't look at it.'

In the light of what happened later, these are not only hard words but unfair ones, too. They were also unstatesmanlike and ignorant. There is good reason to believe that Operation Ebb-Tide might not only have worked, but might have saved hundreds of thousands of lives. It would have been welcomed by the Congress Party and, with some reservations, by Jinnah and the Muslim League. The battle cry of Congress was still 'Quit India!' and, as Gandhi's biographer and close associate, Pyarelal, says, Gandhi would have welcomed it as a very fair challenge 'provided the British Government were ready to transfer full power to Indian hands and withdraw their forces from Indian soil with grace and goodwill'. It is true that the Muslim League's watchword was 'Divide and Quit!' But Wavell's plan would have made adequate arrangement for the protection of minorities during the period of withdrawal and the predominantly Muslim areas of India would be those to which the British would retreat, thus protecting the Muslims until some *modus vivendi* could be reached during the interim period. Among some of the British concerned with Wavell's plan, it was estimated that to preserve peace in India while it was in operation would cost some 30,000 lives. The enormity of this figure caused a number of them to have second thoughts, though it would seem like a mere drop in the ocean of Indian mortality a little over a year later.

In any case, the Labour Government would have none of it. So far as Mr Attlee was concerned, it was the end of Wavell as Viceroy. On the morning of 19 February 1947 the Viceroy was having breakfast with George Abell, when the dispatches were brought in. One of the cables marked 'private and confidential' was handed to the Viceroy, who opened it, read it through, and then went on eating his egg. Abell was on sufficiently close terms with his Chief to realize, from the set of Wavell's face, that something had happened, and he waited to be told. There was five minutes' silence. At last, Abell said:

'Anything important, sir?'

Wavell: 'They've sacked me, George.' A long pause, and then: 'They were quite right, I suppose.'

I doubt if history will agree with him.

On 20 February 1947, Mr Attlee announced in the House of Commons that power would be transferred into the hands of a responsible Indian Government by a date not later than June 1948. He also announced the resignation of Lord Wavell as Viceroy and his replacement by Admiral Viscount Mountbatten. His tribute to Wavell's unrelaxing efforts was polite but cool. As he said afterwards, 'I came to the conclusion that Wavell had shot his bolt.' There was no mention of Operation Ebb-Tide, or of the fact that Wavell had faced the implications of the Indian dilemma long before Attlee. He announced simply that in return for his services, the retiring Viceroy had been raised in the peerage (that usual British reward for failure or disagreement) to the rank of Earl. Wavell characteristically was too polite to refuse the preferment. For the next few weeks, he went on doggedly with his job in Delhi, still listening to the Indian leaders, still exhorting the Congress to be generous, still urging the Muslims to be statesmanlike. The only comment he ever made (and that was in private conversation) was, bitterly: 'I always get the dirty end of the stick, don't I, George?'

June 1948. A definite date had now been set by the Labour Government for the transfer of British power in India. For Congress, it was a matter for jubilation.

'The clear and definite declaration that the final transference of power will take place by a date not later than June 1948', declared Nehru, 'not only removes all misconceptions and suspicions, but also brings reality and a certain dynamic quality to the present situation in India ... It is a challenge to all of us, and we shall try to meet it bravely in the spirit of that challenge.'

Mr Jinnah's reaction was shorter. 'For the moment I refuse to comment,' he said, 'except to say that the Muslim League will not yield an inch in its demand for Pakistan.'

There were those in Britain who condemned the announcement of a time-limit as, in the words of Sir John Anderson, 'a gamble and an unjustifiable gamble'. Viscount Templewood forecast rioting and bloodshed and Lord Simon that 'the end of this business is not going to be the establishment of peace in India, but rather that it is going to degrade the British name.' For Winston Churchill, to whom the Congress Party had always been a rabble and Gandhi a little agitator in a nightshirt, the announcement had the effect of an incendiary bomb on a load of hay. 'In handing over the Government of India to these so-called political classes,' he said, 'we are handing over to men of straw of whom in a few years no trace will remain.' He suggested that instead of fixing a date for withdrawal, the aid of the United Nations should be called in. 'Many have defended Britain against their foes,' he ended, 'none can defend her against herself. But at least let us not add—by shameful flight, by a premature hurried scuttle—at least let us not add to the pangs of sorrow so many of us feel, the taint and smear of shame.'

Those were extravagant words which, for once, stirred few hearts in Parliament and fell on deaf ears throughout the rest of the world, where the attitude would be summed up in the words: 'So Britain's giving away India in June 1948. Thank goodness that's over.'

But it wasn't over, of course. And for those who, as the Hindu historian V. P. Menon has pointed out, 'even in India . . . considered it a leap in the dark,' and a hurried one too, there were shocks to come.

Mr Attlee had chosen Lord Mountbatten as the new Viceroy because 'he was an extremely lively, exciting personality. He had an extraordinary faculty for getting on with all kinds of people, as he had shown when he was Supremo in South East Asia. He was also blessed with a very unusual wife.'

He had another quality, too. When he was given a job, he did not like to dawdle on it. Other men might hesitate or cautiously ponder the problem. Mountbatten believed in driving things through, by short cuts if there were any. He approached the problem of Indian independence by June 1948, rather in the manner of a time-and-motion-study expert who has been called into a factory to knock off the wasteful minutes and get out the product before the target date.

CHAPTER THREE

THE MEN WHO MATTERED

JUST WHO WERE the men who mattered in India in 1947?

So far in this narrative we have been catching up with events and have spent little time studying the character and background of the men who made them. It might be useful at this juncture to do exactly what Lord Mountbatten did before he departed for India, and consider with just what sort of leaders and organizations he would have to deal.

There are, of course, many personalities and parties who played their part in the drama of independence who have not yet even been mentioned. They will now begin to figure increasingly in this story, for better or for worse, and it would be as well to know what they were, in order to understand what they did and why.

As must have become clear by this time, the fight for Indian freedom had become by 1947 not so much a battle between Indians and British, but between Indians (Congress) and Indians (the Muslim League), with the British acting as a sort of combatant referee—sometimes intervening in an effort to ensure fair play, sometimes surreptitiously planting a rabbit punch of their own. In addition (to continue the boxing metaphor) the corners of the ring were manned by seconds who were also belligerently inclined, and who, at frequent intervals, dived in to mix it with the two main contenders and turn the title-fight into a free-for-all.

The most frequent and pusillanimous of these were undoubtedly the Sikhs, though their numbers (4,500,000) were small compared with many of the other bodies and organizations involved. The Sikh people were concentrated in the province of the Punjab, the land of the Five Rivers, in the North West of India, and though they were outnumbered in the province by 16,000,000 Muslims and 7,500,000 Hindus, psychologically, economically and socially they could always be relied upon to make their presence felt. They have always been India's most martial race and were the last to be subdued by the conquering British; since which time (until Independence) they supplied some of their bravest soldiers to that remarkable instrument of the might of the British Raj, the Indian Army. In the Punjab they built a system of canals, which spread out from the Five Rivers in a great irrigation network which made the land smile and turned the province into the granary of India. They were not only good farmers but, unlike their neighbours, good with machines; and they had a corner in most of the transport (as well as providing drivers, mechanics and policemen for the rest of India).

Religiously the Sikhs differ both from the Muslims and the Hindus and are fiercely proud of the difference. They believe in an indefinable Super Being or God whose principles and tenets have been brought to earth by a succession of ten holy men or *gurus*, most of whom were also extremely doughty fighters. The places where the *gurus* breathed their last (usually in battles against the Moghuls and Muslims) are principally in Northern India, the most important being in Western Punjab at Nankhana Sahib. Their Rome, Mecca, Canterbury, call it what you will, is the fabulous Golden Temple at Amritsar, set in a holy lake or tank filled with enormous carp and orfe. But like the other temples or gurdwaras where the Sikhs go to pay their religious respects, the Golden Temple is open to anyone of any religion and a pilgrim can always find food there and shelter for the night (though in times of trouble, a Muslim would have been foolhardy to go near one). Anyone can join the Sikhs by conversion. It is not a 'difficult' religion in the sense that there is a great deal of ritual or dogma to be learned, but of its male converts it demands five things and the rejection of another. These are known as the five 'K's'—*kes* or the long hair and beard which distinguishes Sikhs from all other Indians (and makes a male swimming pool filled with bathing Sikhs a wondrous sight to behold); *kanghi* or a comb to be worn in the hair; *kach* or short underdrawers; *karra* or a steel or iron bracelet on the right wrist; and *kirpan* or a short but highly lethal knife. These, except possibly the *kanghi* when swimming, must be worn at all times.[1]

A Sikh may drink any liquor he likes, but he is expressly forbidden to smoke. There was a riot in Bombay some years ago when a newspaper published a cartoon showing a Sikh smoking a hookah. There are some Sikhs who have started to cut their hair and shave their beards, but they usually live in the big cities outside the Punjab and are wryly known as 'mechanised Sikhs'.

---

[1] This naturally created a crisis whenever there were riots in an area which included Sikhs, for they could always cry religious persecution if the authorities forbade them to carry their knives, or *kirpans*.

On the eve of Mountbatten's arrival, the Sikhs felt themselves to be the odd men out in the struggle for Indian independence. Most of their four and a half millions were spread throughout all parts of the Punjab, and some of their most costly irrigation canals and richest farming lands were in the extreme West of the province. Their relations with their Muslim neighbours were already strained and there had been a massacre of Sikhs in Rawalpindi shortly before Mountbatten's arrival. The Sikhs made no bones about their antipathy to the Muslims; the Muslims were equally plain in their envy of the Sikhs. *What is going to happen to us*, asked the Sikhs, *when independence comes? If Jinnah gets Pakistan, the Punjab—or, at the least, Western Punjab—will go to him. We could never live as a minority under the Muslims. But if we don't what will happen to our lands, our houses, our canals—and our shrines? Or if freedom comes in the form of the Cabinet Mission Plan, what then? The Punjab will go into the Group B provinces, which will be Muslim dominated. They will grind us down.*

The two political leaders of the Sikhs in the Punjab were Baldev Singh, who had been given the portfolio of Defence in the interim Government, and Gianni Khartar Singh. But the man to be reckoned with in the days to come was neither of these, but an old man with a white beard, twinkling brown eyes, a voice like a dove in conversation and like a hawk in public speech, with a fierce hatred of the Muslims and an ambition to be the first head of a new independent State called Khalistan. His name was Master Tara Singh. 'Whatever is decided in Delhi,' cried Tara Singh, 'will leave my people like no man's children in no man's land!'

Tara Singh was a *guru* who had earned the courtesy title of Master for his knowledge of the Granth Sahib, the Sikh scripture which is lodged in the Golden Temple, and for his teaching of the Sikh way of life, which he once summed up as: 'To eschew idolatry, caste exclusiveness, the burning of widows (suttee), the immurement of women for adultery, the immoderate use of wine and drugs, tobacco smoking, the killing of infants, slander, bathing in the sacred tanks of the Hindus; and to promote loyalty, gratitude, philanthropy, impartiality, justice for all, truth, honesty, decency and gentleness.'

It will be seen later in this story that Master Tara Singh did not always follow these tenets himself, and could, when the occasion presented itself, be an extremely bloodthirsty old man. He was 71 years old in 1947.

Dr Bhimrao Ramji Ambedkar was 54, and, as representative of 50,000,000 Indians or one-seventh of the population of the country, might be thought to be one of the most powerful politicians in the land. The Indians whom Ambedkar led were, however, the Untouchables or, as they were dubbed by the British, the 'Scheduled Castes',[1] and it was one thing to have them as followers and another to persuade them to utilize their undoubted strength at the polling booths. The lot of the Untouchables is somewhat better in India today; they can get jobs in the Government and, in the towns, are allowed to go to school; and there is even an ordinance which provides them with carts so that they need no longer carry away 'night soil,' as excrement is called, on their heads. But in 1947 the lot of the bulk of India's Untouchables was frightful.

In the caste society of the Hindus, they were literally the outcasts. They believed in Hindu gods, but no temple was open to them in which to worship. Their children were not allowed in the schools. They could not use the burning *ghats* to cremate their dead, but had to put them on their own meagre fires, for which there was never enough fuel; so the vultures got them. Theirs were always the menial jobs—the sweepers, the laundry-men, leather workers (all religiously despised trades)—and the future for them and their children was predestined. They could never hope to rise to better things. In country districts, where caste was strictly observed, they had to retreat to a safe distance whenever a man of caste came by, in case their shadow should fall upon him and defile him. In the South, such was their power to defile that they were only—on pain of beating, starvation, or denial of left-over water from Hindu households—able to move out of their huts at night.

Most Englishmen who watched the caste system at work in India, particularly its appalling degradation of the lowest orders, wondered why the Untouchables never left their religion and became Christians or Muslims. In fact, many of them did. But the bulk of India's 50,000,000 Untouchables were, in spite of everything, devout Hindus who believed in their religion; and therefore believed that if only they bore the sufferings and humiliations of this life with patience, they would be born to better things in the next reincarnation.

Such a cowed and submissive section of humanity would hardly

[1] Gandhi called them *Harijans*, or Children of God.

seem fertile material for an ambitious politician, and, until Dr Ambedkar came along, it was not. Most of the Untouchables did what the local Hindu politicians told them to, and voted for Congress. And then in their midst appeared a man who was a living proof that there was hope of improvement in this life, even for an Untouchable. Ambedkar was an Untouchable himself. As a child begging at a race meeting he caught the eye of one of the Gaekwars of Baroda, who was touched by his brightness and quick intelligence, paid for his schooling, and eventually sent him to Columbia University, New York. Thereafter, he studied in Germany and Britain (at the London School of Economics) and returned to India a lawyer (yes, another!) with an ambition to rise in the Civil Service. He got a job as a clerk. Immediately, all the other clerks boycotted him. He roamed around Western India doing a variety of jobs, all of which ended (sometimes abruptly, with a beating) when it was discovered that he was an Untouchable.

By this time he was an embittered man. Burning with hatred against the Hindu Caste system, he resolved to attack it through the Untouchables and he formed a party to represent them, which soon gained large support in the bigger cities. The British began to take an interest in him. They sent him to London to represent the Untouchables at the Round Table Conference, a move which shrewdly cut across Congress's claims to represent all Indians, or even all Hindus.

Ambedkar's aim was to draw the Untouchables away from Hinduism and turn them into a party which, like the Muslims, would be put on a separate electoral roll at the elections and given 'weightage'. This would have immediately turned them into a Third Force along with the Congress and the Muslim League and have made them a power in the land. He succeeded to the extent that in 1932 the British administration announced that a separate roll for the Scheduled Castes was about to be established.

Congress awoke to the danger, for they did not want 50,000,000 Hindus in an anti-Congress camp—and Ambedkar's inclinations were definitely anti-Congress. Gandhi was called in. He began his famous fast for the Untouchables which, though ostensibly for religious purposes to better their lot, certainly had the added political purpose of persuading them that Congress was for them. The British called off their decision to give the Untouchables a separate electoral roll, and Gandhi called off his fast; but Ambedkar got an increased representation for his people.

By 1947 he was a quick-tempered, surly and suspicious leader, who had lost some of his hold on the Untouchables, thanks to Gandhi's efforts, but was in the market to make a deal with whichever side—Muslim League or Congress—could offer him the best position of influence.

Even before Independence there were two Indias, not one. There was British India, ruled by the Viceroy from Delhi and with British Governors in all its eleven provinces, but with an interim Government composed entirely of Indians elected by the people at the polls. This was the India where Congress and the Muslim League wrangled, and where Gandhi, Nehru and Jinnah moved freely, spoke freely, worked freely—though not yet as freely as they wished.

There was also the India of the Princely States. In area, the States covered two-fifths of the sub-Continent. In population, they contained something over 80,000,000, or just under a quarter of India's total population. There were 601 Princely and native States in all, ranging in size from the vast kingdom of Hyderabad in Central India, with 14,000,000 people and a territory bigger than Britain minus Scotland, to several small States in Kathiawar, West India, with only 900 people and less than ten square miles of land. They were ruled by maharanas, maharajahs, nawabs, rajahs, jagadirs, and by a Gaekwar (of Baroda), a Jam Sahib (of Nawanager), a Nizam (of Hyderabad), and a Wali (of Swat). They were rich and they were poor. The Nizam of Hyderabad was so rich that he could afford to be a miser. The Maharajah of Kashmir was so rich that he bought hundreds of concubines and dancing girls at £20-£50,000 apiece and once paid £150,000 (in blackmail) for one hour with a female crook in a London hotel bedroom. The rajahs and jagadirs of the Deccan States were so poor that they lived on less than £80 a year.

There were good princes and there were bad princes. The Maharajah of Mysore ran a model state on such civilized lines that the standard of living of his people was far above that of the rest of India. The Maharajah of Travancore was so enlightened that he opened his Hindu temples to Untouchables—a bold step indeed in caste-ridden Southern India. The Maharajah of Kashmir on the other hand, though 95 per cent of his people were Muslims, ran his state as a strictly Hindu kingdom and the beef-eating Muslims got seven years in jail if they were caught killing a cow.

The Nawab of Junagadh spent more money per year on his kennels of dogs than on hospitals. The Maharajah of Alwar once poured petrol over a race horse and set fire to it when it failed to win. And a large portion of the princes spent more time in Monte Carlo, Paris and London than they ever did in their own palaces.

Yet all these Princes had one thing in common. They were independent of Delhi and of any laws passed by the Government in Delhi. They acknowledged only one paramount authority, and that was the British Crown, whose foreign policy they agreed to accept and follow; and though the British retained the right to intervene in the affairs of the Princely States, they rarely did so unless a Maharajah created a public scandal—and even then, it all depended upon what kind of a public scandal. He could spend most of his country's income on wild living, so long as he did not flaunt his extravagance too boldly in the state, but saved them for Bombay and points abroad; he could dally with cocottes abroad, so long as he did not bring them back with him (though Indian cocottes were allowed); he could even burn racehorses, so long as he did not do it too often; and get away with murder, so long as it was not too openly committed. He had his own private army, he ran and took the revenues from the Customs between his state and British India, the profits from the post-offices (sometimes he printed his own stamps and minted his own money), the rents from the railways which passed through his state. He decided what system of justice should prevail in his courts (which often meant none at all), what taxes his people should pay, what schools and hospitals they might attend, what jobs they might have.

He ruled, in fact, like a feudal monarch of olden times, and, even in the more enlightened States, he was the absolute arbiter of his people's destiny.

This anachronistic agglomeration of Princes had another thing in common besides its separation from British India, and that was fear—fear that when freedom came to British India, the States would be absorbed against their will, their titles abolished, their personal power and privileges lopped away, their vast private fortunes suddenly made subject to taxes. In the circumstances, few of them wished for freedom to come to India at all, though the more enlightened of them realized that it was inevitable. For self-protection they had formed themselves, some years before the war, into a Chamber of Princes by which they hoped to present a combined front in face of the political agitations and developments germinating just beyond their frontiers. The Chancellor of the Chamber of Princes in 1947, when Mountbatten arrived as Viceroy, was a Muslim, the Nawab of Bhopal, and in this royal trade union Bhopal was the chief shop steward with whom the new Viceroy would have to deal.[1] He was a shrewd and able negotiator who had inherited his throne from his mother in 1926 (she abdicated in his favour to prevent another claimant from getting it), and had since run his State with a firm but autocratic hand. India's Princes usually counted their importance in terms of the number of gun salutes they were entitled to receive on ceremonial occasions. There were five 21-gun States, Hyderabad, Mysore, Baroda, Kashmir, and Gwalior. Bhopal was a 19-gun prince, which put him above such rivals as Jaipur, Jodhpur and Bikaner, and this, plus a driving personality, made him a potent influence in a body whose members were apt to be as lackadaisical and apathetic as some trade union members in Britain and America.

Bhopal realized the inevitability of independence, regrettable though that might be. He set out to use the Chamber of Princes as an instrument through which he would make the position of the States *vis-à-vis* an independent India absolutely clear when the transfer of power came. This he achieved when the Cabinet Mission came to India in 1946. Sir Stafford Cripps (and subsequently Lord Wavell) confirmed that the day Britain left India and British India was set free, the paramountcy or allegiance which the Princely States owed to the British Crown would not automatically be transferred to the newly independent State. In other words, the Princely States would get back all those powers which they had formerly turned over to the British; they would be completely independent; and they would be completely free to make their own arrangements, on their own terms, for federation with the newly-freed India beyond their frontiers. In this way, Bhopal hoped to put the Chamber of Princes in an immensely strong position to bargain for their thrones, their privileges and their fortunes. In the event of a unitary India as envisaged by the Cabinet Mission Plan, he saw the Princely States as a powerful Third Force (it would never have occurred to Bhopal to think of

---

[1] Though it should be pointed out that certain States preferred to stay out of the Chamber of Princes—notably Hyderabad, Mysore and Travancore. They had their own highly-skilled prime ministers (hired administrators, paid a fixed salary) through whom they preferred to put their case. The Nizam of Hyderabad also retained Sir Walter (now Lord) Monckton to advise him.

the Untouchables as a Third Force) which could ally itself with the Muslim League and challenge, and possibly even outvote, the Congress Party. He was intensely anti-Congress himself, and rightly suspected that most of the Hindu princes were too. If partition came, and Pakistan was formed, Bhopal hoped to persuade a number of States to band together to form an independent Princely Federation which would connect itself with Hindustan and Pakistan on only the loosest terms.

In this strategy, however, he miscalculated in three ways. He forgot (or did not sufficiently take into account) the feebleness, the lack of cohesion and the irresponsibility of most of the Indian princes. He did not realize how determined was Congress, once it got India, to get the Princely States too; for which purpose they had infiltrated Congress agitators into most of the States and formed unofficial parties which could organize an agitation or riot at any moment they chose. And he was not prepared for the blandishments of Lord Mountbatten, who, as one Indian commentator later on put it, could 'not only talk the hind leg off a donkey but also the throne from under a prince'.

There were other States which, as has previously been mentioned, stayed aloof from the Chamber of Princes, preferring to fight their own battles or make their own arrangements with independent India when the time came.

Of these, Hyderabad and its remarkable Nizam was to prove the most important. In addition to being a miser with a private fortune which was reputed to make him the richest man in the world, the Nizam was a Muslim of distinguished lineage, who traced his ancestry back to Ghazi-ud-din Khan Feroz Jang, one of the generals of the Moghul Emperor, Aurangzeb. He succeeded to his throne in 1911, and in 1918, as a reward for the soldiers from his private army and the money he provided to help Britain in the Great War, he was granted the hereditary title of His Exalted Highness. To this was added an autographed letter from King George V giving him the additional title of 'Faithful Ally of the British Government'. Of these titles he was inordinately proud. He ran Hyderabad as a completely separate entity from the rest of British India and the other Indian States, printing his own stamps, coining his own money, and running an efficient private army (under British officers) which was armed and equipped from his own factories. He maintained quasi-diplomatic offices in several countries. In Hyderabad, most of his officials and advisers were Muslim, as also were all the richest manufacturers and land-holders in the country. But 90 per cent of his people were Hindus.

The Nizam had no intention of seeing them or himself in even the loosest federation with an independent India, particularly with Congress, whose members he loathed and despised. Congress agitators who came to his State were quickly clapped into jail (though there were, nevertheless, powerful underground Congress and Communist organizations functioning, in spite of the vigilance of his police). Nor, as some Hindus charged later, had he any idea of acceding to Pakistan if it came into being—a situation which would, in Sardar Patel's phrase, have created 'an enemy country in the belly of India'. His sympathies were wholly with Jinnah but his ambitions for Hyderabad were otherwise engaged.

The Nizam made it clear to the British authorities long before Mountbatten arrived that he would have no part in an independent India. In 1946 he sent his regent, the Nawab of Chhatari, and his legal adviser, Sir Walter Monckton, to see Lord Wavell in Delhi, an occasion on which he stressed that Hyderabad would assume complete independence after the transfer of power (though he hoped to be allowed to remain as a Dominion in the British Commonwealth) and the only approach he would make to his Indian neighbours would be to lease through them a passage to the sea. He hoped, by an arrangement with the Portuguese Government, to make the Portuguese Indian possession of Goa into Hyderabad's port.

There was one other personality who played a large part in the struggle of the Indian Princes to preserve their rights and privileges, but he was not a maharajah but an English knight. Sir Conrad Corfield, the son of the Vicar of Finchhampstead in Berkshire, was head of the Political Department in Delhi whose task it was to look after the interests of Princely States. It was he who appointed the British Resident to each State to advise the rulers. It was he who acted as liaison between the Chamber of Princes and the Viceroy. It was he who had the power to intervene in the affairs of the States when he considered it necessary and, as late as 1946, he had a ruler removed from his throne for flagrant maladministration. Corfield was, however, a power behind the scenes who rarely intervened unless it was vitally necessary. But his influence on the Princes was considerable, and in the struggle that lay ahead the part he played was dramatic indeed.

By virtue of his position, Sir Conrad Corfield took no overt part in Indian politics, though it can be taken as certain that his sympathies were cool towards the Congress Party and not much more than lukewarm towards the Muslim League. His principal activity in the days before the arrival of Mountbatten was to try to persuade the Princes to bring a measure of democracy and modernity to their States, and to introduce at least some semblance of popular representative government, so that when freedom came to India they would be in a stronger position to resist agitation from the politicians across their frontiers. He was finding it rather like hitting an elephant with a feather.

In the earlier pages of this book, some reference has been made to the character and characteristics of the leaders of the Muslim League and Congress. But a further word is necessary to fill in the picture, to put the flesh on the bones of the men who were to play such a vital part in the drama of the days ahead.

In a physical sense, there is little flesh to put on Mohammed Ali Jinnah's bones. He was probably the thinnest man ever to lead a political party; he was over six foot in height and he weighed less than 140 pounds. He clothed his spare figure in Savile Row suits of the most immaculate cut, liked to wear the white and brown footwear which used to be known as 'co-respondent's shoes', and occasionally sported a monocle. His leathery, cadaverous face (he had sunken cheeks, even in early middle-age) and bright, burning, luminous eyes gave him the appearance of an emaciated brontosaurus, but when he smiled his face was transformed, and the expression was of gentle amiability. He was immensely proud of his appearance and he could never avoid a sneer when he had to mix with the khaki-clad members of Congress, who made a fad of their peasant clothes.

'You like this, don't you?' said Gandhi to him once, when the photographers crowded round them after a meeting.

'Not as much as you do,' replied Jinnah.

There were more similarities between Jinnah and Gandhi than either of them liked to admit. Both held power over their followers by sheer personality. 'You have mesmerized the Muslims,' Gandhi once accused Jinnah. 'And you have hypnotized the Hindus,' he replied.

Though Jinnah was actually born in Karachi, his background was the same as Gandhi's. Both their families were Gujeratis from Kathiawar, that proliferation of Princely States which, until Independence, spread like pieces of an unsolved jigsaw puzzle across the slab of Western India to the North of Bombay. As has been mentioned before, Jinnah's grandfather was a Hindu. He was from the same caste as Gandhi's family, the Vaisya, which is third down the scale from the Brahmins. But something happened—no one seems to know quite what—which caused Jinnah's parents to embrace Islam and move to Karachi.[1] There Jinnah was born, on Christmas Day, 1876, and brought up a Muslim. But the parallels with Gandhi continued. He was betrothed to a Kathiawar girl and married to her when he was fifteen and she eleven. (Gandhi was thirteen and his wife twelve when they married.) He left her to go to England to study law, as did Gandhi, but Jinnah's wife—unlike Gandhi's, who lived on to bear him children—wasted and died while he was in London.

Jinnah was only sixteen when he began his studies as a law student in London, and he passed his examinations in the incredibly short period of two years, though due to the formalities he was not admitted to Lincoln's Inn until he was twenty. He returned to Bombay to build himself a reputation as an astute pleader before the courts, where he soon made a considerable fortune. It was during this time that his friends and enemies alike gave two handles to his name, which never left him for the rest of his life: they began calling him 'the arrogant Mr Jinnah', and also 'the honest Mr Jinnah'.

At the age of thirty, now comfortably off, he joined the Congress Party. A few years later, he also joined the Muslim League. There was no incongruity in this. His main aim was to bring about Hindu-Muslim unity and co-ordinate the drives of both parties towards the goal of Indian independence. He continued to preach Hindu-Muslim unity and continued to rise in the hierarchy of the Congress Party until 1920. But by this time a new star had begun to dazzle the eyes of Congress Party followers —a star which beckoned them along new and dangerous paths to Indian freedom. The star was that of Gandhi, who had come to India fresh from his battles for the rights of Indians in South Africa and convinced that the methods he had experimented with there—of civil disobedience against the authorities—would succeed in India against the British. After one such demonstration

[1] The Vaisya caste in Kathiawar was very strict, and once expelled Gandhi for going to England. Caste Hindus are not supposed to travel 'over water'.

of civil disobedience in which the 'peaceful' demonstrators indulged in a riot of violence and destruction, Jinnah decided that neither Gandhi nor his methods were for him. He arrived at the Nagpur session of Congress in December 1920, and made what was, for him, a fervid plea to the delegates to show their abhorrence of civil disobedience and stick to constitutional methods to get what they wanted from the British. It was a fellow-Muslim who secured the cheers of the assembly by jumping to his feet and repudiating him by saying: 'You talk too much of the constitutional way. It reminds me of a story of a young Tory who came out of the Carlton Club one evening and walked up to Piccadilly Circus, where there was a Salvation Army meeting in progress. The speaker was saying, "Come this way—it is God's way." The young Tory interrupted him and said, "How long have you been preaching this?" "Twenty years," replied the Salvationist. "Well," said the Tory, "if it's only got you as far as Piccadilly Circus, I don't think much of it".'[1]

From that moment on, Jinnah faded out of the Congress Party. He not only did not agree with Gandhi's 'rabble rousing', as he called it, but also realized that his personality would have no chance of succeeding with Congress and securing him the leader-ship he coveted so long as its members were dazzled by Gandhi's 'Hindu revivalism'. But as late as 1928 he was still pleading for a union between the two great communities in India, and some time before that he said: 'Foreign rule and its continuance is primarily due to the fact that the people of India, Hindus and Muslims, are not united and do not sufficiently trust each other . . . I am almost inclined to say that India will get Dominion responsible government the day the Hindus and Muslims are united.'

What made him change his mind?

Ambition, say the Hindus. After his parting of the ways with Congress, Jinnah departed for England, where he began to prac-tise before the Privy Council. While there he was seen by Nawab-zada Liaquat Ali Khan, a member of the Muslim League, who was in Europe on his honeymoon. Liaquat had always been an admirer of Jinnah and had writhed in furious frustration when he had seen him humiliated and sneered at by Congress leaders, particu-larly the Muslim members of it. He painted an unhappy picture of the state of the Muslim League in India, wallowing in the

[1] Related by Hector Bolitho in his book, *Jinnah*.

trough for want of a strong guiding hand, and asked Jinnah to return and lead it. Jinnah considered, and then said that if Liaquat could find sufficient support he was to cable him and he would return. Forty-eight hours after he got back to Bombay, Liaquat cabled the single word, 'Come'.

According to Mr Nehru,[1] Jinnah accepted only because the leadership of the Muslim League gave him a chance to lash back at Gandhi and those Congress delegates who had snubbed him. And, Nehru added, he subsequently directed the Muslim League's policy along the road of separatism and anti-Hinduism not because he really believed in Islam and Pakistan, but because it was a policy which would win him easy attention and secular power. This, I think, is an unfortunate misreading of Jinnah's state of mind, of the same kind which was to lead Nehru into grave errors in dealing with him in 1946–7. He could not believe that Jinnah was sincere. Yet there was always one thing certain about Mohammed Ali Jinnah. He could be arrogantly, stupidly, infuriatingly wrong, but he was always honest and he was never insincere. By the same sort of contemptuous mental process which persuaded Nehru that Jinnah left the Congress Party 'only because it ceased to be a party for gentlemen, and he was a snob', the Congress leader chose to go on convincing himself that the Muslim League leader was a sham, that this campaign was illogical and, therefore, easily destructible, that Pakistan was not viable and, therefore, impossible. It was a misjudgement which was to cost India a heavy toll in lives in 1947.

In between his departure from Congress and his assumption of the leadership of the Muslim League, Jinnah married again. He was forty-one when it happened. For some time his name had been linked with the Indian poetess and Congresswoman, Mrs Sarojini Naidu (who was to be the first woman provincial governor in independent India). She was madly in love with him and sent him love poems, in which she wrote such phrases as, 'in the desolate hours of midnight . . . my soul hungers for thy voice', which embarrassed him considerably (he was never a man to read poetry). It was not to Mrs Naidu's blandishments that his heart opened. At a reception in Bombay he was introduced to a beautiful girl. Her name was Rutten Pettit. The fact that she was a Parsee and only seventeen years old—and the daughter, moreover, of one of his friends and business associates—did not swerve

[1] In a conversation with the author.

Jinnah from his determination to marry her. Nor did furious parental opposition.

The couple stole away, and the first Rutten's father knew of the event was an announcement in the *Times of India* that she had been received into the Islamic faith and was now the wife of Jinnah. Her parents forgave their daughter, but not Jinnah. Nor was the marriage a great success. One child was born, a daughter. Shortly afterwards, quarrels began. The young wife yearned for gay parties, but was soon cringing under the lash of Jinnah's tongue. After four years, she left his house and went to live in the Taj Mahal Hotel in Bombay. Shortly after that, she departed with her parents for Europe, a few months before Jinnah himself went to England to practise law. When the reconciliation for which she had hoped did not eventuate, she attempted suicide and Jinnah rushed to her in Paris, arranged for doctors, and stayed with her until she recovered. But their reunion did not last long, and Rutten sailed back to Bombay and Jinnah returned to England, where his devoted sister, Fatimah, was looking after him. In 1928, Rutten died under mysterious circumstances in the Taj Mahal Hotel. Thereafter, his sister was Jinnah's sole companion, and she cared for him with passionate devotion.

Jinnah had no vices—unless you can call Pakistan a vice. He neither smoked nor drank. His temper was short and he never hesitated to insult his opponent if he thought he was being snubbed or neglected. He suffered from chronic bronchitis, and possibly lung cancer, and one of his doctors said: 'He must always have been exhausted, weak, tired.' But no one who faced him, in interviews or at conferences, would have thought so. He had the vigilance of an owl and, on occasion, the sting of an electric eel. In 1947, he was 71 and looked it. But not once you heard him talk. He was known as *Quaid-i Azam*, or great leader, and the title was deserved.

There were several members of the Muslim League Working Committee whose names began to crop up in the communiqués from 1946 onwards, but none of them needs concern us here with the exception of Liaquat Ali Khan. He was the Muslim Leaguer who persuaded Jinnah to assume leadership of the League, and in that action he epitomised his own lack of ambition and willingness to take second place. He was born a subordinate and had no wish to lead but only to serve,[1] and he was just as much of a rubber stamp as the rest of the League Working Committee when it came to endorsing the wishes of Jinnah. But he nonetheless played an important part in the apotheosis of Pakistan, and was a right-hand man to his leader and without him much less might have been accomplished. He revered Jinnah to such an extent, with such a schoolboy 'crush', that he would never relax when he was present, and though Jinnah would often designate him as spokesman and remain silent, Liaquat would never speak unless he first got a nod of approval from his chief.

In appearance, Liaquat was short, podgy, pudding-faced and bespectacled, and he looked very much the dumpy proletarian when seen beside the tall, lean, aristocratic Jinnah. In fact, he came from a far more distinguished lineage, and had graduated from the famous Muslim University of Aligarh, near Amritsar, to Exeter College, Oxford, after which he became—or need I say it?—a lawyer. He was twenty years younger than Jinnah and an enthusiastic debater and one of those public speakers who loves to 'mix it' with a hostile or restive audience. Jinnah never managed to get to a university, and had no great love for anything but practical learning; yet on the public platform he spoke like a rather distant and contemptuous don. It was rare for him to show heat or emotion; he always viewed his opponents with a frigid contempt. Liaquat, on the other hand, was a reader and scholar, but a great popular orator too. It was he who took Jinnah's message of Pakistan to the villages and drove it home, and he who kept the local organizations fed with money, enthusiasm, and promises of glory. For this he never asked any more than the opportunity to go on serving Jinnah. Whether he was as eager for Pakistan as his leader is something we will never know; nor will we know whether he would have preferred to have seen a federated India with the Muslims assured of their rights and freedoms. All that is known is that he loved Bombay (which became Indian), and absolutely hated Karachi, Lahore, and Rawalpindi (which became Pakistan).

Liaquat Ali Khan once said of Lord Mountbatten: 'I hear that he has come to India most reluctantly and his real ambition is to be Admiral of the Fleet. If he will grant us Pakistan at once, we will devote our first budget to building him a battleship and will

[1] His instincts may have been right. The moment he exchanged second place for first, and became leader of Pakistan, after Jinnah's death, he was assassinated.

even supply him with a crew—Azad as laundryman, Nehru as steersman (which means he will never come within miles of us), and Gandhi for hot air to breathe into the boilers.'

So much has been written about Mohandas Karamchand Gandhi that no more than a few paragraphs are necessary here to bring back the image of this good and remarkable man. Of all the personalities—statesmen, politicians, soldiers, administrators—involved in the last chapter of Britain's Indian story, he alone emerges with his stature undiminished. It is true that there were times when his behaviour was questionable, his statements equivocal, his actions disingenuous, but in the last days his achievements were immeasurably, triumphantly and devotedly for the good of his people, no matter what their caste or religion.

A psychologist given Gandhi's history without clues to his identity or nationality would almost certainly say that his career was motivated by the suppression of an unusually strong sex-drive. (They would probably say the same about most other prophets and holy men, too.) In his long autobiography, *The Story of My Experiments with Truth*, Gandhi writes in intimate and sometimes embarrassing detail of his obsession with sex, which first raised its ugly head for him when he was married by his parents in Porbander, a small princely state in Kathiawar. He was thirteen and his bride was twelve (though Gandhi maintains that she was only ten), and although Kasturbai, his wife, was illiterate and he was anxious to teach her, 'lustful love left no time'. Gradually, but not until after he had sired three children, Gandhi's sense of guilt over the potency of his sexual urge crystallized into a determination to eschew it. He came to an agreement with Kasturbai that their relationship would henceforth be on a non-physical plane, an arrangement she may well have found harder to bear than he did, since she had no means of sublimation. Gandhi's zeal on behalf of his people increased, but so did his sexual needs; he quenched them by adopting a diet of goat's milk, as being the food least likely to stimulate him; and slowly, painfully, and always conscious of temptation, he learned to live and work in celibacy. It is Gandhi's own confession of this weakness in him, and his lifelong struggle with it, which helps to make him so much more human and his achievements so much more remarkable.

Gandhi was a lawyer (British trained, of course) like the rest of them. He gave up a prosperous barrister's practice in South Africa to work for the betterment of the Indians there, and after the Great War returned to India to help in the fight for Indian freedom. Until his arrival, the waxing personality in Congress, the party principally engaged in the fight, was Mohammed Ali Jinnah, whose goal was Dominion status and whose method was strictly constitutional agitation. Gandhi changed all that. He changed the name of the Home Rule Association to Swaraj (or *Our* Raj). He spoke passionately against the British and advocated Civil Disobedience—and though he was cast down when the Indian people proved to be anything but civil in the way they disobeyed, he gradually turned the act of national non-co-operation into a massive weapon.

He had a great sense of drama, and his leadership galvanized Congress (and drove Jinnah out of it). He led the great March through India which culminated in a ceremonial making of salt on the seashore at Dandi—a protest not so much against the Government salt monopoly as a symbolic gesture against their very existence. He went to jail, and enjoyed it. He began his first great fast in an effort to bring Hindus and Muslims together, and his closeness to death so gripped the nation that the two peoples jointly pleaded with him—on promise of permanent brotherliness —to eat. He fasted many times after that. He went to jail again. By the time the war came in 1939, he was the greatest influence in the nation.

In many ways, Gandhi was a saint. The three great aims of his life were Indian freedom, the unity of his people, Hindus and Muslims, and the betterment of the lot of the Untouchables. For these three goals, he was willing to suffer and die.

But Gandhi was also a politician and a lawyer. Like Lord Wavell, Jinnah found him impossible to deal with 'because I can never pin the fellow down. He is as wily as a snake.' Once he came to an agreement with Gandhi over the issue of a joint statment, but Gandhi subsequently went back on his promise because he said, his 'inner light' had told him to change his mind. 'To hell with his "inner light,"' exploded Jinnah. 'Why can't he be honest and admit he made a mistake?'

As we have seen, Gandhi was never above using his spiritual influence to do a little recruiting for the Congress Party, as in the case of the Untouchables. When there were awkward questions to be answered, he often took refuge in a pencilled message saying: 'This is my day of silence.' And though his official connexion with Congress ended in 1941, his influence behind the scenes was great until the last—although, unfortunately, not great enough. He often disagreed with the actions and statements of Congress in the final days, but when there was a memorandum to be written it was to Gandhi that the Congress leaders came and asked him to draft it. Congress memoranda were all written by Gandhi, even those he was against; and they are all masterpieces.

In 1947, when Mountbatten arrived in Delhi, Gandhi was on a peace mission in Bihar, where Hindus had been savagely murdering Muslims and destroying their property. Congress called him back. The Working Committee had a shrewd idea that Mountbatten, unlike Wavell, would be hypnotized by Gandhi's personality.

In the book which he wrote while imprisoned by the British from 1942–5, *Discovery of India*, Pandit Jawaharlal Nehru discussed the campaigns and infiltrations by which the British became masters of India, and commented:

'Looking back over this period, it almost seems that the British succeeded in dominating India by a succession of fortuitous circumstances and flukes. With remarkably little effort, considering the glittering prize, they won a great empire and enormous wealth . . . It seems easy for a slight turn in events to have taken place which would have dashed their hopes and ended their ambitions.' After which he adds: 'And yet a closer scrutiny reveals, in the circumstances then existing, a certain inevitability in what happened.'

They are words which could be used, simply by changing 'British' to 'Nehru' (and perhaps eliminating the phrase 'and enormous wealth'), to describe his own apotheosis in the Congress Party and India. His road to supreme power, to benevolent autocracy, over the Indian people was a pilgrim's progress full of pitfalls and side-roads, any one of which, but for coincidence and flukes, might have sidetracked him.

It was a coincidence which got him into Congress agitation in the first place. The formative years of his life were spent in an atmosphere calculated to turn him into a copy of a typical, cultivated English gentleman. At home in Allahabad, where his father was a prosperous lawyer, Jawaharlal was brought up in surroundings of great luxury and of continuous English influence.

He had a succession of English tutors. The house was always filled with guests, mostly British, although Hindus and Muslims came frequently too. (Nehru's father ran three separate kitchens to cater for their tastes.) He made only scanty progress in Hindi and Sanscrit, but was quickly fluent in English; and from the age of fifteen, when he went to Harrow, until the age of 22, when he returned from Cambridge via London, a lawyer himself, he was soaked in English background and tradition. 'In my heart I rather admired the English,' he wrote later, and his hatred of 'the alien rulers of my country' was against those who misbehaved. 'I had no feeling whatever, so far as I can remember, against individual Englishmen.' He was called to the Bar in 1912, and when he returned to India he was practically a stranger in his own land, but an aristocrat in every sense of the word—a Kashmiri Brahmin with all the culture and education (and habits) of an English peer. 'I am afraid I was a bit of a prig,' he wrote of himself, 'with little to commend me.' He did not, however, like Jinnah, take to a monocle.

And then occurred the Amritsar massacre, in which troops under the command of General Dyer cut down and slaughtered Indians demonstrating for Congress on 13 April, Hindu New Year's Day, 1919. There is no doubt that the Indians were there illegally, for martial law had been declared in the city some days before (after riots in which five Europeans had been killed), and certainly the Congress leaders who incited them to demonstrate in such conditions must share the blame for the tragedy that followed. But General Dyer's method of keeping order was of just the blunderingly ruthless, unimaginative kind to provoke rather than quiet a tense city. It was enough for him to order curfews and rigid enforcement of the laws against assembly; but he did more than that. An Englishwoman, Miss Alice Sherwood, who had done great work among the Indians as a medical missionary, had been criminally assaulted during the rioting of the previous days, a lamentable act of violence against a real friend of India. But Miss Sherwood would have been the first to protest against the result of her appalling experience: General Dyer enforced an order that all Indians who passed the spot where she had been attacked must do so on hands and knees.

  Amritsar is a city of narrow streets where gossip, rumour and alarm can spread (as we shall see) like fire among dry kindling wood. The city simmered into revolt. The Congress leaders—with foolhardy recklessness and criminal stupidity, considering how well they must have known the workings of General Dyer's 'whiff of grapeshot' mind—still called out their followers despite the martial law. And in Jallianwalla Bagh, a public park from which there was only one exit, 20,000 of them were suddenly confronted by 150 British soldiers, read the Riot Act by a British officer, and ordered to disperse, an impossibility since the soldiers blocked the only way out. In the subsequent shooting 379 were killed and over 1,000 were wounded.

As late as 1961, to judge from letters which appeared in the *Sunday Times*, London, there are still those who defend the Amritsar shootings. It was, of course, a tragic dilemma in which the British found themselves—and, as I have said, the guilt of Congress for it is great—but more flexible British soldiers in the past have coped with such problems without having to resort to massacre. What is certain is that the Amritsar shootings turned most Indians, including those who had co-operated willingly before, into resentful and mistrustful minions, conscious that the British who ruled them regarded their lives as unimportant and their race as inferior.

It was the greatest recruiting poster for Congress ever to be waved before the Indian people, and they joined up in their thousands. Among them was Jawaharlal Nehru. Nehru was returning from a holiday in Simla, the hill station, where he had undergone an experience which was, for him, extremely humiliating. It so happened that he and his wife (whom he had married in 1916) were staying in the same hotel as the one in which an Afghan delegation was housed while it discussed a peace treaty with the British. Nehru was visited by a British magistrate and crisply informed that his presence was unwelcome—presumably because he was already a member of Mrs Annie Besant's Home Rule League. He was asked to give an undertaking that he would not contact the Afghans. It was the first time he had heard of them, but Nehru was immediately on his dignity. He refused to give any such pledge.

'In that case,' said the magistrate, 'we give you four hours to leave Simla—or we escort you out.'

On the train going South, a number of British officers joined the train at Amritsar and three of them shared Nehru's coach. In the way some Britons have when in foreign parts, they talked freely about India and the Indians on the journey to Delhi and did not bother to mind their tongues because there was an Indian present. They took a great pleasure in reciting all the details of the Amritsar killing, and one of them remarked that 'this will teach the bloody browns a lesson'. By the time the train reached its destination, Jawaharlal Nehru had undergone a transformation. He smouldered with resentment, humiliation, even hatred of the British. From that moment, he threw himself wholeheartedly into the Congress movement and solidly behind Gandhi. Less than a year later, he served his first jail term. Thereafter, he was whole-heartedly a campaigner and fighter for freedom from the English yoke, and all the more sensitively aware of his peoples' 'inferiority' because his own sense of kinship with the English had been so rudely shattered.[1]

His burning sense of insult developed into a fierce resolve to rid India of the English after an incident in the Princely State of Nabha, in 1923. He and some companions, who had gone to investigate conditions there, were arrested and thrown into jail. To Nehru's indignation they were first handcuffed together and marched through the streets of the town like common criminals. The prison cell was verminous and alive with rats, and the nights in which they scampered across his face stayed in his memory for all time.

The next morning the British Resident, who was in charge of the State, came to see them and offered to let them free if they would apologize publicly. Nehru refused. Thereafter, a trial began. Their applications to import lawyers from British India were refused. The magistrate was obviously ignorant of any known legal system. Nehru's indignation was wafted to fever heat by the sight of the British Resident sitting idly by while the farcical trial went on; a trial which resulted in sentences of eighteen months in prison each. They were subsequently suspended and Nehru and his companions expelled from the State, but Nehru was seriously ill with typhoid for some months afterwards.

These were the events which turned him from a dilettante, carbon-copy Englishman into a Congress fighter.

In 1936, an equally fortuitous sequence of circumstances got

---

[1] Gandhi always took the rudeness of ignorant Englishmen in his stride. Once, when one of them in South Africa called to him on a railway station, 'Hey, coolie, pick up that bag', he obediently trotted with it to the man's carriage. He rather treasured Winston Churchill's description of him as 'a half-naked fakir'.

him the leadership of the party. It was the year when the first general elections were to take place in India, following the introduction of the reforms of 1935. Before going to the polls, Congress met and decided that it must elect a dynamic leader. For most of the party, there was one obvious choice. This was Sardar Vallabhbhai Patel, the strong man from Bombay. Patel was the man who ran the Congress Party machine, held rebels and recalcitrants in line, and kept the policy of the party respectable enough to keep the contributions flowing in from pro-Congress millionaires. He was eager to lead his party into the elections and determined to have the presidency, especially since his views, though similar to those of Nehru so far as Indian independence was concerned, were diametrically opposed so far as what should be done in India once freedom was won. He was a middle-of-the-road capitalist. Nehru was a socialist. There is little doubt that, by use of the party machine, he could have swung enough support behind himself to win the day. But at the last minute, on the eve of the Party Congress Gandhi called Patel to a conference and pleaded with him to withdraw his candidacy and support Nehru instead, because Nehru's personality would make more appeal to the people. Patel at length agreed, but with great reluctance. He had neither liking nor admiration for Nehru—and his feelings were to grow stronger as the years passed—but he gave way, for such was Gandhi's tremendous hold over his followers.

Patel told the Congress delegates that 'on some vital matters my views are in conflict with those held by Jawaharlalji', and he gave a warning to Nehru not to try him too far by adding: 'The Congress does not part with its ample powers by electing any individual, no matter who he is.' But he ended by asking the delegates to elect Nehru.

From Nehru's point of view, it could not have come at a better time. He swung into the election campaign and stumped the country, speaking with great fervour and brilliance, gathering mass support for himself and his views. Before, he had been one of the intellectuals behind the scenes. Now the people had a chance to see him. He met the people and the people met him, and thereafter he never looked back.

Once more, when there was a chance that Nehru's star might wane, fate stepped in to keep it shining, and that was in 1946. As has been briefly mentioned in this story, that was the year when Maulana Abul Kalam Azad, the Muslim President of Congress, decided that the time had come to resign his office. There was a strong contingent in the party which urged him to continue as leader of the party. 'But I sensed that there was some difference of opinion in the inner circles of the Congress High Command.' he wrote in *India Wins Freedom*. 'I found that Sardar Patel and his friends wished that he should be elected President.'

This was indeed the case. Patel had waited a long time for power, and this, he felt, was his moment—the moment when negotiations for freedom were beginning to bear fruit. Unfortunately, Azad did not like Patel. In personality, background and culture, they were completely opposed. Azad was the studious, scholarly advocate of reason and logic, an apostle of patience and compromise. Patel was the iron fist of Congress, which rarely even bothered to wear a velvet glove. He believed in hammering out agreements by sheer force and weight of numbers. At this moment, Azad believed he would be the wrong man to face the crises looming ahead; and he decided to back Nehru, a subtle man like himself (or so he thought) instead.

'I was anxious that the next President,' Azad wrote, 'should be one who agreed with my point of view and would carry out the same policy as I had pursued. After weighing the pros and cons, I came to the conclusion that Jawaharlal should be the next President. Accordingly, on the 26 April 1946, I issued a statement proposing his name for the Presidency and appealing to Congressmen that they should elect Jawaharlal unanimously.'

It was not necessarily a *fait accompli*, as all Congress knew. Until this moment, Patel had been sure that Gandhi favoured his election, for when they had talked of it previously, the Mahatma had indicated that he would welcome it. Now, like the rest of the Congress delegates, he waited for Gandhi to give a sign; and he was sufficiently confident that the sign would be against Nehru and for him that he made no overt move himself to secure it.

But the day of the Congress elections came, and Gandhi made no sign. Mortified, well aware that, at his age, the chance would never come again, Patel had to sit back and watch his rival once more take the presidency from him—and this time at the most important moment of all. He never forgave Azad for the events of 1946. He moved away from Gandhi, whose devoted disciple he had always been. And he resolved to bide his time, let Nehru make his mistakes, as he had no doubt he would, and wait for the

opportunity to reassert his domination over Congress, Nehru
and all.

It was Lord Mountbatten who eventually provided him with
his opportunity.

Jawaharlal Nehru was 57 years old in 1947. He rarely wore
his smart English clothes any more, but dressed almost invariably
in a Gandhi cap and khaddar breeches and tunic, but there was
always a red rosebud in his lapel. His figure had already begun
to be slightly bent and his face in repose looked weary, with
smudges of dark brown skin under his eyes. His temper was short
(as it still is) and he suffered fools badly; but he was highly susceptible to those who flattered him, those who talked to him
about poetry, or a pretty woman. He liked a sherry in the
evening, could not stand the vegetarian diet of the Hindu
extremists (though for Gandhi's sake, he had tried hard to follow
it) and fretted because one of his favourite English papers, the
New Statesman, was always late in arriving or did not arrive at all.
He was still incredibly handsome and extremely proud of his
appearance. Prison had left its mark upon him for, unlike Gandhi,
he had hated every moment of it,[1] and it had certainly increased
his suspicions of everything British. His attitude towards the
latest developments could perhaps be summed up in a passage
from a favourite work, Euripides' *Alcestis*:

> There be many shapes of mystery;
>   And many things God brings to be,
>   Past hope or fear.
> And the end man looketh for cometh not,
>   And a path is there where no man thought.

Or perhaps in a passage he wrote in prison:

'There was a time, many years ago, when I lived for considerable periods in a state of emotional exaltation, wrapped up in
action which absorbed me. Those days of my youth seem far
away now, not merely because of the passage of years but far
more so because of the ocean of experience and painful thought
that separates them from today. The old exuberance is much less
now, the almost uncontrollable impulses have toned down,
and passion and feeling are much more in check. The burden
of thought is often a hindrance, and in the mind where there was
once certainty doubt creeps in. Perhaps it is just age . . .'

[1] Though it produced one of his best books, *Discovery of India*.

Nehru in 1947, as I have said, was 57. Sometimes he sounded much more.

And yet there were also moments when his spirits rose and he looked and acted like a matinee idol, bestriding the Indian political scene like a sunburned Ivor Novello. He was still subject, no matter what his self-conviction, to the same uncontrollable impulses which had got him (and his party) into trouble in the past. His blunder over the Cabinet Mission Plan was not an isolated one. He could not take Mr Jinnah and the Muslim League seriously, and though members of Congress warned him repeatedly that the Muslim League strength was building up throughout India and the Muslim friends of Congress were deserting them for Jinnah, he angrily refused to believe it.

'How can we be losing our Muslim supporters,' he said, 'when Congress still rules in the North West Frontier Province, where they are all Muslims?'

It was suggested to him that Congress' hold there was loosening rapidly, that the Party machine there was running down fast.

'Then I will go and wind it up again,' he said, and told his secretary to prepare for a journey to Peshawar. He was convinced that a wave of his hand and a few rallying speeches would revive the fortunes of the flagging local Congress administration. What he got instead were rioting crowds, a threatening situation in which revolvers had to be fired, and a shower of bricks from the mob. He returned to Delhi chastened, but still not convinced —he never would be convinced—that the power of the Muslim League was anything but a confidence trick.

For Nehru, there was one welcome personal aspect about the arrival of Lord Mountbatten as the new Viceroy. Someone had told him the story of how, during the 1945 election, a Labour Party canvasser arrived to interview Lord and Lady Mountbatten. 'Oh, you don't have to convince us,' said Mountbatten. 'But you're going to have a devil of a job in the kitchen. The butler and the staff are all out-and-out Tories.'

'After all these Hindus,' said Nehru, with a patronizing wave of his hand towards his fellow Congressmen, 'it will be good to meet a straightforward English Socialist again.'

There is not much more to say about Sardar Vallabhbhai Patel than has already been mentioned in these pages (for the moment that is) except to stress his importance in the Congress Party and his iron control over the Party machine. He was a man of great personal ambition, but, as has been seen, such was Gandhi's influence over him until 1946 that he twice allowed himself to be superseded by Nehru in the leadership of the Party, though convinced that Nehru was a temperamental dreamer and he himself was the better man.

It is a curious coincidence, and perhaps food for the psychiatrists, that the three most important political leaders in India in 1947—if you discount Gandhi—were all widowers. The story goes that Patel was in the middle of a final speech for the defence in a Bombay court case when a messenger came in with a telegram announcing the death of his wife. He read it, stuffed it in his pocket, and went on with his speech. Like Nehru, he was thenceforward looked after by a devoted daughter.

Patel was well aware that he was regarded by the Left Wing of the Congress Party as a die-hard capitalist whose constant attention to the practical side of Congress administration was the typical activity of a *non-idealist* and *non-intellectual* (the terms are from Congress documents, not from me). Congress sometimes took more pride in the scholastic achievements of its hierarchy than it did in its relations with the masses. Of the eleven members of the Party who were imprisoned by the British in 1942, Nehru wrote:

'Nearly all the principal living Indian languages as well as the classical languages which have powerfully influenced India in the past and present were represented and the standard was often that of high scholarship. Among the classical languages were Sanskrit and Pali, Arabic and Persian.'

Nonetheless, it was Patel—who spoke only Gujerati and English—who kept the Party going with regular infusions of money from the big Hindu millionaires, and with frequent purgings and oilings of the political machine of a nature with which Nehru would never have been asked to soil his hands.

When it was announced that Mountbatten would be the new Viceroy, Patel sent for a report on him from his correspondents in London. He was told that Mountbatten was 'a Liberal aristocrat with revolutionary leanings'. His reaction to the news was: 'He will be a toy for Jawaharlalji to play with—while we arrange the revolution.'

It turned out to be somewhat different from that, but it still went the way that Sardar Patel was thinking. He was 72 in 1947.

There were other distinguished names in the Congress Party, but, in the context of the fight for independence, they played minor roles. Rajagopalachari of Madras had pleaded, from the start, for some sort of recognition of the Muslim League that would give them at worst a securely protected role in a federal India, or at best, their own independent Pakistan. Like the premature anti-Fascists of pre-war Europe and America, he spoke too forthrightly and too soon to be heeded. But he remained, quick-witted, Churchillian in manner and speech (though he never smoked a cigar or drank a brandy in his life), an influence behind the scenes, though never quite strong enough to tip the scales towards common-sense when the rest of Congress were plumping for excess.

Maulana Abul Kalam Azad's influence on Congress, while President, had been great and his influence upon Congress-Muslim League negotiations did much to hold religious antipathies in check. It was only after he relinquished the presidency that the floodgates of hatred opened. There are those in India today who still believe that if only Azad could have been persuaded to keep the leadership of Congress during the last days of the negotiations for independence, most of the melancholy events which followed could have been avoided.   His eclipse, according to these students of Indian history, signalized for the Muslims the end of Muslim influence in the Congress Party and the certainty that independence would be independence for the Hindus only. There is little doubt that his decision to resign the leadership of the Party in 1946 was a cardinal error; and though Azad himself realized it afterwards, there should have been some members, at least, in the Congress Party who realized it before—and realized, too, that they had no better card to play in their claim to represent all parties, all races, and all creeds in India than a distinguished and perfervidly pro-Congress Muslim at their head. So long as Azad was their President, how could anyone claim that Congress was anti-Muslim?

Perhaps more than any other subordinate member of Congress, Azad still continued to play his part. He remained from first to last a firm believer in a unitary India, in a nation which need not be divided by religious factions, in the need to compromise to achieve independence. When Wavell was sacked by the Labour Government, he found himself in a minority in Congress in his feelings of sorrow. Nehru, particularly, believed that Wavell was under the thumb of pro-Muslim League influences. Patel thought Wavell's anxiety to prevent civil war in India and establish a common feeling between the peoples would keep the British in power for another ten years. Only Azad shared Wavell's desperate wish to bring the warring factions together, to negotiate, wait, argue, negotiate, wait, argue and then negotiate again, in a determined and wholehearted effort to make the Hindus and Muslims learn to live together. To a great extent, he shot his bolt as an important Congress leader by issuing a statement when Wavell's resignation was announced. It was not endorsed by any other Congress leader. It said, in part:

'I do not know what communications passed between Lord Wavell and H.M.G. in the last two or three weeks. Obviously there were some differences which led to his resignation. We may differ from his appraisement of the situation. But we cannot doubt his sincerity or integrity of purpose. Nor can I forget that the credit for the changed atmosphere in Indo-British relations today must be traced back to the step which he so courageously took in June 1945. After the failure of the Cripps Mission, Churchill's Government had made up their mind to put the India question in cold storage for the duration of the war. Indian opinion could also find no way out and events after 1942 had further increased the bitterness. To Lord Wavell must belong the credit for opening the closed door . . . I am confident that India will never forget this service of Lord Wavell and when the time comes for the historian of independent India to appraise the relations of India and England, he will give Lord Wavell the credit for opening a new chapter in those relations.'

Maulana Abul Kalam Azad was born in Mecca in 1888, which made him 59 in 1947, a year-and-a-half older than Nehru. He was a distinguished scholar in Arabic (he had studied at Al Azhar, in Cairo), Urdu, Hindi, Sanskrit and English. Nehru once said of him: 'Maulana Abul Kalam Azad, whose vast erudition invariably delighted me but sometimes also rather overwhelmed me.'

He had fought the British all his life, but admired them greatly. He had an abounding faith in their honesty and goodwill. Until the new Viceroy arrived, that is.

This is the place, I think, to mention two other Indians who played a significant part in the struggle for independence, particularly since the shape of it would have been different had it not been for them. Neither of them was a member of Congress or the Muslim League, though one was a Hindu and the other a Muslim.

Both were members of the Indian Government Service, but not the ICS. Chaudri Mohammed Ali was a Muslim, born near Lucknow in the United Provinces, who went to London University and the London School of Economics and also (need I say?) was called to the Bar. He joined the Indian Audit and Accounts Service as a junior clerk and worked his way through the Finance Department until, in 1946, he was assistant head of the department, and, in the words of his English chief, 'a most expert, able administrator, as well as a damned good economist'.

Chaudri Mohammed Ali now maintains that he always believed in the idea of Pakistan right from the days of his youth in England. Be that as it may, it was not until he met Mr Jinnah in 1946 that he allowed Muslim League politics to obtrude into his work in the Indian Government. Influenced by Jinnah's personality and League propaganda, he soon became such a partial member of the Finance Department that his chief began to greet him, whenever he came into the office, with the cry of *Pakistan Zindabad!*[1]

'Actually,' said Chaudri, 'my conversion had taken place before this. I knew my worth as a financial expert and I was pleased when my chief, who is now a director of one of the great English banks, proposed me as a director of the Federal Bank of India, whose board at that time was composed of Hindus and Parsis. I would have been the first Muslim director. They agreed to have me enthusiastically at first. But then my chief made the mistake of pointing out how skilled I was at finance, how much experience I had, how valuable and perceptive I would be. The more he advanced my credentials, the less warm they grew, until finally they found an excuse to reject me. You see, they wouldn't have minded a Muslim so long as he was stupid or amenable. It would have given the show a semblance of racial and communal unity. But the moment they thought I might be efficient, they backed down. It was the same with Congress. They didn't mind Muslims. What they were afraid of were intelligent or able Muslims.'[2]

The big moment in Chaudri Mohammed Ali's career, so far as the fight for freedom was concerned, came shortly before Lord

[1] Which did not, as some facetious correspondents later translated it, mean 'Pakistan's in the bag' but 'Hail to Pakistan'.
[2] In a conversation with the author.

Mountbatten's arrival. The Muslim League had by this time taken up its five places in the interim Government and there was discussion between them, Congress and the Viceroy as to the chief Cabinet post which should be given to them. Jinnah had signified that he would take no part in the Cabinet himself but he had assigned Liaquat Ali Khan and expected him to be given a position of some consequence. The Viceroy suggested that Liaquat should be appointed Home Member (the equivalent of a British Home Secretary) with power to deal with judicial and police affairs, as well as other matters of domestic administration. It so happened that Sardar Vallabhbhai Patel had made himself Home Member and found it a useful post for controlling Congress Party patronage and policies. He was urged to give it up to Liaquat but angrily refused; it was rather like asking an old-time Postmaster General in an American administration to hand over to a Republican. He suggested instead that Liaquat should be given the portfolio of Finance Member (or Chancellor of the Exchequer in British parlance). Patel thought this would give Liaquat a high-sounding post, but no say in the politics of the interim Government.

It was a monumental error which was to have Himalayan repercussions. Liaquat had no sense of the job's tactical and strategic importance when he took it. But then Chaudri Mohammed Ali stepped in. He pointed out that the Congress Party, through Nehru, proclaimed its sympathy for Socialism and its eagerness to promote the welfare of the people and share the wealth of India among them. But the financial backing of the Congress Party came almost entirely from millionaires, who had made fortunes during the war. Chaudri proposed to Liaquat that he should draw up a Budget which would squeeze the rich backers of the Congress Party until, as Geddes once said, 'you could hear the pips squeak'.

It did more than that. It made Nehru and Patel scream with rage, too. And, as will be seen, it profoundly changed their attitude towards the question of India's future.

Chaudri Mohammed Ali subsequently became one of Pakistan's prime ministers and is now head of an insurance company. He is at present writing his own history of Indian independence, and it should contain some fascinating revelations. The only man he really admired in the Congress Party was Gandhi. 'He had great subtlety of mind and a lawyer's wiliness behind all that simplicity,' he said. 'I am told that some people also considered him a saint.'[1]

V. P. Menon[2] has the happy distinction of having played a major role—some would say the all-important role—in the drama of India's independence without having been (a) to school in England, (b) to university anywhere and (c) without being a lawyer.

He was Reforms Commissioner and Constitutional Adviser to Linlithgow, Wavell and Mountbatten, the highest position in the Indian Government Service ever to have been held by an Indian, and an even more remarkable achievement when you consider his background. He was born in Malabar in 1889, a member of one of those Jain family tribes which farm the fertile slopes of this loveliest corner of India. At the age of fifteen he fell seriously ill with typhoid and was away from school for several months. He still sat for his matriculation examination, however, and passed; but he had, through his illness, not put in the requisite time at school and he was not allowed to receive his certificate without attending for another year. It so happened that this was a time when his family was going through a period of grave financial crisis; his father, the head of the clan, had died and there were innumerable brothers and cousins still be to educated. Menon decided that there was only one thing to do: leave home, earn his own living, and send back money to help his family. He set off, unmatriculated, into a land where a certificate of education can mean the difference between a comfortable living and starvation. Time and again he demonstrated to Hindu employers that he could read and write, was fluent in English, good at figures; and time and again he was thrown out of their offices when he could not produce the all-important scroll. He was down to work in the railway shops and rapidly wasting away on a thin diet when an Englishman rescued him. Menon saw an advertisement in the Madras *Mail* for a clerk to work in the Kolar Goldfields, in Mysore; beneath it, another advertisement from the same organization for a contract overseer to work in the mines themselves. He decided to apply for both jobs and was told to come for an interview.

The English manager took a fancy to young Menon and waved

---

[1] In a conversation with the author.
[2] No relation to Krishna Menon, K. P. S. Menon or any of the other Menons who figure so frequently in Indian politics.

away the confession that he was uncertificated. He advised Menon to take on the safe, steady job as a clerk in the office and promised him good prospects if he worked hard; but Menon had heard stories of the huge sums to be made by contract overseers and was determined, despite warnings that there were hazards, to have a try. He was given a sum of money by the manager, told to go out and hire himself a gang of coolies, and get to work in the mine. He would be paid a percentage of all the gold his gang brought up. 'The harder you work them,' the manager said, 'the more you'll make. But don't work them too hard, or you'll kill them.'

Menon was not the type. For the first few weeks, his coolies laboured splendidly for him. He was making nearly a thousand rupees a week and sending most of it home. Then he made the error of increasing the rations of his coolies and giving them time off with pay when they fell sick. The coolies decided that he was an easy mark. They would descend to the second or third level of the mine, where it was cool, and go off to sleep instead of to work. Week after week, the amount of gold dropped below Menon's quota. At the end of three months, he was heavily in debt to the management, and hourly waiting for the summons that would turn him into an employee himself until he had paid off what he owed. Instead, the Englishman called him in to his office.

'I told you not to be a damned fool,' he said. 'Too bloody nice, that's your trouble. Well, it's all up, my lad. Here, take this—and get out and don't come back.'

He handed Menon an envelope. Inside were two 100 rupee notes, and a letter to a tobacco firm manager in Bangalore. He was never asked to repay his debt.

It was an Englishman, too, who gave V. P. Menon his start in the Government Service. Years later, once more on the verge of starvation, Menon had borrowed sufficient money to take the train back to Malabar and was on his way to the station when an Englishman he had met while clerking in Bombay crossed the road to greet him. He was head of the Home Department in Delhi. When he heard of Menon's plight, he got him a job in the department and encouraged him to study at night school.

By 1940, Menon had made himself an expert on Indian affairs and well-nigh indispensable to the administration. In 1941 he drew up a scheme for the Federation of the Princely States with the rest of India in which the States would have acceded to British India on a limited basis, retaining their own internal administration but passing Defence, Foreign Affairs and Communications to the Central Government. It was a plan which would have laid the foundations for a Unitary India of the future. Lord Linlithgow, the Viceroy, locked the plan away in his famous Little Black Box (which he was reputed to take with him to the toilet, in case someone tried to look inside) and never even acknowledged it.

'It's all very well for you to hang around, Menon,' he said on one occasion. 'You expect me to make you Reforms Commissioner when the job comes up, don't you? You had better get it out of your mind. It is not a job for an Indian.'

When the office fell vacant, H. V. Hodson was jumped into the position over Menon's head. Menon never held it against him, and they became firm friends; nor did it cool Menon's warm regard and admiration for the British, though he did not necessarily learn to love Lord Linlithgow. But he bided his time. In 1943, H. V. Hodson quarrelled with the Viceroy and departed for Britain (where he subsequently became the distinguished Editor of the London *Sunday Times*) and Linlithgow looked around for an Englishman to fill his place. His advisers informed him that there was none in the whole of India who could approach V. P. Menon in the breadth of his knowledge of Indian affairs, law, civil administration and relations with the Princely States. Linlithgow righted the earlier injustice and summoned Menon. He got one of the best Reforms Commissioners in the history of the Indian Government and he and his successors leaned heavily on his shoulders from that moment on. Few of them, however, ever realized how much he did for them, just as few people realize how great was his part in the achievement of independence.

One thing is certain. V. P. Menon was certainly the most unusual Indian ever to rise to the top of the Government Services. He had no university degree. He came into the service by the backdoor. He was outspoken. He was, also unlike many Indians, a man completely without guile and would never genuflect to anyone, no matter what their position, if he thought they were in the wrong. He could, over India's wrongs (though never over his own), work himself into quite a state, one of the few characteristics he shared with Nehru. 'Your only weakness,' Mountbatten was to write to him later, 'which is shared by so many of the greatest in India, is that you lose your sense of balance in emotional periods. Fortunately, unlike many others, you yourself recover your balance long before any wrong decisions have been taken. You have been kind enough to attribute this recovery of your balance to my influence but unless you had inherent stability in you, I could not have helped you. If ever you find yourself under great emotional strain and are about to fly off the handle, pause for a moment and say: "What would Mountbatten have said?" '

With the attainment of the office of Reforms Commissioner, V. P. Menon fulfilled the personal ambition of his life. He wanted to see only one other thing come about—Indian independence during his lifetime.

In 1946 he met Sardar Vallabhbhai Patel for the first time, and the two men swiftly became close friends and (so far as Menon's job made it possible) collaborators. It was an association which had much more to do with the shaping of India's future than has hitherto been realized.

CHAPTER FOUR

THE LAST CHUKKA

VISCOUNT AND VISCOUNTESS Mountbatten arrived in New Delhi on 22 March 1947, and were installed as the last Viceroy and Vicereine[1] of India forty-eight hours later. It is a ceremony which is as near to a Coronation as you can get without a king, and since there would be no more after this one, the Viceroy's Staff made sure that it lacked nothing in pomp, circumstance and splendid colour. At Mountbatten's suggestion it was also photographed for the first and last time, and, for the benefit of the assembled Congressmen, Muslim Leaguers and bejewelled and sparkling Princes—as well as an international radio hook-up—he made one break with tradition. He delivered a short speech in which he emphasized his role as a passer-on of, rather than a clinger-on to, power. His manner was crisp and confident and there was no sign of any emotion as he spoke of the approaching twilight of the British Raj. His voice and bearing caused a quickening of interest among the leaders of both parties, and gave several of the Princes shudders of apprehension, for he had the air of a man who had come to make a deal—and no nonsense about sentiment.

In marked contrast was the expression of dismal gloom on the face of Field Marshal Lord Ismay, who had volunteered to accompany Mountbatten to India as his Chief of Staff. Ismay's formative years had been spent as a young soldier in India and the land truly was, for him, a precious jewel in Britain's Crown. He was depressed by the changes he had found in modern India compared with the glorious Raj he had known in his youth. (His state of mind can be guessed from the remark he made to Field Marshal Sir Claude Auchinleck, Commander in Chief of the Indian Army, when he met him at the airport. Auchinleck was wearing a beret. 'Good God, Claude,' exclaimed Ismay. 'Where's your topee?')[2] He did not share Mountbatten's opti-

---

[1] 'Isn't it delicious?' commented Lady Mountbatten to a friend. 'Some of the old hands around here refer to me as the Vice Queen. It makes me feel like Mrs Meyrick.'
[2] *The Memoirs of General Lord Ismay.*

mism, and he described his task as 'one of the most delicate and perhaps distasteful assignments imaginable'. He added: 'We would be going out to the last chukka twelve goals down.'

The Staff the new Viceroy had brought to India with him was a powerful one. In Ismay himself he had an ally of enormous influence, for as Churchill's wartime aide he was admired and trusted by just those elements who were apt to suspect Mountbatten's technique. The new Viceroy was too well aware of his own skill and charm to doubt his ability to handle relations between himself, the public and the Labour Government. But he was not so sure of his skill with the Tories. He was relying upon Ismay to handle them.

Second-in-Command to Ismay was Sir Eric Mièville, another old India hand but one rather less romantic about it than Ismay. He had once been Private Secretary to Lord Willingdon when he was Viceroy, and had served, thereafter, as Assistant Private Secretary to King George the Sixth, and had given up his job as Something in the City to accompany Mountbatten.

There were four other members of the Staff: old-time aides of Mountbatten in Burma and at Combined Operations during the War, unswervingly loyal subordinates, a talented quadrumvirate of 'front men', whose main task was the projection of their chief's personality as the image of achievement. They were Captain Ronald Brockman, RN, an ex-submariner, Commander George Nicholls, RN, Lieut.-Colonel Vernon Erskine Crum, Scots Guards, and Alan Campbell-Johnson, in charge of Public Relations. Campbell-Johnson was perhaps the most important of them. He was an expert on publicity. During the War he had been the keeper of Mountbatten's diaries and the defender of his policies. It had not escaped the new Viceroy's notice that the Viceregal Staff had never hitherto possessed a wholetime spokesman, and much of Wavell's remoteness from the public could possibly be explained by the fact that there was never anyone available to 'interpret' or 'project' him to the Press. Mountbatten had no intention of hiding his own personality under any bushel, Indian or otherwise. It was Campbell-Johnson's job to keep ramming home, to Press and public alike, that the name of Mountbatten was synonymous with success.

These four Mountbatten men were all on intimate, first-name terms with their chief, and, at times, were derisively known among other members of the Administration as 'the Dickie Birds'.

In addition, Mountbatten had taken on some of the senior members of Wavell's staff, the two most notable being Mr George Abell, a distinguished scholar and triple Blue whose knowledge of India and Indians was great, and Rao Bahadur V. P. Menon, the Reforms Commissioner, a remarkable Hindu to whom reference has already been made.

Each morning these members of the Viceroy's entourage (with one exception) met after breakfast for an informal conference at which the day's tactics were decided. It was very much a Mountbatten speciality, modelled on his wartime conferences in Burma, at which the others were expected to indulge in a game of verbal ping-pong, batting the problems of Indian independence back and forth across the table, while the Viceroy looked on and acted as a sort of amiable umpire. It was a cosy, British oasis of badinage and cross-talk of a kind which would have appalled any foreigner who listened to it. On serious subjects, it was almost mandatory to be flippant. The Indians were referred to as 'the bods', Gandhi as 'His Nibs' and Jinnah as 'Gimlet'. V. P. Menon was not at first invited to these meetings, at Abell's suggestion, because 'continual consultation with him, a Hindu, will convince the Muslims that we are becoming too partial to Congress'. Menon, fuming in the anteroom, retorted that the presence of Abell 'will convince anyone who knows the way his mind works that there is already a pro-Muslim League element at the meeting—so why not a Hindu to balance it?' It was not until much later that he was called in, and then only infrequently, and on these occasions the proceedings became much more serious and formal.

It was the time of the year when the energies of most Indians begin to flag. The temperature in March in Delhi mounts every day from 100 degrees to 103, and from 103 to 106, until, soaked with sweat, the newcomer asks himself: 'Surely it can't get any hotter than this?' But it does. The bare red bones of the Delhi landscape shimmer as if they were boiling in some enormous cosmic stewpot. In Old Delhi, there is bustle in the pink coolness of early morning, and again at night when an occasional breeze fans the skin, but otherwise people make for shade and uneasy sleep. In New Delhi, the walls of Lutyens' Secretariat building suck in the heat, ready to throw it out again at night-time, and inside, the Civil Servants work amidst a mad hurricane of flailing fans flapping weighted-down papers, and envy their wives gone to summer in the hills.

It is in the summer that Indian politicians lose their grip, their resolutions, and their tempers. It is to be remembered that the leaders of both Indian political parties were elderly men of whom Nehru was the youngest at 57. Mohammed Ali Jinnah was already suffering (though he did not know it) from the cancer of the lung which would eventually kill him. Nehru confessed that, in spite of early morning yoga exercises, he was 'tired and dispirited'. None of them lived in air-conditioned houses or worked in air-conditioned offices, and for many of them—Maulana Abul Kalam Azad, for instance—the prospect of fighting another battle for independence in the stupefying heat of New Delhi was almost too much to contemplate.

Heat was, on the other hand, something upon which the new Viceroy thrived. He was not, of course, the first or even the last Englishman who found the dizzy heights of Delhi's summer temperatures—anything from 115 to 120 degrees—stimulating and challenging, but as Lady Mountbatten once said: 'I think both Dickie and I have something the matter with our glands. We never seem to get tired. But I get headaches and swollen feet, whereas Dickie only has a mild hangover if he has had too many drinks the night before.'

Delhi's furnace heat acted like a blow torch on his skin, and galvanized him into activity. True, he had air-conditioning for all the rooms in which he did his most important work. He had his study and his bedroom redecorated and refurnished in his favourite shade of cool green. He had a staff of no less than 7,500 (including 250 gardeners and a permanently-employed plucker of chickens) to look after the Viceregal House and attend to his every request.[1]

But his energy was, as Campbell-Johnson remarked, demonic. To Ismay and Miéville there were days when they felt like old retainers who were putting a great and ancient house in order, ready for the sale of itself and all its treasures; and on those days, the workmanlike attitude of the Viceroy, bustling through the corridors, reminded them uncomfortably of an auctioneer with a mallet in his hand. 'By God,' said one of his Staff later, 'you would be surprised how cut-and-dried he made it all seem.'

He had written to Gandhi and Jinnah to come and see him

---

[1] Except the most menial ones. The hoariest story is only too true of how Lady Linlithgow's dog, just before a banquet, made a mess on the carpet. She summoned servants to wipe it up. It took so long to find a servant of low enough rank that she was cleaning it up herself when the first guests arrived.

even before he was sworn in as Viceroy, but it was, in fact, Nehru who was his first official visitor. They had met once before, in Malaya shortly before the end of the War, when Nehru had flown out to visit troops of the Indian Army, and the attraction between the two men was mutual. They had, of course, much in common. Both were proud men. Both were aristocrats who had espoused popular causes and believed in public welfare rather than inherited privilege. The deeper thought and sensitivity belonged to Nehru; he was a man, even in triumph, who was often consumed by doubt and self-accusation. It was therefore natural, perhaps, that he should be enormously attracted to the personality of the new Viceroy, so serenely self-confident, so utterly devoid of doubt so completely in control of himself and all who came into his orbit.

He found it easy to talk to Mountbatten, and he talked without stint or reservation. The Viceroy was shrewd enough to spot from the start one of Nehru's weaknesses; he cannot help, when encouraged, being gossipy and malicious about his friends and colleagues. It was from Nehru that Mountbatten obtained much of the ammunition which he subsequently used upon other Congress leaders, and when he led Nehru on to talk of Jinnah, he found him no less frank. 'A mediocre lawyer with an obsession for Pakistan,' said Nehru contemptuously. Not one of us, he seemed to infer.

By the end of their three-hour talk, Nehru was completely won over and Mountbatten had the measure of his man. He could be flattered. He could be persuaded. 'Mr. Nehru,' he said, as they parted, 'I want you to regard me not as the last Viceroy winding up the British Raj, but as the first to lead the way to the new India.'

Nehru was intensely moved. 'Now I know,' he said, 'what they mean about your charm being so dangerous.'

But he was Mountbatten's man from that moment on, and his attachment to the Mountbatten ménage was much increased by his subsequent contact with Lady Mountbatten. He had long been a widower, and he was a lonely man. Lady Mountbatten filled an important gap in his life. He began by admiring her for the way she queened it over the great Viceregal banquets or vast garden parties; but it was her obvious sympathy for India and her practical desire to help the Indian people which stirred in him emotions which were soon much stronger than mere admiration.

The combination of Mountbatten's charm and Edwina's

sympathy was not so successful on Gandhi, but even he was not impervious to it. The Mahatma was in Bihar on a pilgrimage of penance in the riot-areas when the Viceroy's invitation arrived.

'You have rightly gauged my difficulty about moving out of Bihar,' he wrote in reply, 'but I dare not resist your kind call. I am just leaving for one of the disturbed areas of Bihar. Will you therefore forgive me if I do not send you the exact date of my departure for Delhi? I return from this third Bihar tour on the 28th inst. My departure will therefore be as quickly as I can arrange it after the 28th.'

For this meeting, which Mountbatten considered all important, he was prepared to give all the time Gandhi desired. In fact, they met on two consecutive days. On the first day, Gandhi talked for almost three hours, but it was almost entirely about his early life and struggles. For Mountbatten, who believes that no man needs more than an hour in which to explain himself, it must have been something of a strain to give it his whole attention as he thought of the wreckage of his timetable. On the following day, Gandhi became (for him) more practical. He produced a plan—but it was just the kind of plan which was apt to make Wavell writhe in agony and call him an 'obscurantist'. He proposed that the Congress-Muslim League deadlock might be solved by a simple solution: the Viceroy should call upon Mr Jinnah to set up a Government immediately, leaving him to decide whether it should be all Muslims or contain both Muslims and Hindus; and this Government should be allowed an absolutely free hand, with the exception of a Viceregal power of veto, to rule India.

The Viceroy replied at once that he found the plan 'attractive', and promised to regard it sympathetically if Congress, too, agreed to its feasibility. He posed for smiling portraits with Gandhi and Lady Mountbatten, and introduced his daughter, Pamela. 'I shall be sending her to your prayer meeting tomorrow,' he said. Gandhi returned from the meeting, in the words of his biographer, Pyarelal, 'greatly impressed by the Viceroy's sincerity, gentlemanliness and nobility of character'. He was not so impressed a little later. He found his plan rudely rebuffed by Congress, and the Viceroy wrote to him to point out that there had been a 'misunderstanding' about his own reception of it. What happened, in fact, was that immediately after the meeting Mountbatten and his staff set to work to sabotage the plan, which they (and many Congress leaders) considered unworkable. The sabotage was so effective that Gandhi shortly afterwards informed Congress that he would take no further part in the discussions with the Viceroy or play anything other than a minor advisory role in Congress affairs, and he departed once more for his healing mission in Bihar. Within a fortnight of his arrival, the Viceroy had eliminated him from the negotiations for Indian independence. It was an elimination of enormous importance and gravity for India. For Gandhi was one of the only two members of the Congress Party who, despite all propaganda and pressure, remained unshakably against the partition of India into Pakistan and Hindustan.

Of his first meeting with Jinnah, the Viceroy afterwards said: 'My God, he was cold! It took all my efforts to unfreeze him.' He quickly discovered that here was a man completely impervious to his charm. Jinnah began the interview by brusquely saying: 'I will enter into this discussion on one condition only . . .'

The Viceroy 'immediately saw,' as one of his Staff put it later, 'that this was an occasion for the old soft soap.' He interrupted with the smiling remark: 'Mr Jinnah, I am not prepared to discuss conditions, or indeed the present situation, until I have had the chance of making your acquaintance and hearing more about you, yourself.'

It was an approach which would have dissolved most suspicions and breached most defences, but Mr Jinnah at seventy had reached a stage when he was not prepared to lower the drawbridge to anyone, least of all to someone whom he suspected of being a playboy, a pro-Hindu and an anti-Muslim. The Viceroy may have imagined that he was unfrozen by the end of the interview, but the icicles were still visibly clinging to him when he emerged from the Viceroy's House to say to reporters: 'The Viceroy just does not understand.'

That, however, is unfair. The Viceroy understood only too well. No matter what else may be said about the Mountbatten Mission to India, this should be emphasized at the beginning. Within three weeks of his arrival in India, Mountbatten never had any doubt as to what should be done in order to turn his mission into a success. Even earlier than that, V. P. Menon wrote of him after his first meeting (on 28 March):

'Even that early, only four days after his arrival, I got the feeling that he had decided which way he was going, what solution he had in mind. I told him on this occasion that in my view, Jinnah and the Muslim League would be willing to accept even a truncated Pakistan rather than go into a central Government. He seized upon the point right away. I left him feeling that he had come to India armed with plenipotentiary powers and if the parties were not able to come together, the decision would ultimately have to be given by His Excellency. The decision, I think, will not be palatable to either party.'[1]

Mountbatten had one great strength—a strength which enabled him to make it clear, immediately upon arriving in Delhi, that though a caretaker Viceroy he was master in the house so long as he remained. Mr Attlee, the Labour Prime Minister, had given him the straightforward direction for which his predecessor, Wavell, had repeatedly asked in vain. He brought with him to India a message from Attlee which set out the terms and scope of his mission in such a way that he never had any doubt of the extent of his discretion.

'It is the definite object of His Majesty's Government,' the Prime Minister had written, 'to obtain a unitary Government of India within the British Commonwealth, through the medium of a Constituent Assembly, set up and run in accordance with the Cabinet Mission's Plan, and you should do the utmost in your power to persuade all Parties to work together to this end, and advise His Majesty's Government, in the light of developments, as to the steps that will have to be taken.'

But he went on:

'Since, however, this plan can only become operative in respect of British India by agreement between the major Parties, there can be no question of compelling either Party to accept it. If by October 1 you consider that there is no prospect of reaching a settlement on the basis of a unitary Government for British India, either with or without the co-operation of the Indian States, you should report to His Majesty's Government on the steps which you consider should be taken for the handing over of power on the due date.'

There was more to the Instruction than this, but this was the kernel. He had been given both authority and room for manœuvre, and he made the speediest possible use of it. By the end of his first three weeks in India, the Viceroy may not have decided that a unitary India was impossible, but he had certainly reached the conclusion that the attainment of it would be a long and ticklish job, fraught with danger and uncertainty. And Lord Mountbatten

[1] V. P. Menon, *The Transfer of Power in India.*

was in India not to risk failure but to achieve success, and quickly. As V. P. Menon puts it in *The Transfer of Power in India*:

'Lord Mountbatten was required by his directive to find an agreed solution for a united India on the basis of the Cabinet Mission Plan and he set about most expeditiously and zealously on this path. But in the course of his talks with the party leaders, particularly with Jinnah and his colleagues, he became more and more convinced that there was no prospect of an agreed solution on that basis and that an alternative plan for the transfer of power had to be found and implemented without loss of time.'

The only alternative was, of course, partition—and Pakistan. But how to sell partition to the Congress leaders and particularly Gandhi and Nehru, who were adamantly against it? How to sell it to the Government at home? And how to sell it to soldiers and civil servants who would have the dreadful job of cutting the country in two?

With Gandhi, the problem was not a difficult one. The Viceroy's clever manœuvring after his first two meetings with the Mahatma had already exiled him to the periphery of the Congress movement. 'He is not a practical man,' Mountbatten said in effect to the Congress leaders. 'Look at the silly plan he produced to hand India over to Jinnah. This is no time for idealistic gestures—this is the time for action.' From this time onwards Congress began more and more frequently to take important decisions without consulting him. One of those decisions was contained in a Resolution passed by the Congress Working Committee at the beginning of March, and it played straight into the Viceroy's hands.

The author of the Resolution was Sardar Patel, and he alone, perhaps, of all his colleagues was aware exactly what he was doing. For the Resolution, proposed by Patel and adopted by the Congress Working Committee, recommended the partition of the great granary-province of the Punjab into two communal states, Muslim and Hindu, with freedom to the Sikhs to choose in which community they would live and work. The significance of such a decision was surely obvious: that if Congress was willing to accept partition of a province, then it could not claim any longer to be against the partition of the country. Patel saw it in no other way. For he had made up his mind. So far as he was concerned, the Muslims could go and take their majority territories with them. As organizer and controller of the Congress Party machine, he saw nothing but trouble ahead if independent India included the Muslim League as Opposition, thwarting his plans, holding up legislation. The actions of Liaquat Ali Khan—the Muslim League deputy leader—as Finance Member of the interim Government had given him the fright of his life, for, it will be remembered, Liaquat's Budget had heavily soaked the millionaire backers of Congress and shown up the hypocrisy of the Party's claim to be Socialist. Patel not only campaigned to get the Budget modified (which, with the help of the Viceroy, he succeeded in doing) but he resolved never to be trapped into a such situation again.

Not that Patel explained his attitude to his colleagues with quite such brutal clarity. For them he had another line of reasoning more calculated to appeal to their desire to preserve Indian unity at all costs.

'If the League insists on Pakistan,' he wrote to one of the Working Committee, 'the only alternative is the division of the Punjab and Bengal ... I do not think that the British Government will agree to division. In the end, they will see the wisdom of handing over the reins of Government to the strongest party. Even if they do not, it will not matter. A strong Centre with the whole of India—except E. Bengal and part of the Punjab, Sind and Baluchistan—enjoying full autonomy under the Centre will be so powerful that the remaining portions will eventually come in.'

It was this line of reasoning which particularly appealed to Pandit Nehru. It was no use; he could not take Jinnah and the Muslim League seriously. The aim was to discredit them once and for all, and to demonstrate to India's Muslims that only Congress could protect their future welfare.

To him, Patel's Resolution was a stratagem rather than an admittance of the fact of partition. It was with his active connivance that the Congress Working Committee met and signified their approval of a partition of the Punjab. It was far from representing the crossing of the Rubicon, he thought; it would merely show the Muslims what must be faced if they insisted upon their agitation for Pakistan. Even Mr Jinnah himself would realize that his agitation could only lead to a truncated State so painfully mutilated that it could never be viable. A date was chosen for the passing of the Resolution when Gandhi was immersed in his healing mission in Bihar and when the only important Muslim member of the Congress hierarchy, Maulana Abul Kalam Azad, was ill and absent, for Patel and Nehru knew that both of them would be against it and would use all their influence to stop it from going through. And even after it was passed, steps were taken to keep it secret and no message was sent to Gandhi to tell him what had taken place.

'I have long intended to write to you asking you about the Working Committee resolution on the possible partition of the Punjab,' he wrote to Nehru, nearly three weeks later. 'I would like to know the reason for it. I have to speak about it. I have done so in the absence of full facts with the greatest caution. Kripalani (who had now taken the Congress presidency from Nehru) said in answer to a question in Madras that it was possible that the principle might also be applied to Bengal. I was asked by a Muslim Leaguer of note . . . if it was applicable to the Muslim-majority provinces why it should not be so to Congress-majority provinces like Bihar. I think I did not know the reason behind the Working Committee's resolution. Nor had I the opportunity. I could only give my own view which was against any partition based on communal grounds and the two-nation theory. Anything was possible by compulsion. But willing consent required an appeal to reason and heart. Compulsion or show of it had no place in voluntariness.'

He wrote at the same time to Sardar Patel asking him to explain the 'Punjab resolution'.

Patel was the first to reply, and it was a response disingenuous in the extreme:

'It has been difficult to explain to you the resolution about the Punjab. It was adopted after the deepest deliberation. Nothing has been done in a hurry or without full thought. *That you had expressed your views against it, we learned only from the papers.*[1] But you are of course entitled to say what you feel right. The situation in the Punjab is far worse than in Bihar. The military has taken over control. As a result, on the surface things seem to have quietened down somewhat. But no one can say when there may be a bust-up again. If that happens, I am afraid even Delhi will not remain unaffected. But here of course we shall be able to deal with it.'

Pandit Nehru's reply, which followed a day later, was much more lame.

[1] My italics—L. M. Gandhi had never left anyone—least of all Patel—in doubt of his objection to *any* form of partition.

'About our proposal to divide Punjab,' he wrote, 'this flows naturally from our previous decisions. These were negative previously, but now the time for a decision has come and merely passing resolutions giving expression to our views means little. I feel convinced, and so did most of the members of the Working Committee, that we must press for this immediate division *so that reality might be brought into the picture. Indeed, this is the only answer to partition as demanded by Jinnah.*'[1]

He still could not be convinced that Jinnah would rather have a 'moth-eaten Pakistan', as he was to call it later, than no Pakistan at all.

Neither George Abell nor V. P. Menon were slow in drawing the Viceroy's attention to the Congress Resolution and stressing the fundamental change which it represented (whether the members realized it or not) in Congress strategy. He at once sent for Patel and carefully sounded him on the motives which had been behind the Punjab Resolution. It was no part of Patel's technique to play the game of Indian independence with his cards face up on the table, and for most of the interview he was the somewhat naive Hindu politician only half aware of what the Resolution meant. There were far too important stakes in the games ahead for him to worry about being thought a sucker in this one. It was with surprise and a small show of dismay that he allowed it to be demonstrated to him that by accepting the division of the Punjab he had recognized the principle of Indian partition; and it was even more slowly and unwillingly that he appeared to accept Mountbatten's contention that this was, perhaps, the way out after all. Think of the peace if the Muslims could be banished once and for all to their own (very small and unworkable) country. No opposition to Congress plans. No cunning campaigns against the owners of the Congress money-bags. A free India under a one-party regime, free to carry out its plans without interference.

Grudgingly, Patel allowed himself to be persuaded that here, perhaps, was the way out. Jubilantly, Mountbatten emerged from the meeting to tell his Staff: 'It worked! He seemed like such a hard nut—yet once I cracked the shell, he was all pulp inside!'

Neither V. P. Menon, who heard this remark, or Patel himself, ever revealed to the Viceroy that they had talked of the real meaning of the Resolution long before it was submitted; that, in

[1] My italics—L. M.

fact (as it will be seen), while ostensibly walking innocently into Mountbatten's parlour, Sardar Patel was busily spinning a web of his own.

'As soon as Sardar Patel had been convinced,' wrote Maulana Abul Kalam Azad later, 'Lord Mountbatten turned his attention to Jawaharlal. Jawaharlal was not at first at all willing and reacted violently against the very idea of partition, but Lord Mountbatten persisted till step by step Jawaharlal's opposition was torn down. Within a month of Lord Mountbatten's arrival in India, Jawaharlal, the firm opponent of partition, had become if not a supporter at least acquiescent towards the idea.'

Azad added: 'I have often wondered how Jawaharlal was won over by Lord Mountbatten.'

There were, in fact, a great many factors involved in his astonishing change of front, but one of them was certainly Lady Mountbatten.

From the very beginning, the Viceroy and his Staff worked as a team, and very much part of the team was his wife and—in a lesser way—their daughter, Pamela. Each day, in addition to their ordinary administrative duties, the Staff proliferated over Delhi to spread Viceregal goodwill and oil the wheels of negotiation. Campbell-Johnson maintained a fairly close liaison with the Nehru household and became a welcome guest at the Nehru breakfast table, a firm friend of Nehru's daughter, Indira—whose influence on her father was considerable—and a successful lubricant of the Nehru-Mountbatten axis. He also moved with notable effect among those Indian intellectuals, like Pannikar, who were not officially members of Congress but had a great deal of influence on Congress thinking.

Lord Ismay's job was the rather more difficult one of advocating the Viceroy's good intentions among the Muslims, and in this he was aided by George Abell. Most of Ismay's military life in India had been spent among Muslim troops and he made no secret of the fact that he vastly preferred them to the Hindus. He was a manifestly good and well-meaning man,[1] and though he never did succeed in penetrating Mohammed Ali Jinnah's armour

[1] It is typical of him that he had, for more than twenty years, been supplementing his old Muslim batman's Army pension with one of his own. Just before he arrived in India, his bank manager wrote to tell him that the pension hadn't been collected for weeks. He realized why when he reached Delhi. His batman, hearing of his appointment on the radio, had set out on foot and walked for weeks—and was waiting in Delhi to serve him again.

of reserve and suspicion, he was much more successful with Liaquat Ali Khan. All the other members of the entourage worked like eager beavers, nibbling their way into Indian hearts.

For his own family, the Viceroy had tasks assigned, too; although, if the truth be told, Lady Mountbatten did not need assignments. She responded immediately to the challenge of India, and had no intention of confining her activities to the running of the Viceroy's House and its 7,500 servants, or to the occasional banquets and garden parties which were part of the programme of a Viceregal year, even as exceptional a one as this. She briefed her daughter, Pamela, in Indian politics and then told her to go out and 'breathe friendship and goodwill on everyone'. Pamela became a familiar figure at Gandhi prayer meetings when they took place in Delhi and an animated speaker at Young Indian discussion groups.

Lady Mountbatten's chief stock-in-trade, as she well knew, was charm and sympathy. She shared with her husband a need to be liked, to be successful, but hers was an ambition which got its impetus much more from the heart than from the head. She was shrewd enough to realize that even the most anti-British Indians dearly love a Lady and are dazzled by even the reflected light of royalty, and she used her background, her personality and her beauty for all they were worth in making contacts. But once made, she genuinely enjoyed them. She liked the Indians and was completely devoid of the colour-consciousness and class-consciousness of so many British memsahibs. She made friends of most of the Indian leaders and their wives, and much of her enthusiastic support of her husband's policies and ideas communicated itself to them in the most subtly convincing way.

One of her closest friends now was Pandit Nehru, and, in the words of Maulana Abul Kalam Azad, more than the influence of Patel or Mountbatten upon him 'was the influence of Lady Mountbatten . . . She admired her husband greatly and in many cases tried to interpret his thought to those who would not at first agree with him.'

It was not Lady Mountbatten alone, however, but a combination of circumstances in which she played her part which eventually turned Nehru's troubled and uncertain mind to the solution of Pakistan. He had himself travelled to the Punjab and seen something of the communal riots which, in March and April, caused the deaths of at least 2,000 people. India was rapidly becoming an unholy mess of bloodshed and hatred, and Nehru was consumed with a sense of hopelessness in the face of it. 'I have seen ghastly sights and I have heard of behaviour by human beings which would degrade brutes,' he wrote. A few years before it would not have daunted him; rather would he have accepted it as a challenge to his own leadership and Congress policy, and gone out personally to fight it. But now . . . he was tired. He felt out of touch with the people.

'Conditions all over India to some extent are very unsatisfactory,' he wrote to Gandhi. 'There is a certain disruptive tendency at work which affects our work in every direction. The whole Congress organization is suffering from it and we, who are in the Government, have not time at all to give to any work except the immediate problems which confront us . . . What I am worrying about is the rapidly deteriorating state of the Congress organization. Those of us who are in the Government have given and can give no time at all to the Congress work. We are losing touch with the people.'

It was while he was in this state of mind that Lady Mountbatten came back from a tour of the Punjab, which she had made by plane and car through most of the worst riot areas. It was the first time she had really ventured out of the air-conditioned coolness of the Viceroy's House into the dust-filled furnace of an Indian summer, and she was appalled by what she saw and felt. 'This summer', she wrote in a report to the St John Ambulance Brigade, 'has been the most trying on record, the temperature varying from up to 114 in the shade (with a night temperature rarely dropping below 95) to the middle nineties where it now seems to have settled, but with humidity rising all the time . . . This has made active work, particularly out in towns and villages where there are often no such things as fans, very trying indeed, and I have often found myself wringing out my hair two or three times in the day, in fact one forgets what it is to be dry.'

In her visits to hospitals and riot-wrecked villages, she encountered all the horrors of communal savagery—a child with its hands chopped off, a pregnant mother disembowelled, a family wiped out save for a small baby. She came back to Delhi in great distress, appalled by her confrontation with communal hatred and convinced that her husband and his advisers were right and that partition was the only way. It was while she was in this wretched state of numbed horror and despair that Mount-

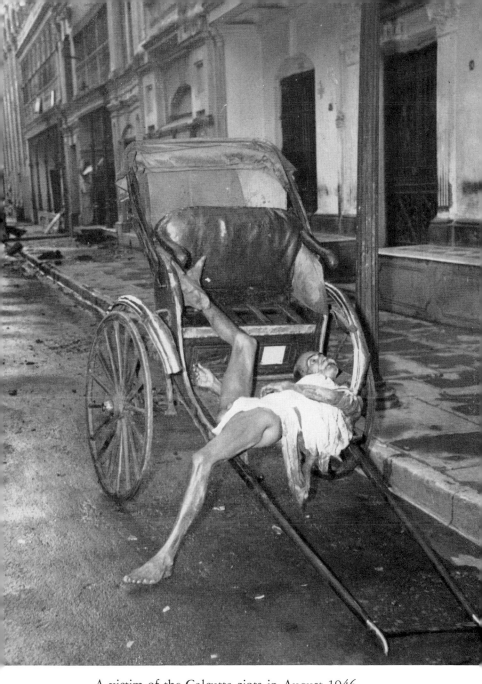

A victim of the Calcutta riots in August 1946

Pandit Nehru with Mahatma Gandhi at a committee meeting in
Bombay, July 6, 1946

Field Marshal Lord Wavell talking to Lord Mountbatten in March 1947

Lord Mountbatten being greeted by Pandit Nehru and Liaquat Ali Khan on his arrival in New Delhi to take up his post as Viceroy.

The Nizam of Hyderabad

Princes and representatives of Indian states discussing plans for independence with Lord Mountbatten and Lord Ismay

Pandit Nehru, Lord Ismay, Lord Mountbatten, and Mohammed
Ali Jinnah at the conference in New Delhi on June 7, 1947 when
the British plan for partition was accepted

Lord Radcliffe

Lord Mountbatten with Sardar Patel

Pandit Nehru being sworn in as first Prime Minister of India, August 15, 1947

Mohammed Ali Jinnah making his first speech as President of Pakistan

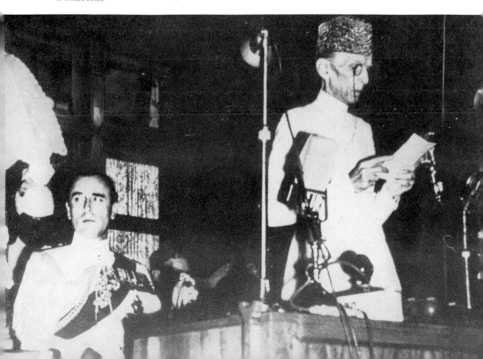

Muslim refugees crowding a train leaving for Pakistan

Victims of the riots in New Delhi

batten sent her to see Nehru. They grieved together over India's misery. A few days after this Nehru went round to see Maulana Abul Kalam Azad. 'Jawaharlal asked me in despair', wrote Azad afterwards, 'what other alternative was there to accepting partition . . . He recognized that partition was evil, but he held that circumstances were inevitably leading in that direction . . . and asked me to give up my opposition to partition. He said that it was inevitable and it would be wisdom not to oppose what was bound to happen. *He also said that it would not be wise for me to oppose Lord Mountbatten on this issue.*'[1]

It was done. The man who had fought so long for a free and unitary India, who had mocked Jinnah and despised the Muslim League, had been won over by Mountbatten's charm and Lady Mountbatten's distress in less than a month; and though, of course, there were other factors involved—particularly the weariness of many Congress leaders and Sardar Patel's determination to be rid of the Muslims once and for all—there was no doubt in anyone's mind in India that the Viceroy, in persuading Nehru, had performed the confidence trick of the century. For Nehru's conversion was the key. Without his consent, the Congress would never have accepted the idea of partition.

Mohammed Ali Jinnah preserved a cool and dignified attitude in public and accepted Nehru's *volte face* as a tardy recognition of undeniable facts; but in private, he could hardly contain himself. His satisfaction was as great as the Viceroy's. He had never expected recognition of Pakistan by Congress to come so soon. In fact, many who knew him maintained that he had never really expected Pakistan to come, either. And now here he was, standing on its threshold.

On 11 April 1947 Lord Ismay sent the following letter to V. P. Menon, the Reforms Commissioner, from the Viceroy's House:

'My dear Menon,—I send you herewith the bare bones of a possible plan for the transfer of power. The Viceroy would be glad if you would *a.* amend the draft in any way you think right and put some flesh on it; *b.* consider what the procedure would be immediately after HMG had made their announcement. For example, would a general election throughout India be necessary? How would we set about the partition of the Punjab, Bengal and Assam? Presumably, the decision will be left to HE and will

[1] My italics—L. M.

not be open to argument. What will be the machinery for those groups who wish to get together to frame their constitution and so on and so forth? *c.* Work out a rough timetable. I ought to explain that nothing very precise is required at this stage but only to give HE an idea of how this plan would be implemented if adopted, and how long it would take. Yours very sincerely, Ismay.'

Menon's draft was circulated a few days later to the Governors of India's eleven provinces who had been summoned to Delhi for a conference with the Viceroy. The moment they read it, they realized that their days were numbered. 'The blighter's pulled it off,' one of them said. 'What is he—a swami or something?' But even Sir Evan Jenkins, the Governor of the Punjab and a fervid opponent of the partition of that province, raised no objections to the draft. Only Sir Frederick Burrows, Governor of Bengal, who was absent owing to illness, indicated his opposition and hinted that he was lending his support to agitation in Calcutta for a separate State of Bengal, independent of both Pakistan *and* Hindustan (and, of course, led by that cheerful political boss, Mr Shaheed Suhrarwardy).[1] Otherwise, the Governors gave the Viceroy *carte blanche* to go ahead. The main concern of a considerable number of them was not the future of India but the safety of British nationals once independence was proclaimed; they appeared to believe that a massacre of the sahibs would automatically follow.

The Viceroy dined them and their ladies in the great banqueting hall on Viceregal silver, and though the food was frugal (for Lady Mountbatten had initiated an austerity régime as a gesture to 'starving India') the reminiscences were rich and sentimental, for all were aware that there would never again be such a function. From the walls, the portraits of past Viceroys looked down on the farewell supper, and as he glanced up at them occasionally, at least one Governor wondered, sadly, what Lord Curzon would have thought about it all.

It was, nonetheless, a triumph of no mean order for the Viceroy. It may have been charm, it may have been confidence trickery, it may have been a ruthless use of snobbery and salesmanship on the susceptible Indians, but it had certainly changed the situation

[1] 'I'll probably stay on to run the railways,' joked Sir Frederick. (He was fond of reminding the Indians that he was an old railway worker. 'The folks you usually get out here are experts on huntin' and shootin',' he told them. 'Well, I'm an expert on shuntin' and hootin'.')

in less than a month from hopeless deadlock to hopeful settlement.

For personal reasons, Mountbatten had good reason to be satisfied. To the world, the choice of 1 June 1948 as the date when power would irrevocably be handed over to the Indians had been chosen by the Prime Minister, Mr Attlee, as one which would best shock the Indian leaders into a sense of reality. So, if official spokesmen have their way, will the date go down in history. In fact, it was not Mr Attlee who chose the date but Lord Mountbatten, and it was not chosen for reasons of Indian policy but to conform with the Viceroy's personal plans. When the Labour Party premier first asked him to assume the task of being India's last Viceroy, Mountbatten refused for the genuine reason that he felt it was time he got back to the Navy and resumed his career[1]. Attlee pleaded with him. He said that he had been thinking along the lines of giving the Indians a time limit to put their house in order, and had thought that they should be told that two years would be as much as the British Government would be prepared to endure the present situation.

Mountbatten replied that two years was far too long for him to be away from the Navy. The Prime Minister then asked him how long he would be prepared to give to the task if the Government guaranteed that his rank, seniority and opportunities for promotion in the Royal Navy were preserved. Mountbatten asked permission to think it over, and went off to talk about the prospects of the job to a number of his friends—and to the King.

Next day, he saw Mr Attlee again and asked him whether the job could not be done in twelve months, which was the maximum time he felt he could spare, even for the disposal of the Indian Empire. The premier replied that, after some thought, he had come to the conclusion that eighteen months would be long enough—but perhaps a compromise could be arranged.

The compromise resulted in a ring round the calendar for 1 June 1948, fifteen months after the assumption of office. Within thirty days of that date, Mr Attlee assured Mountbatten, he would be back in the Navy.

---

[1] Mountbatten's father, Prince Louis of Battenberg, was forced to resign as First Lord of the Admiralty during the Great War because of his name and German parentage. His son was determined to vindicate him by becoming First Lord himself, an ambition which he has since achieved and surpassed.

'Too soon, too soon,' Churchill had cried, when the date of 1 June 1948 was first mentioned in the House of Commons. But the way things were going, one month after Mountbatten's arrival, it looked like being even sooner.

Thanks to his methods, the opposition to his plans was just melting away.

CHAPTER FIVE

NEW DEAL AT SIMLA

IT IS PERHAPS significant that in the last few days of April and the first week of May 1947 Mountbatten was able to give two hours a day to work on his family tree; while Nehru's daughter, Indira, reported that her father was talking loudly in his sleep again. With the former, a compilation of his more remote ancestry was a favourite hobby when things were going well, and with the latter somniloquy was a symptom that things were going badly.

Having proved to his own satisfaction that the Indians were largely paper tigers when confronted by the right kind of bluff, the Viceroy gathered his British Staff around him and told them to rush through details of the Draft Scheme for Independence without delay. The idea was to jostle a settlement through before either Congress or the Muslim League had too much time to think about it, and before any really effective opposition to the partition of the country had time to develop.

It might have been expected that either Lord Ismay or George Abell, two great lovers of India, would have protested against the sudden unseemly rush to reach a settlement. Ismay had agreed to accompany the new Viceroy to India because he knew the task was one of fantastic difficulty and responsibility and because he suspected that Mountbatten might be inclined to rush it. 'You'll be a fool to go,' Churchill said to him, when Ismay told him of his decision. 'You'll get nothing out of it.' The idea that he might be going in order to get himself a decoration or a preferment in the peerage had filled Ismay with unaccustomed rage, and for once he had lashed out at his old chief with the angry remark: 'I'm going anyway, and you can go to hell!' It was always his idea that he would be Mountbatten's counsellor of caution, the hand upon his shoulder, the foot upon the brake when the juggernaut seemed to be moving too fast.

But a month in India had changed all that. Far from counselling hesitation and reflection, his was the voice which urged Mountbatten to make haste. 'The communal feeling I found', he said

later to Hector Bolitho, 'I just did not believe possible. It tore
at you, all the time. There was slaughter everywhere. We British
had all the responsibility and none of the power. The police force
was already undermined, and the civil service were frustrated
and madly anxious. They were blamed by both Nehru and Jinnah
for everything that went wrong. This was one reason why to
delay partition would be to increase the disasters. There was
another reason: the Viceroy's Executive Council, which had been
composed of six or eight wise men, had disappeared. We had
instead a Cabinet of nine Congress leaders and five Muslim
League leaders who could agree on only one thought—that the
British should quit India.'[1]

To George Abell, too, the spectre of an India torn by civil war
was very real. The news from the Punjab and the North West
Frontier Province was very bad: private armies forming in the
former, Muslim League agitation (against the tottering pro-
Congress Government) in the latter. June 1948 seemed a very
long way away and when it came, the whole of India might well
be in chaos.

So the Viceroy's two chief advisers believed. It was a panicky
state of mind which made them easy prey for the Mountbatten
policy of 'let's get it over with and get out quickly'. They were
embittered and disillusioned. For neither of them was this any
longer the India they had known and loved, and their attitude
was rather like that of a madly doting father whose daughter has
run away with the wrong man. 'After all I've done for her!'
mourned Ismay. 'Call the lawyer—I'm going to change my will!'
said Abell.

What they were doing was not so much handing India her
freedom but washing their hands of her; and once the mood of
disillusion was upon them, they would listen to no voices which
counselled calm, reflection, deliberation. They were at one with
Mountbatten in agreeing 'that the need for the political solution
is much more pressing than was apparent when we were in
London, and that the June 1948 limit, far from being not long
enough, is already too remote a deadline'.[2] The Viceroy, Ismay,
Abell, Mièville and 'The Dickie Birds' formed a tight circle
around the anvil in the Viceroy's House and set to work with a
will and an almost desperate eagerness to hammer out a detailed

[1] H. Bolitho, *Jinnah*.
[2] Quoted by Alan Campbell-Johnson, *Mission with Mountbatten*.

Plan for Indian Independence for Ismay to take to London. It was to be an all-British plan in the drawing up of which all Indians, including V. P. Menon, the Reforms Commissioner, were excluded; and this was to prove important in the days to come. They worked at it night and day and in great secrecy. This was the great Plan which would solve everything.

Until this moment, V. P. Menon had been frequently consulted by the Viceroy and his Staff, but for the present he had, in Campbell-Johnson's phrase, 'suffered a period of eclipse'. It was difficult to explain why. There was, of course, the obvious reason that being a Hindu his too-close connexion with the conception of the Plan might arouse Muslim suspicions (though this becomes ridiculous in the light of what happened later). The more likely reason is that some of the Viceroy's Staff considered him rather too sure of himself and not subservient enough for their liking. The position of Reforms Commissioner and Constitutional Adviser to the Viceroy had, when held by an Englishman, always been one of the most important in the Indian administration, but to some of the most senior officials there is little doubt that the influence diminished now that an Indian held it. Menon knew, for example, that one of the problems which troubled Mount-batten and his Staff was the question of Dominion status for a divided India. Congress had always made it plain that when they asked for independence, they meant complete independence, with absolutely no connexion with the British Commonwealth. To the great mass of Indians, the status of a Dominion within the Commonwealth meant—in spite of how things had changed —a continuance of British subjection. The idea of owing allegiance to the British Crown was anathema to them.

On the other hand, Pakistan not only was willing to remain in the Commonwealth but Jinnah actively insisted on it. But what was to happen when India was divided? The Viceroy's view was that Dominion status could not possibly be given to one of the two new States (Pakistan) if the other (Hindustan) did not want it. That would immediately start the whole thing off on the wrong basis and create suspicion between the two States.

Ismay replied that you couldn't chuck Pakistan out of the Commonwealth just because the Hindus didn't want to come in. Think of the effect on the Muslim world in the Middle East if we insulted Jinnah in this fashion.

Mièville mentioned at this point that Menon had said *en passant* that he had talked with Sardar Patel on this very problem, and the Congress wasn't so hostile to Dominion status, after all; they might even consider it.

This remark was made with such lack of emphasis and with such obvious ignorance of its vital importance that no one on the Viceroy's Staff took any notice of it. Who cared about what Menon said, anyway? They went on with their drafting of the great Plan, carefully skirting the difficult question of Dominion status and presuming that Congress policy was still that of complete independence from Commonwealth and Crown. They did not realize that they were digging a pit for the Viceroy to fall in; nor did it occur to them to call in Menon and ask him what he meant when, in putting 'the flesh' on the Draft Plan, as he had been asked to do by Ismay, *he had appended his own opinion that the Plan was a bad one and certainly would not work.*

From his dunce's stool in the anteroom, V. P. Menon made an attempt to rescue his British colleagues from the consequence of their stupidity, and also to restore his own position. He wrote to George Abell to complain:

'Dear Abell,—I have been thinking of writing to you about the difficult position in which I am placed as Reforms Commissioner. I would not have raised this issue but for important practical reasons of great urgency. Since power has to be transferred not later than June 1948, it is essential that there should be some organization to evolve a plan of operation and then implement it. I have so far assumed that the Reforms Office acting under HE's orders would be that organization. However, if the Reforms Office is to do this work it is essential that I should be kept in touch with all the relevant developments. Unless I am able to view all issues in their true mutual relationship and have sufficient background information, I cannot advise HE with full knowledge . . . Surely our general approach has to be settled before we start settling the details. There is very little time and a great many problems to solve. There is a grave danger of lack of co-ordination if departments work in water-tight compartments . . . It is essential that there should be an automatic procedure by which I am kept informed of developments.'

It should in fairness be pointed out that Menon's interest in what was happening inside the Viceregal parlour was not entirely disinterested. He was a devoted civil servant and a loyal admirer of the British. But he was also, naturally, a passionate believer in

Indian independence and, much more important, a close friend
and fervent admirer of Sardar Patel, the Congress Party strong-
man. He was surely not the first civil servant, however, to have
strong views and partialities, and there is certainly no evidence
that he ever let them affect his work for the Government of India.
What is surprising is that the Viceroy's Staff should, at such a
critical moment, have excluded from their counsels a direct channel
of communication with the Congress Party who could have
warned them when they were going wrong. But for some members
of Mountbatten's staff, an Indian was still an Indian.

On 2 May 1947 Lord Ismay and Mr George Abell departed
for London with what might be called the 'Dickie Bird Plan' for
Indian independence.

As V. P. Menon described it in *The Transfer of Power in India*,
in a chapter headed 'Lord Mountbatten's Draft Plan', the Viceroy
had revised his tentative plan 'in the light of his discussions with
the Governors and party leaders and sent this revised plan to
London with Lord Ismay and George Abell on 2 May . . . In all
his discussions with party leaders and others, despite the divergent
views which he was forced to adjust and reconcile, there was
nowhere any evidence of an attempt to question either his own
impartiality or the bona fides of His Majesty's Government.'

But Menon added: 'I had always been opposed to the plan
which Lord Ismay and George Abell had taken to London. The
theory that the provinces should become initially independent
successor States was particularly abhorrent to me. But my protests
and my views in the discussion with the Viceroy's advisers went
in vain.'

The Mountbatten Draft Plan was, in fact, an adaptation of the
Cabinet Mission Plan—in this instance, to transfer power uni-
laterally, without the willing consent of the party leaders, and
with a federal rather than a strong central government.

The task of the two senior members of the Viceroy's Staff was
to go over the Plan clause by clause with the Cabinet in London
and secure their approval of it. They took with them assurances
from Mountbatten that this was the Plan which would be
accepted by both parties, and that all that was needed was the
approval of Mr Attlee and his colleagues to set the machinery for
independence in motion.

It is true that the Viceroy did have a sudden qualm, after Ismay's
departure, that perhaps the Plan might run into trouble after all—

not from Congress, but from the Muslims and particularly Mr Jinnah. He sent an urgent message by telegram to Ismay saying:

'In recent conversations which Miéville and I have had with Jinnah, the latter did not appear seriously to contest the idea of a truncated Pakistan. In fact, the general impression which Jinnah has given me throughout, and I think you will confirm he gave you before you left, was that he did not intend to reject the Plan contained in the draft announcement. In my interviews with Jinnah and Liaquat Ali Khan I have always watched them carefully for any indication of an intention to reject the Plan, and I have seen no such indication. In fact, every test which I have applied has passed off successfully and has led me to believe that they are likely to accept the Plan. If Jinnah intends to spring a surprise on me by rejecting the Plan at the last moment, he could not have played his part better towards making this surprise complete. I am of the opinion that the statement issued to the Press by Jinnah on 30 April opposing the partition of the provinces was a counterblast to extreme Hindu and Sikh demands, but it would be unwise to bank on this assumption. I have purposely refrained from asking him outright whether he would accept a truncated or 'moth-eaten' Pakistan, as he calls it, because I have felt he could certainly have said no, in the mistaken belief or hope that I would go further and recommend to HMG the full Pakistan that he desires. Therefore, we must still be on our guard against this contingency. I know full well that Jinnah is a hard bargainer and the possibility of his intention to lead me up the garden path has got to be catered for.'[1]

It should be remembered that, at this juncture, neither the Muslim League nor the Congress (nor, of course, the Sikhs) had so far seen the 'Dickie Bird Plan' but had only been told in broad outline of its nature. The Viceroy seemed to have no fears at all of its reception by Congress, but the possibility of trickery by Jinnah nagged at him. A few hours after sending his cable to Ismay, he asked his Staff to prepare a memorandum for him as to what action could be taken if Jinnah did, in fact, doublecross him at the last moment. He received the following document:

1. If Mr Jinnah does not accept the draft announcement proposed by Your Excellency there are two alternatives for parting with power:

[1] Government of India Records.

a. That power will be parted with to the Central Government as at present constituted, on a Dominion basis.

N.B. This will be attacked by the Conservative Party as handing over Jinnah to the tender mercy of the Hindus. It might also attract the attention of Muslim countries outside India, particularly if it is followed by Muslim League propaganda.

b. To transfer power to the existing Central Government on a Dominion status basis subject to one stipulation. The Muslim demand for a Provincewise Pakistan could not be sustained on any equitable argument. We came down as a defensible proposition on a truncated Pakistan. Jinnah has rejected this proposition. Therefore in order to meet the possible attack both from the Conservatives in England and outside India, I would include a condition in the Government of India Act 1935 or in the Treaty that will be concluded between Great Britain and India, that in the event of the Muslim League changing their opinion within 3 years and demanding a truncated Pakistan, it will be open to the Governor-General under the procedure laid down in the Announcement, to authorise legislation by which Muslim majority areas could form a Government of their own. Till that takes place the power will be parted to the existing Central Government who will be responsible for the administration of India, including Pakistan.'[1]

But as the days passed, the Viceroy became cheerfully confident that this hypothetical plan to counter Jinnah would not be necessary, and that all would go through smoothly. Even Gandhi was not powerful enough any longer to dam or divert the course of events. The Mahatma had, in fact, hurried north from Bengal when he heard of the changed trend of Congress thinking on the question of partition; but he had come too late. Patel, who normally gave way before Gandhi's persuasion, had made up his mind and had the power to make Congress conform. Nehru saw no other way but partition, though he admitted to Gandhi that it was 'tragic and evil'. In an interview with the Viceroy, the Mahatma pleaded with him to fight at all costs for a unitary India and to revise the Cabinet Mission Plan once more. Mountbatten told him that it was out of his hands and that his only hope was to convince Mr Jinnah and the Muslim League. He had arranged his talk with Gandhi so that it overlapped one with Jinnah, and the two former Congress colleagues met again

[1] Government of India Records.

for the first time for many years. They greeted each other cordially, if warily, and under the Viceroy's prodding agreed to have a conference together at a future date. They met at Jinnah's house in Aurangzeb Road, New Delhi, on 6 May 1947, in a room on the wall of which was a silver map of India, with Pakistan painted on it in green. The two old men talked together for three hours (all Indians always seem to talk for three hours at official meetings) and a communiqué was issued afterwards. It said:

'We discussed two matters. One was the question of the division of India into Pakistan and Hindustan, and Mr Gandhi does not accept the principle of division. He thinks that division is not inevitable, whereas in my opinion not only is Pakistan inevitable but is the only practical solution of India's political problem.

'The second matter which we discussed was the letter which we have both signed jointly appealing to the people to maintain peace; we have both come to the conclusion that we must do our best in our respective spheres to see that that appeal of ours is carried out and we will make every effort for this purpose.'

In other words, the conference had got Gandhi nowhere. Little wonder that the Viceroy began to have diminishing fears of any slip-up. It was just a question of waiting for the decision of the Cabinet in London—and he had not much doubt that Attlee would be behind him.

It was time, the Viceroy decided, to get away from the exhausting red-hot atmosphere of New Delhi to the coolness of the hills, and he instructed Campbell-Johnson to announce that he was leaving for a few days' rest at the Viceregal Lodge in Simla. It was to be more than a rest, in fact, for Mountbatten planned to take the next step towards independence while in the hills; and when the Viceregal cavalcade set out, no fewer than 350 servants and retainers accompanied him. For two days, Mountbatten and Lady Mountbatten—who was increasingly subject to headaches and neuralgia at this time—luxuriated in the fresh breezes and chilly nights of Simla, breathing the cold air blowing down upon them from the snowcapped Himalayas which ran, a rampart between India and Tibet, along the blue horizon.

But among those who had accompanied the Viceroy to Simla was V. P. Menon (and also Sir Eric Mièville), and for Menon this was the first opportunity since Mountbatten's arrival in India when he could talk to him freely and openly. On all previous occasions, the interviews had been formal, arranged by Ismay, stop-watched by Abell, and carefully screened by Mièville, and little deviation had been allowed from the prescribed line of talk.

In Simla's relaxing air, with the watchdogs called off,[1] Menon at last found an opportunity to expound his ideas and his theories. When Mountbatten raised the vexed question of the future status of India as a member (or not a member) of the Commonwealth community, Menon raised his bushy eyebrows in pained surprise. 'Did no one ever tell you', he said to the Viceroy, 'that I have already drawn up a scheme to solve the problem? Surely you must know about it? I told Lord Wavell about it. I told The India Office about it. I told Sir Eric Mièville about it.'

Well, yes, Mountbatten finally admitted, Mièville did say *something* but exactly what he couldn't really remember.

At which point V. P. Menon came into his own.

It was late in December 1946, he told the Viceroy, that he had a long talk with Sardar Vallabhbhai Patel about the Cabinet Mission Plan. In spite of what everyone else thought, Menon considered that the Cabinet Mission Plan would never work; the three-tiered constitutional set-up offended his orderly mind as unwieldy and unworkable; and it was certainly not the Plan which he visualized for an independent India. In addition to this, he believed, from a long association with Jinnah and an assessment of the way his mind worked, that he would never back down from his claim to a separate Pakistan.

'I told Patel that he had better face the fact that Jinnah had the support of influential British opinion in his claim to Pakistan,' Menon told the Viceroy, 'and, more important, he was supported by most of the high officers of the Army in India. My personal view was that it was better to divide India rather than let it gravitate towards civil war. If we agreed to partition, Jinnah could obviously not ask for those portions of the Punjab, Bengal and Assam which were predominantly non-Muslim. The crucial problem was the basis on which power could be transferred.'

'In a divided India', Menon went on, 'this could best be two central governments—and here', he told Mountbatten, 'is the point which should interest you—*on the basis of Dominion status*. By consenting to accept Dominion status, the Congress would be gaining three great advantages. Firstly, it would ensure a peaceful transfer of power. Secondly, such acceptance would be warmly welcomed in Britain, and Congress would by this single act

[1] They were in London with the 'Dickie Bird Plan'.

have gained British friendship and goodwill. Thirdly, the civil services in India were manned, in the higher posts, largely by Britons, and they would be encouraged to help if India stayed in the Commonwealth. Fourthly, the Indian Army, Air Force and Navy were mainly officered by Britons, and they would be persuaded to stay and help in the interim period. Fifthly, the Princely States, which are so fond of their connection with the Crown, would be reassured and more willing to federate.'

'And what have we got to lose?' Menon asked Patel. 'Whatever constitution India eventually makes for herself will be unaffected by Dominion status. If we get Dominion status, we can have power immediately, and when we are on our own feet, we can walk out of the Commonwealth at any time we like.'

Sardar Patel was at once impressed with Menon's scheme. 'He assured me,' Menon told the Viceroy, 'that if power could be transferred at once on the basis of Dominion status, he would use his influence to see that Congress accepted it.'

Menon, in Patel's presence, dictated an outline of the plan and sent it by special messenger to the Secretary of State for India— omitting only the detail that Patel had seen and approved it.

He had never heard anything about it since.

In the face of this revelation, the Viceroy behaved rather like a small boy who is ecstatically happy playing with a round pink balloon until he sees another boy playing with one that is sausage-shaped, and green. His confidence in his own Plan at once began to wane a little.

'What do you think of my Plan which Ismay has taken to London?' he asked Menon.

'I wish you had asked me that before,' his Reforms Commissioner replied. 'I don't like it a bit.'

On 8 May, Pandit Nehru and a friend and confidant, Krishna Menon, arrived in Simla to stay at the Viceregal Lodge as the Viceroy's guests. This was the period when Krishna Menon was busily fighting and intriguing his way from the junior to the senior ranks of the Congress Party hierarchy, and he, too—having nostrils sensitive to every change of wind—had sensed that the question of Dominion status might loom large in the discussions to come. He had, therefore, been propagating a scheme of his own with Nehru for some sort of sovereign state within the British Commonwealth. When Mountbatten heard about it, he quickly summoned V. P. Menon and told him to talk to Nehru at once about his Dominion status formula. 'But under no circumstances', ordered the Viceroy, 'are you to say anything at all about the Plan which Ismay has taken to London.'

V. P. Menon had a long talk with Nehru the next morning. It was a meeting which began extremely frigidly, for Nehru had learned that this was a scheme which Menon had discussed with Patel over four months earlier, and the revelation that the Sardar had been intriguing behind his back was a hard one for Nehru to swallow. But he was so impressed that he agreed to attend a formal meeting the next day, 10 May, to discuss it further in the presence of the Viceroy. They met the following morning in Mountbatten's green-walled, air-cooled study, and in addition to the Viceroy, Nehru and V. P. Menon, Sir Eric Mièville and Lieut.-Colonel Erskine Crum were also present.

The Viceroy formally explained that Menon had been working on a scheme for the early transfer of power on a Dominion status basis long before he, the Viceroy, had come to India. He said he would like to give Menon an opportunity of explaining it in some detail to himself and Pandit Nehru.

Menon, thereupon, repeated much of what he had already said to Mountbatten and Nehru. The broad outlines of the scheme were that the Muslim majority areas should be separated from India. The transfer of power should then be made to two Central Governments, one Pakistan, one Hindustan, each having its own Governor-General. Pending the drafting of a Constitution by the respective Constituent Assemblies, the interim Constitution for each of the two Dominions should be based on the Government of India Act of 1935, suitably adapted. And from that moment on, the two new countries would be ready to go.

The Viceroy underlined the simplicity and the importance of the scheme by pointing out that with such straightforward arrangements there would be no need to wait until June 1948 to hand over power. It could be passed on the moment that the Cabinet in Britain agreed to the scheme.

Nehru was obviously more impressed than ever, though he could not resist a series of reservations. 'You must realize', he said, rather testily, 'that there is an overwhelming opinion in India in favour of complete independence. The words "Dominion status" are likely to irritate people because of their past association. I know that in theory it can be shown that Dominion status is equivalent to complete independence, but such fine points are not, however, understood by the people.'

V. P. Menon interrupted. 'There would be an arrangement in my scheme to drop the word "Emperor" from the title of King-Emperor, by an Order in Council.'[1]

Nehru replied that he was afraid that such phraseology might still mean to many the continuation of indirect domination. And then he perked up. 'Still,' he said, 'I myself have always been most anxious for sentimental reasons to have the closest possible relationship with the British Commonwealth. I am still not clear what form the relationship should take, but I think and I hope it will be possible for the relationship to continue—but without the offending phraseology.' And then he added: 'But, of course, under Dominion status India would always have the power to leave the Commonwealth when she wished.'

Mountbatten: 'I agree. I also think that this fact should be emphasized, as well as a target for the termination of Dominion status.'[1]

One would have thought that, from all this discussion, the next step would have been the formal adoption of the Plan as the formula for the transfer of power. But how could that be? There was already another Plan in existence. It had been taken to London by Ismay to be approved by the Cabinet. It was this Plan—the 'Dickie Bird Plan'—upon which the Viceroy was resting his hopes for a settlement of the Indian deadlock and the handing over of power.

One wonders what can possibly have been passing through his mind that, in such circumstances, he allowed V. P. Menon's Plan to be put on what was a semi-official basis and to have a formal discussion about it, to be recorded in the Viceregal Minutes, with Pandit Nehru. It was asking for trouble—and trouble is what he got.

Among the other qualities which Lord Mountbatten possesses, however, in addition to intelligence, shrewdness, a formidable memory, a genius for organization, and charm, charm, charm was also luck, luck, luck.

And luck was certainly with him at Simla.

The meeting with Nehru over, the Viceroy called in his Press adviser, Campbell-Johnson, and told him to announce to the world Press that a vital meeting would be held in New Delhi

[1] Government of India Records.

on the morning of 17 May 1947. To this meeting the Viceroy
had invited the leaders of all the organizations vitally concerned
with the transfer of power—Nehru and Patel for the Congress,
Jinnah and Liaquat Ali Khan for the Muslims, and Baldev Singh
for the Sikhs. 'On that morning', the announcement said, 'the
Viceroy will present to the five leaders the Plan which
His Majesty's Government has approved for the transfer of
power to Indian hands.'

This plan was, of course, 'the Dickie Bird Plan'. For the moment, the Viceroy had banished V. P. Menon's scheme from his
mind. He was basing his future on the Plan which he and his
British advisers had cooked up for themselves. And, even at this
stage, having talked to Menon, having talked to Nehru, he was
still confident enough in it to send a digest to London of the
remarks he would make to the five Indian leaders when they met
him on 17 May. He would say that, 'since both parties have
not seen their way to accept the Cabinet Mission Plan, it is clear
that the Indian people, through their elected representatives in the
Provinces, must be given the opportunity of deciding on their
own future. When I first arrived as Viceroy with the mission of
transferring power, I thought that the beginning of 1948 would
be early enough to reach a settlement, but you have all in our
individual discussions pressed upon me and convinced me of the
necessity of speed. In consequence I and my staff have been working night and day to achieve a quick and right decision. We
have produced the plan which I am about to read to you. It is
the best we have been able to produce in the time. We have
embodied as far as possible all the suggestions which have been
put forward in our individual conversations. The Plan was taken
back by Lord Ismay to London a fortnight ago to be examined
closely by the Cabinet. HMG has given it priority over all other
matters of State and has approved of it in quicker time than any
matter of this importance has ever been dealt with before. Lord
Ismay arrived back with HMG's approval a few hours ago.
Parliament rises for the Whitsun recess on 23 May, so it is essential that the plan should be announced before 22 May. I wish to
make it clear that this plan is and will remain even after it is
announced open to amendment on any point.'[1]

This, remember, was only a precis of the remarks he *intended*
to make at the meeting of the Indian leaders on 17 May. Its

[1] Government of India Records.

intention was to keep the Cabinet, and Lord Ismay and Abell, in the picture.

The fact that it was cabled to London is, however, a proof of the Viceroy's confidence, even at this last moment, in the 'Dickie Bird Plan'. The Plan had by this time (10 May) been cabled back to him from London. It contained a number of amendments which had been inserted at the insistence of Mr Attlee and the Cabinet, but its basic principles had not been altered, and certainly Mountbatten did not consider them important enough to hesitate about his schedule. On top of the announcement of the forthcoming conference with the leaders, he approved a Press conference which was given to Indian and foreign correspondents on the morning of 10 May by Sir Eric Mièville, in which he stressed the importance of the 17 May summit meeting and the agreement which it would bring forth. The political prospect seemed to be as fragrant with hope and as idyllically calm as the scented Simla afternoon. Nehru accompanied the Viceroy and Vicereine to Campbell-Johnson's house, an eyrie called 'The Retreat' tucked at the end of a mule-track in a fold of the hills, and he was in high spirits. He showed the company how to save breath and muscle by walking up steep hills backward, romped with the children, laughed at the antics of the local apes, and only wrinkled his brow with distaste when he passed through Simla itself on the way back to the Viceregal Lodge.[1]

On the evening of 10 May 1947 Mountbatten asked Nehru to join him in the Viceregal study for an after-dinner whisky-and-soda. Nothing had happened over dinner to cause him anxiety. But as the two men talked, Mountbatten had what he afterwards called a 'sudden hunch'. He was not supposed to show the Plan which, with its amendments, had now been cabled back from London, to anyone until the meeting on 17 May. The Viceroy, however, had an impulse. He went over to his safe, opened it and took out the Plan, and asked Nehru to read it.

The next thirty minutes were probably the most uncomfortable

[1] It was said that Nehru hated Simla because its principal form of passenger transport is coolie-drawn rickshas, which he considered an affront to human dignity. In fact, the whole conception of Simla aroused his contempt, for it was so determinedly pseudo-English and suburban. The main street was known as the Mall. One of its loveliest slopes was called Elysium Hill 'as a compliment to the sisters of Lord Auckland, who resided there with their brother'. The granite, red-roofed Secretariat was called 'Gorton Castle', and the Army Commander's house was known as 'Snowdon'. This within a hundred miles of the borders of Tibet.

of his life. Nehru has a transparent face and never dissimulates
when he is in the grip of strong emotion. Mountbatten had the
unhappy experience of watching the Indian leader's face go first
red with anger and then green with distress. At the end of his
reading, he made as if to fling the Plan on the ground, then
recollected himself and tossed it on to the Viceroy's desk.

'It won't do,' he said. 'I will never accept a plan like this!
Congress will never accept it! And India will never accept it,
either!'

Mountbatten looked at him in bewilderment and distress. 'I
thought that I knew what was in Nehru's mind,' he said (to the
author) later. 'But the Hindus are strange. You can never tell.
I had talked to all of them, and then I sat down and drafted a Plan
which I thought expressed their ideas. I was completely wrong.'

But what was to be done now? After riddling the 'Dickie Bird
Plan' with some of his choicest grapeshot, Nehru departed for
his bedroom, no doubt to talk louder in his sleep than ever before.
Mountbatten stayed behind to contemplate the warm drink in his
glass and the ruin of his hopes and ambitions. It is likely that even
his unfailingly peaceful sleep was somewhat troubled on this
occasion.

Nor did the following morning produce a political prospect
to match the sunshine outside. Nehru had obviously brooded and
worked through most of the night, and to the Viceroy's breakfast
table came a memorandum, couched in heated words, condemning
the Plan. 'The picture presented by the proposals in the Plan is
an ominous one,' wrote Nehru. 'Not only do they menace India
but they endanger the future relations between Britain and India.
Instead of producing any sense of certainty, security and stability,
they would encourage disruptive tendencies everywhere and
chaos and weakness. They would particularly endanger important
strategic areas . . . The inevitable consequences of the proposals
would be to invite the Balkanization of India; to provoke certain
civil conflict and add to violence and disorder; to cause a further
breakdown of the central authority, which could alone prevent
the growing chaos, and to demoralize the army, the police and
the central services . . . If it was indeed His Majesty's Government's sole purpose to ascertain the wishes of the people of India
and to transfer power with the least possible dislocation, the
purpose would not be advanced or achieved by these proposals.
Before the people chose they should have a proper picture of what

they were choosing. [This plan] with no clear background would produce nothing but confusion, and the transfer of power, instead of being made without dislocation, would be obstructed by violence, by a mass of complications, and by weakness of the central Government and its organs . . . I have no doubt that Congress will not accept the proposals.'[1]

The Viceroy might have been forgiven if he had given vent to a schoolboyish 'phew!' after reading this document. His Staff had well and truly dropped him in the mire.

But Lord Mountbatten, as will have been seen from his Indian adventures alone, was not without resilience and bounce and audacity. With the mud still plastered in his hair, he at once crawled back into the fight. He was certainly not ready to admit defeat yet.

First, he sent out an immediate call for V. P. Menon. Menon was having morning coffee with Nehru and finding the going difficult. The Indian leader was resentful because Menon had not told him beforehand what was in the 'Dickie Bird Plan'; Menon could not explain that the Viceroy had ordered him not to; it was all very sticky, and Menon was glad to hurry away to the Viceregal Lodge. There he found Mountbatten in a state as close to panic as he is ever likely to be. He explained what had happened and desperately asked what he should do next.

'I told him', said Menon, 'that the most promising line of action was to proceed on the basis of my plan. This proposition was almost certain to be accepted by Congress, because it would ensure an early demission of power. The only question was whether Jinnah would accept a truncated Pakistan—and I reminded the Viceroy that he himself had gained the impression that Jinnah was reconciled to the idea of the partition of the Punjab and Bengal.'[2]

Before Menon had finished speaking, Mountbatten had made up his mind. The panic was gone and he was full of confidence again. He told Menon to summon a Staff meeting at once, and to send an invitation to Nehru to attend it. At this meeting, Nehru's objection to the 'Dickie Bird Plan' was formally read into the Minutes. Then both the Viceroy and V. P. Menon once more expounded the benefits of the Menon Plan for Dominion Status, and the Viceroy ended the meeting by saying:

[1] Government of India Records.
[2] In a conversation with the author.

'I would like to ask you a straight question, Pandit Nehru. Will Congress accept a new draft Plan if it is amended in the light of these discussions?'

Nehru: 'I cannot say. I would prefer to see the new draft first.'[1]

The meeting adjourned and Nehru departed, but the Viceroy and V. P. Menon stayed behind to talk. Menon had anticipated that there would now be some delay while a draft of his Plan was drawn up; but Mountbatten was determined that no more time must be lost. He explained to Menon that Nehru was leaving that evening for Delhi, and it was vital that he should see and approve a draft of the new Plan before he left—otherwise it might be impossible to pin him down for weeks, and everything would be ruined. Could V.P. get out the draft in time for Nehru to see and read it before his train departed?

It was by now 2 p.m. V. P. Menon walked to his hotel, poured himself a stiff whisky (he had never before had a whisky before six in the evening) and settled down to work. Meanwhile, the Viceroy was busy. He had called Campbell-Johnson and told him to put out a second communique to the Press announcing the postponement of the 17 May meeting. 'Give any excuse you like,' he said. Campbell-Johnson replied that the announcement would have to be co-ordinated with London, and urgent cipher cables ripped back and forth through the lunch hour. One of them from Mountbatten to Mr Attlee said, in effect: *The Draft Plan which you have approved is hereby cancelled. Please stand by for revised plan.* Another came back from Ismay saying, in effect: *What in hell is going on?* Eventually, Campbell-Johnson put out an agreed communique which said: 'Owing to the imminence of the Parliamentary recess in London, it has been found necessary to postpone HE the Viceroy's meeting with the Indian leaders announced to begin on Saturday 17th May to Monday 2nd June.' It deceived no one, for, as Campbell-Johnson remarked, 'the weakness of our position is that we have told the truth, but it is not the whole truth and nothing but the truth'.[2]

At 6 p.m. V. P. Menon finished the last sentence of the Draft Plan and had it snatched from his hands by Sir Eric Mièville, who was leaning over him.

Menon, who now had a splitting headache, took four aspirins and went to bed. It was not until nine o'clock that evening, at a

[1] Government of India Records.
[2] *Mission with Mountbatten.*

banquet at Viceregal Lodge, that he got the first hint of the result of his labours. His wife was at one end of the receiving line when the Viceroy and Vicereine came in and he was at the other. He watched the Mountbattens make a bee-line for Mrs Menon and warmly greet her. Then he had to wait for another five minutes, until Lady Mountbatten came up to him, gave him an affectionate peck on the cheek while she whispered in his ear:

'He accepted it, V.P.'

It had taken one man exactly four hours to draw up the Plan which was to change the face of India, and the world.

It was not, of course, as easily accomplished as all that. Nehru might be satisfied. Mountbatten was confident now, with this hurdle surmounted, that he could take care of the Indians. But in the meantime, from London, urgent requests were coming in for explanations.

The Viceroy returned to New Delhi on 14 May to find a message from the Cabinet summoning him to London. There were also personal cables from Ismay pleading for guidance. Mountbatten called in V. P. Menon and said: 'They want me to come back to London and explain myself. I've decided not to go. I shall cable them that either they accept the new Draft Plan which I have cabled to them, as it is, and without me there, or I shall resign.'[1] He was in a defensive mood and, unlike him, ready to bluster.

Menon told him not to be too precipitate. In his view, the Viceroy's best course was to tell the Cabinet in London the whole truth about what had happened, keeping back absolutely nothing; and to signify his willingness to return and stand by the new Plan.

To this Mountbatten eventually agreed, but only after some hesitation plus a lecture from Lady Mountbatten on the necessity of presenting a bold front.

But the attack of nerves was short, and he told Attlee on the evening of 14 May that he was returning to explain the new Plan personally. He cabled Ismay to send back his personal aircraft.

On 18 May 1947 Lord and Lady Mountbatten left Palam Airport for London, and they took V. P. Menon with them.

Ismay and Abell were there to meet them on arrival, and they fought long and hard against the Menon Plan. They still preferred their own. Mr Attlee and the Cabinet, however, accepted it at a meeting at 10 Downing Street which lasted exactly five minutes.

[1] In a conversation recalled by the participants.

It had been a remarkable combination of patience, brilliant planning and remarkable flexibility of mind on the part of V. P. Menon (with Sardar Patel always in the background) which had got the new Plan through. Little wonder that Mountbatten wrote to him later: 'It was indeed fortunate that you were Reforms Commissioner on my Staff, and that thus we were brought together into close association with one another at a very early stage, for you were the first person I met who entirely agreed with the idea of Dominion status, and you found the solution which I had not thought of, of making it acceptable by a very early transfer of power. History must always rate that decision very high, and I owe it to your advice; advice given in the teeth of considerable opposition from other advisers.'

The Viceroy had reason to be grateful. Otherwise, as he said to Campbell-Johnson: 'Dickie Mountbatten would have been sunk, and could have packed his bags.'

But it is all very well to draw up a plan to divide India in four hours and accept it in five minutes.

How, in a land consisting of 250,000,000 Hindus, 90,000,000 Muslims, 10,000,000 Christians and—particularly *and*—5,000,000 simmering Sikhs, do you implement it?

CHAPTER SIX

'PLEASE, MR JINNAH!'

ON THE EVENING of 3 June 1947 the leaders of the three parties mainly concerned, the Congress, the Muslim League and the Sikhs, followed Lord Mountbatten to the microphones of All India Radio to broadcast—not to the nation, for from now on there was no longer an Indian nation, but to their peoples to tell them what was in store for them a little over two months ahead.

The intervening days since the Viceroy's arrival back in India with the Cabinet's approval of the new Plan had not been without their bluff, counterbluff and political hurly-burly. Jinnah suddenly announced that he would need a thousand-mile long corridor through Indian territory to link the western and eastern territories of Pakistan. Congress reacted to the demand with the startled yelps of a pack of dogs among which a firecracker has been thrown, but they quickly regained their composure on discovering that it was all noise and no damage. Gandhi was still vehemently proclaiming his adamant opposition to the partition of the country. 'Let it not be said that Gandhi was a party to India's vivisection,' he said. 'But everyone today is impatient for independence. Congress has practically decided to accept partition. They have been handed a wooden loaf in this new plan. If they eat it, they die of colic. If they leave it, they starve.'

He made yet one more journey from Bihar and Bengal to Delhi to appeal for time and reflection before the irrevocable decision was made. On the journey north, while he slept, someone stole his watch from under Gandhi's pillow. It was almost symbolic. If they could rob the Mahatma of his beloved watch—he had treasured it for years, and it was one of his few worldly possessions—they could also steal India from him. At Delhi station, he said: 'I have been a fighter all my life. I am come to Delhi to fight a losing battle.'

At this juncture, Gandhi's arrival was the one thing Mountbatten feared. It is true that in the past few weeks he had, by playing on the hopes and ambitions of Nehru and Patel, successfully manœuvred the Mahatma out of the main stream of Indian politics; but there was no knowing with this shrewd, able, magnificent old man. By the exercise of his remarkable personality and the potent projection of his fundamental goodness, he still had the power to hypnotize his colleagues in the Congress. By a word or by a fast, he could wreck all the Viceroy's schemes. Mountbatten dreaded his coming. He need not have done. When Gandhi came to see him, he announced—by writing on a scrap of paper—that this was his day of silence, and that he had nothing to say. 'You don't really want me to say anything, do you?' he wrote. The crisis was past, and there would be no trouble with Gandhi.

With the Muslim member of the Congress hierarchy, Maulana Abul Kalam Azad, there was less to be feared. Azad's stubborn fight against partition and his repeated warnings of its evil consequences had by this time become monotonous and irritating to his colleagues, eager as they were for the prospects of power. His dire forebodings fell on deaf ears.

In desperation, just before the final decision was taken, he went to the Viceroy to plead with him to think again about partition.

'I also asked Lord Mountbatten to take into consideration the likely consequences of the partition of the country,' he wrote afterwards. 'Even without partition, there had been riots in Calcutta, Noakhali, Bihar, Bombay and the Punjab. Hindus had attacked Muslims and Muslims had attacked Hindus. If the country was divided in such an atmosphere there would be rivers of blood flowing in different parts of the country and the British would be responsible for the carnage.'[1]

The Viceroy gave him the verbal equivalent of a reassuring slap on the back. Mountbatten certainly had no forebodings about the future. And then he made a remarkable statement which, in view of what was to happen a few weeks later, appears to have received amazingly little attention from those historians who have so far dealt with the period.

'At least on this one question [carnage],' said the Viceroy, 'I shall give you complete assurance. I shall see to it that there is no bloodshed and riot. I am a soldier, not a civilian. Once partition is accepted in principle, I shall issue orders to see that there are no communal disturbances in the country. If there should be the slightest agitation, I shall adopt the sternest measures to nip the

[1] M. Azad, *India Wins Freedom*.

trouble in the bud. I shall not use even the armed police. I will order the Army and Air Force to act and I will use tanks and aeroplanes to suppress anybody who wants to create trouble.'

For the moment, the Viceroy had good reason to feel optimistic. Why should there be trouble? At the meeting on 2 June, about which he had previously worried so much, everything went off more smoothly than he could have hoped. He had gone to great trouble to damp down the blaze of publicity with which most of his activities had been associated since his arrival in India, and there was only one photographer (an Indian) present when Congress, Muslim League and Sikh leaders met him, though there were echoes of the furious quarrel going on in the anteroom as members of the world Press protested furiously at their exclusion. The leaders sat around the round table in the Viceregal study, with Nehru on Mountbatten's right and Jinnah on his left, and the others, Patel and Kripalani, Nishtar and Liaquat Ali Khan, edged close to their leaders, with the Sikh delegate, Baldev Singh, not inappropriately in the middle. He did not seem to be aware that he would shortly be the meat in the sandwich that was being cut.

Behind the table sat the two senior members of Mountbatten's Staff, Lord Ismay and Sir Eric Mièville. In the circumstances, it is perhaps not surprising that V. P. Menon, author of the Plan which the delegates were going to swallow, with varying degrees of satisfaction, was not present.

Lord Ismay's account of the proceedings, in his *Memoirs*, suggests an air of dramatic tension which was really not there. 'I woke up on 2 June feeling rather like I had done on the various D-Days during the war,' he writes, 'but on this occasion I had less confidence in the result.' Mountbatten was, in fact, completely master of the situation from start to finish. He was in the powerful position of having extracted concessions from all of them, even Jinnah (who had had to accept a split Punjab and Bengal to get Pakistan) and with great charm, subtlety and finesse he exploited the weakness of their various positions. By the end of the first meeting, he had already extracted a tentative promise from Nehru, Jinnah and Baldev Singh that they would go on the radio and urge their communities to support the Plan. True, Jinnah made a last effort to preserve his dignity by humming and haa-ing, pointing out that he (of all the Indian leaders!) was only a servant of his people, and that he could not make any definite promises before consulting first the Working Committee of the Muslim League, and then the full League Council. He arranged to see the Viceroy later that evening to convey the Working Committee's opinion—though he knew, and he knew that the Viceroy knew, that his was only a fusspot gesture to make his acquiescence seem harder to get.

On the morning of 3 June, reporting to London on the results of the first day, Mountbatten was far from giving the impression that the day had been a struggle.

'Jinnah saw me for an hour from 11 last night,' he reported, 'and I had letters during the night from Congress and the Sikhs. All three naturally emphasized points which they did not like, but their conclusions were generally favourable. . . . Jinnah reiterated that he would support me personally and promised to do his utmost to get the plan accepted.'

He summed up Jinnah's attitude by saying: 'His delight was unconcealed.'

True, there was some trouble next morning. Congress had inserted two paragraphs in their letter of acceptance, one dealing with Dominion status and the other with the North West Frontier Province, which well illustrated a bitter remark made by Jinnah about them: 'The trouble with the Hindus is that they always try to get seventeen annas for their rupee.' The first paragraph, reported the Viceroy, 'seemed to me so dangerous that it might well have wrecked the whole chance of agreement, since it was clear that Congress wanted HMG to give an assurance that Pakistan would be expelled from the Commonwealth if the rest of India wished to secede. V. P. Menon, whose services in all these negotiations have been beyond price, rushed round to Patel and pointed out that HMG could never be expected to agree to such a proposal which negatives the whole principle of Dominion status, and urged him to drop it. I sent for Nehru half an hour before the meeting and told him the same thing. I told him that I did not even intend to mention at the meeting that this suggestion had been made. Both Patel and Nehru agreed to this course.'[1]

Congress tried a little sleight of hand over the North West Frontier Province by suggesting that the referendum which was to take place there under the terms of the Plan should not be simply to decide whether the population should choose Pakistan

[1] Government of India Records.

or Hindustan, but also whether it should become an independent State. The NWFP was still in the hands of the pro-Congress Muslims, whose leader, Khan Sahib, had begun propagating the idea of a separate Pakhtoonistan or Pathanistan. But he knew, and Congress knew, that the province could not exist independently; and once more the Mountbatten-Menon axis went into operation. 'V. P. Menon pointed out to Patel,' reported the Viceroy, 'and I pointed out to Nehru that since it was at Nehru's own request that I had dropped the original proposal to vote for Pakistan, Hindustan or independence (the basis of the *Dickie Bird Plan*) they could hardly expect me to reintroduce it at this stage. Nehru quite openly admitted that the NWFP could not possibly stand by itself, and it became clear to me that this was a device to free Khan Sahib's party from the odium [in a largely Muslim province] of being connected with Congress during the referendum period, since Nehru spoke about Khan Sahib wishing to join the Union of India at a subsequent stage. I told Nehru I had no intention of raising this at the meeting, and he accepted my ruling on this.'[1]

Jinnah made a feint, too. He wanted a referendum for independence in Bengal, too—for he believed that the Untouchables would vote with the Muslims rather than the Hindus; but the Viceroy talked him out of it.

The only delegate who might possibly have had something of genuine moment to say at the meeting—other than the words, 'I agree'—was Baldev Singh, the Sikh. For in the Plan the partition of the Punjab was implicit. Baldev Singh, who was never one of the most brilliant minds produced by his people, did not seem to realize what this was going to mean. The Sikhs were spread all over the Punjab. They had been there for generations. They owned and tilled the land. They had built the great system of canals. Their shrines and places of pilgrimage were in western rather than eastern Punjab. It might have seemed likely that any far-seeing Sikh, realizing the situation which would probably result from partition, would have cut his throat or gone to war rather than accept it. But then, as an Englishman later on bitterly remarked, 'is there any such thing as a far-seeing Sikh?' Baldev Singh was acting under instructions from his committee, who were obviously as astigmatic as he was. But he kept largely silent during the all-important meeting, except to agree to the Plan

[1] Government of India Records.

that would cut the jugular vein of his people. 'Baldev Singh wanted the instructions to the Boundary Commission', reported the Viceroy, coolly, 'included in the printed plan, and wished them to take Sikh interests more fully into consideration. I rejected this at the meeting and he accepted my ruling.'

He added: 'One of my difficulties has been to prevent the leaders from talking too much. For example, Liaquat started an attack on Gandhi in the second meeting which nearly wrecked the proceedings. When I think of the number of points over which the meeting could have been shipwrecked, I realize how miraculously lucky we have been.'[1]

Confronted by the actual approach of independence—or, perhaps in one or two cases, guilt-ridden by the vivisection to which they were being a party—the Indian leaders were actually too stunned to wreck anything now. The last phase of the second days' meeting was made particularly piquant by a gesture—thought up by an Indian Civil Servant named John Christie—to present them, the moment they agreed to the Plan which gave them their freedom, with a document entitled *The Administrative Consequences of Partition*.

They all suddenly looked like goldfish out of water.

'I have given them copies of the paper to take away with them,' reported the Viceroy, and added: 'It was clear from the reactions at the meeting that none of the leaders present had even begun to think of the complications with which we are all going to be faced.' To which he appended the cheerful postscript: 'Perhaps this is lucky, since it will enable us to hold the initiative in Viceroy's House during the coming difficult period.'[1]

So they trooped to the radio to announce the news to the Indian peoples. 'For more than a hundred years,' said Mountbatten, 'hundreds of millions of you have lived together, and this country has been administered as a single entity . . . It has been impossible to obtain agreement . . . on any plan that would preserve the unity of India. But there can be no question of coercing any large areas in which one community has a majority to live against their will under a Government in which another community has a majority. The only alternative to coercion is Partition.'

Nehru followed, and, as always on an emotional occasion of

[1] Government of India Records.

this kind, was at his best. 'It is with no joy in my heart that I commend these proposals,' he said, 'though I have no doubt in my mind that it is the best course.' And of the part played in the struggle by himself and his colleagues, he added: 'We are little men serving great causes, but because the cause is great some of that greatness falls upon us also.'

Jinnah was clipped, dry and cold. If this was a great occasion for him—and, of course, it was—he was certainly not going to betray it to a radio audience. 'It is for us to consider,' he said, 'whether the Plan as presented to us by His Majesty's Government should be accepted by us as a compromise or as a settlement.' And, except for a crisp cry of 'Pakistan Zindabad!' that was all he was prepared to concede to the drama of the occasion.

Baldev Singh, in spite of what the Plan would do to his people, had no doubts about it. This was not a compromise, he said, but a settlement. 'It does not please everybody, not the Sikh community, but it is certainly something worth while. Let us take it at that.'

There. It was achieved. The Indian leaders had accepted the Plan. The Government at home had accepted the Plan. And even Winston Churchill and the Conservative Opposition had accepted the Plan. But did all of them know exactly what it was that they had accepted?

Did the Government and Opposition in Britain, for instance, realize that in giving the Viceroy permission to go ahead with the Plan, they had also handed him complete freedom to choose the date upon which it would be implemented? It is true that one of the points Mountbatten had made in London, when talking to the Prime Minister about the Plan, was that the Dominion status formula would enable the transfer of power to be made much sooner than had been visualized under the Cabinet Mission plan.[1] There is much evidence to confirm that even Mr Attlee was shocked when the Viceroy announced, at a Press conference held in Delhi on 4 June 1947, that the transfer of power would actually be made on 15 August, only nine weeks ahead—in other words, some ten months earlier than he had first calculated when he first appointed Mountbatten to the Viceroyalty. There is also reason to believe that neither Churchill nor other Tory leaders, when Mountbatten had consulted them in London

---

[1] But the date he indicated was probably 1 October. This is the date he gave Jinnah at an interview on 17 May, the day before he left for London.

about the Plan in May 1947, would have given their promise to back it had they realized what a hell-for-leather rush to implement it would follow. But both parties had publicly announced their support for the Plan, and they were committed to get the Bill passed through Parliament in the next session. The Draft Bill was drawn up in record time and cabled to Mountbatten on 22 June. The British parliamentary machinery had rarely had to revolve so quickly. But in the Draft Bill there was absolutely no mention of 15 August as the exact date for the transfer of power. Was Attlee hoping that it could be quietly forgotten? The Viceroy was certainly not going to let him do so. He cabled back on 28 June to say 'in view of assurance given by me at Press conference and to Leaders I strongly urge that the appointed day should be 15 August. Any later date will psychologically have adverse effect on present delicate position.'[1]

The Prime Minister fell in with his wishes and stuck the 15 August date in the Draft Bill. The Opposition did not vote against it.

'Thus,' wrote V. P. Menon, 'was the plan accepted . . . But acceptance was one thing; its implementation was a different matter altogether. Here was a task which normally should have taken years to accomplish but which had to be compressed into the short space of a few weeks! It was a task before which anybody would have quailed, for it was one which seemed verily to tempt the Gods.'

'Quail?' the Viceroy could well have replied. 'We do not know the meaning of the word!'

But there were others who did and they were quailing all right. Among them was Field Marshal Sir Claude Auchinleck, G.C.B., G.C.I.E., C.S.I., D.S.O., O.B.E., LL.D., Commander-in-Chief of the Indian Army. Sir Claude was a soldier who, like Wavell, had suffered more than his share of setbacks in the fortunes of war. It is the argument of his biographer, Mr John Connell, that he rather than General Montgomery (as he then was) was the architect of victory in Africa in the last war by creating the strategy by which Montgomery subsequently won the Battle of Alamein. He is generally (and genuinely) believed by many to have been one of the great soldiers of the last war who was, unfortunately, always given what Wavell called 'the dirty end of the stick' and never had the right amount of troops or weapons

---

[1] Government of India Records.

or supplies at the right moment. This may well have been true. He was certainly pulled out of the command of the Eighth Army in the Middle East in 1942 by Churchill shortly before the tide turned and we began to win, and to that extent he was extremely unlucky.

Auchinleck was an able administrator and he commanded the Indian Army (a job which he took on after being sacked from the Middle East in 1942) with skill and a sympathetic touch. There is no doubt that he had a great love for the Indians, not only as soldiers but as people, and that he sympathized with their wish for independence though not with the methods they used to attain it. He was a man of considerable humanity but also a stickler for principle. It was typical of Auchinleck's rigid sense of justice that he insisted on the prosecution, after the war, of some of the more brutal and notorious leaders of the so-called Indian National Army, which had been formed from captured Indian soldiers and had fought for the Japanese after the British disasters in Singapore and Burma. Some of the leaders of the I.N.A. (Sikhs, Muslims and Hindus alike) used methods of great brutality—killing, beating and maiming—to force their compatriots to abandon their oaths to the Indian Army and join the Japanese puppet Army. Auchinleck considered that the worst of them should be treated as war criminals for their excesses and tried for their lives.

It was pointed out that, in the climate of Indian politics in 1945, nothing was more likely to give the people the martyrs for whom they were clamouring at the time. The fact is that the I.N.A. war criminals had been guilty of crimes against their own comrades would loom less in Indian minds than the fact that they had been fighting against the British, ostensibly for Indian independence. Auchinleck was urged either to forget the war criminals or to have them quietly disciplined when the smoke had died down. He refused to do either. As a man of principle, he insisted on a full-dress court martial for them, sincerely believing that only by doing so would he keep faith with the majority of Indian soldiers who had remained loyal to their oath, even after capture by the enemy. He had the Indian renegade officers tried, in the full glare of publicity, in the Red Fort in Delhi. The result was disastrous. The Indian Press and village agitators immediately turned the accused into heroes, and changed their squalid acts of brutality into deeds of great valour. The

Indian political leaders all knew as well as Auchinleck that the accused were at best a bunch of opportunists whose acts certainly could never have been excused by patriotism or anti-British hatred. For these, remember, were only those Indian officers who had tortured and beaten and killed their own fellow-soldiers, not those who had simply fought on the side of the Japanese. But if Auchinleck was driven by principle to stage the trials, no such finer feelings stirred in the Indian leaders. Though Nehru, for instance, expressed nothing but contempt for the renegades in private, he quickly jumped on the bandwagon, spoke up for the accused, and even donned barrister's robes to defend the accused at the hearings in Red Fort. So did all the other leaders. Never have so many Indian politicians so quickly remembered that they were lawyers, and rushed to the defence of the 'martyrs'.

The result was that the conviction and imprisonment of the officers was hailed throughout India as yet another example of British oppression of true Indian nationalism. Auchinleck's *amour propre* was satisfied and he could henceforth claim that, in the whole sorry affair, he had been the only honest and straight-forward participant, and that it had been a magnificent justification of the principle of British justice. Pyrrhus had a victory of this kind too . . .

To Auchinleck now, in 1947, came a problem which was possibly more formidable than any which had hitherto confronted him in his gallant but chequered career. That magnificent instrument of war, painstakingly rebuilt by the British after the Mutiny of 1857, the Indian Army, would now have to be split. As Commander-in-Chief, it would be Auchinleck's job to do it. It was not only a heart-breaking task, but one of fantastic difficulty too. After the Mutiny, every Indian regiment was stratified into communal battalions—two Hindu and one Muslim, two Muslim and one Hindu, or one Hindu, one Muslim and one Sikh—so that no sudden upsurge of religious or racial rebellion could get out of hand. There would always be a loyal battalion around to rally round the flag. Moreover, though Indianization had proceeded to such an extent that, by 1947, only 300 Britons remained in the Civil Service, progress had been very much slower in the Indian Army. A number of Indians had, by sheer guts and skill, risen to the rank of brigadier during the war, but the main cadre of officers—and certainly all the General Staff—was British.

The problem of dividing the Army was a task which took Auchinleck aback. At the final meeting of the Indian leaders on 3 June, Mountbatten reported that 'they agreed that Auchinleck should be invited to broadcast in the near future a steadying message to the Armed Forces giving them a broad outline of their future. I told the leaders that the Working Committees would have to give Auchinleck answers on several points, such as whether the Army was to be divided on a geographical or a communal basis, and whether a Muslim soldier living in Bombay would serve in the Hindustan or Pakistan Army, and, of the latter, whether he would have to transfer his domicile.'[1]

But how much thought had Auchinleck himself given to the prospect? It cannot have escaped his attention. The indefatigable General Tuker saw to that. 'On my return to India from the Burma front in 1945,' he said (in reply to a question from the author), 'I soon became convinced that an independent India would have to be divided between the mainly Hindu and the mainly Muslim parts, and that therefore the Indian Army itself should be sorted out—and an impartial force should be kept, so that when the division of the country came there would be no violent commotion or fighting or massacre on the frontiers between the two countries. Those views, and the view that a divided India would be strategically stronger than an India which was unwillingly and riotously welded together were put by me in a Paper at the end of 1945.' This Paper was sent to the General Staff at G.H.Q. Since it came from the second most senior general in India, it can hardly have been ignored. 'Then the Parliamentary Mission came out to India,' Tuker proceeded, 'to look things over and decide when we should give India independence. They got the breeze up their trousers and wanted to give India independence straight away, and that was the view of the Labour Party who were afraid the Indians would chuck us out of the country.'

Tuker went on: 'When the Cabinet Mission itself was coming out in the spring of 1946, G.H.Q. in Delhi suddenly wanted to know if I had been considering the strategy to be followed if India were divided, and would I send them a Paper. I simply bunged in my original Paper, and I think the sole use they made of it was to get the Viceroy [Wavell] to go to the microphone and explain why it would be fatal to divide India for strategic reasons. My argument was that it was better to divide her than

[1] Government of India Records.

to have two contesting peoples within the country, for whom she had to provide all her armed forces to keep the peace.

'It was a pity that the Paper was sidetracked in 1946, because it did forecast all the Punjab massacres of 1947. Imagine, if only they had done something then, the Government and G.H.Q. would have had no less than eighteen months in which to have everything ready—an impartial type of civil service appointed for the border regions, a reclassified army, and it could all have been done surreptitiously, even a lot of it on paper only, so as to be ready at the drop of a handkerchief any time when partition was decided upon. But they chose to set the Paper aside, and the consequences were incalculable.'

The salient points in Tuker's Paper were:

1. India must be partitioned—therefore the Army must be reclassified into communal units;

2. Each communal force must control strong armed police as an internal security force;

3. A central, impartial force must be formed to step in and stop the inevitable row which would blow up in the Sikh-Hindu-Muslim areas, and as a ready force to look after external frontiers;

4. The whole should be within a Commonwealth Defence Region;

5. We should not hurry to Indianize the impartial force, but build it well, militarily and communally, till it became the nucleus of an Army which might, one day, help to reunify the sub-Continent; and

6. That before any decision was made about the form of independence, *all the above forces must be in position and ready to 'take the bump'*.[1]

If a senior member of the Army General Staff could dispatch a Paper of such importance (and, as it turned out, such prescience) to G.H.Q. both in 1945 and 1946, how is it possible that Sir Claude Auchinleck, the Commander-in-Chief, had made no preparations for the contingencies it prophesied as late as May 1947? Through the months Tuker kept pressing his C.-in-C. ever more urgently with suggestions. One of them was the formation immediately of a force consisting of a small number of British troops, plus the forty Ghurka battalions serving in the Indian Army. Auchinleck curtly turned down the proposal. On 2 June 1947, after dinner with the Viceroy, Tuker buttonholed Lord Ismay

[1] My italics—L. M.

and repeated the suggestion to him, pointing out that the troops could be given a proper posting so that they would stay until troubles were over and would not recur.

Ismay shook his head. 'Nehru would never agree to it,' he said.

Nor would Auchinleck agree to divide the Army. After the Indian leaders had decided upon partition, the first thing they demanded was their own armies. Both Mountbatten and Ismay suggested that for the moment, it might be better to retain a single force in the sub-Continent under British command, to ensure impartiality. Jinnah and Nehru bridled at once. It was clear that neither would regard independence as having been obtained until they possessed their own troops, under their own control. August 15 was the day of independence. By 15 August, both Jinnah and Nehru insisted, the Indian Army must be divided and operating under Pakistan and Indian command, respectively.

Auchinleck had already been called in by Ismay and told to prepare a plan for the reclassification of the forces. The Commander-in-Chief had replied that it was impossible, that to split an instrument like the Indian Army would be to ruin it, and that he had no intention of doing anything about it because he did not believe in it. 'Can't you see,' he said, in effect, 'that here we have the greatest Army in the world today? It can't be broken up.'

He was ordered to the Viceroy's House to see Mountbatten. Mountbatten, it should be remembered, had twice assumed positions of superior rank in spheres where Auchinleck operated, despite the fact that he was, substantively, much junior to him.

He had taken over the job of Supremo in Burma. Now he was Viceroy (and therefore in a position to give orders to the C.-in-C.). He had tried to ease the position by writing to Auchinleck shortly before arriving in India and saying:

'My Dear Claude, God knows I did everything in my power to be allowed to go back to sea. Since however the King over-ruled me and I am to come to India I would like you to know that the feeling that I have such a true friend in you makes all the difference to me. I hope we shall see lots of each other. Looking forward to seeing you, Dickie.'[1]

But by the time partition was decided upon, Mountbatten and Auchinleck were no longer friends and certainly no longer

[1] Quoted in *Auchinleck*, by John Connell.

collaborators. The Viceroy ordered the C.-in-C. to get out a plan for the reclassification without delay, 'and no bloody nonsense about it, Claude'.

Auchinleck's supporters, including his biographer, all give the impression that the C.-in-C. India was henceforth little more than a victim of high-pressure tactics on the part of the Viceroy and the Indian leaders. That may well have been so. Certainly, Mountbatten had said only a few weeks before (8 April) that there would be no splitting of the Indian Army because 'the mechanics won't permit it, and I won't'.[1] But that does not account for Auchinleck's failure to have a plan prepared in advance, just the same. Britain was never invaded by the Germans in 1940, but a plan was nevertheless drawn up by the General Staff, as to what should be done in case we were.

'In the end,' said a senior member of Mountbatten's staff to the author, 'Claude had to be ordered to do it, and he was very resentful. You would be surprised how long it took him to realize that it was inevitable . . . The trouble with Claude was that he was a very tender and sensitive plant. Certain letters have been printed from his associates to prove that he was right about everything, and that the praise in these letters proves it. But they don't. Even when things were going well, Claude was so uncertain that he had to be encouraged. One wrote to him to keep his confidence in himself. One would have been much more salutary if one had wanted to keep history straight. What he is supposed to have done and what we saw him do aren't the same at all.'

Of the division of the Indian Army, Mr John Connell writes in *Auchinleck*:

'Without Auchinleck's personal leadership and his selfless devotion to duty, the whole complex enterprise would have foundered at the outset.' In fact, it was not until the beginning of July (six weeks before Independence) that the Commander-in-Chief got around to giving the Armed Forces Reconstitution Committee their terms of reference. In view of the way he had hesitated and delayed, it is somewhat ironic to read the note which he attached to the terms of reference, which read as follows:

'The division of the Indian Armed Forces is bound to be a complicated process. If it is to be accomplished without confusion and without any marked loss of morale and efficiency, it is

[1] A. Campbell-Johnson, *Mission with Mountbatten*.

essential that all the existing forces in India should be under a single administrative control unit until:

(a) they have been finally sorted out into two distinct forces, and

(b) the two Governments are in a position to administer, i.e. to pay, feed, clothe and equip their respective forces.

'2. On the other hand, it is essential that the Union of India[1] and Pakistan should each have within their own territories forces which:

(a) are with effect from 15 August under their own operational control;

(b) are on 15 August predominantly composed of non-Muslims and Muslims respectively; and

(c) are as soon as possible after 15 August predominantly reconstituted on a territorial basis.

'3. The requirements set out in paragraph (c) above necessitate that partition should be in two stages. The first stage would be a more or less rough and ready division of the existing forces on a communal basis. Plans should be made forthwith for the immediate movement to the Pakistan area of all Muslim majority units that may be outside that area, and similarly for the movement to India of all exclusively non-Muslim or non-Muslim majority units at present in the Pakistan area . . .

'4. The next stage would be to comb out the units themselves on a basis of voluntary transfers. All personnel would be entitled to elect which Dominion they choose to serve in. To this, however, there would be one exception, namely that a Muslim from Pakistan now serving in the Armed Forces will not have the option to join the Armed Forces of the Indian Union, and similarly a non-Muslim from the rest of India will not have the option to join the Armed Forces of Pakistan . . .

'5. If both Governments are to have operational control over their respective Armed Forces by 15 August, they must each have heads for the three Services, i.e. the Navy, the Army and the Air Force, and headquarters staffs, through which to exercise

---

[1] It had been anticipated at first that the two new countries would be known as Pakistan and Hindustan. The Congress leaders objected to this. Their standpoint, which was eventually accepted, was that they represented India, from which parts of certain provinces had seceded to form Pakistan; and that they, therefore, continued to be India. This was accepted by the United Nations, which gave India's old representation to the new nation, while Pakistan had to apply for membership as a new country.

their functions. It is therefore important that these six heads should be selected forthwith . . .

'6. So far as central administration is concerned, the Indian Armed Forces as a whole will remain under the administrative control of the present C.-in-C. India who, in his turn, will be under the Joint Defence Council . . . The Commander-in-Chief in India will have no responsibility for law and order, nor will he have operational control over any units, save those in transit from one Dominion to another; nor will be have any power to move troops within the borders of either Dominion.

'7. In order to avoid confusion, the existing C.-in-C. in India might be entitled Supreme Commander from 15 August until his work is completed. His existing staff would of course be reduced progressively as his functions diminish.'[1]

Little wonder that Tuker fumed with frustration in Calcutta and forecast 'a bloody massacre' in the Punjab. (But not in Eastern Command, where his writ ran. He had made his own preparations there to deal with any emergency.) When the trouble came, the soldiers who might have been in a position to prevent it were, as one Army officer bitterly put it, 'playing swops with each other, and were far too busy scrabbling for jobs to bother about communal riots'.

Auchinleck's main concern, from this moment on, was the safety of the British in India. He had by this time become convinced that Indian independence would be followed by a massacre of the British element in the country. Why he imagined this is hard to understand. It was certainly a misreading of the Indian mind. The Indian peoples, Hindus and Muslims, were certainly anxious to end British rule in their country. They had certainly rioted for freedom under the slogan of 'Quit India'. And, in their time, they had certainly killed or injured British officials or the odd Briton who got in the way of their demonstrations.

But the British as individuals were far from being hated and —at best—held in great affection. In spite of this, Auchinleck chose to believe that their blood would flow the moment the British Raj came to an end. Can he really have believed this? Or was it merely a way of trying to persuade Mountbatten to keep British troops in India for other purposes—of which the Viceroy was unaware, but certain elements in the War Office were?

[1] Government of India Records.

Whatever the reason, he wrote to Mountbatten earnestly suggesting that a British armed force should be retained in India until at least 1 January 1948, not, as Tuker had suggested, as a trouble-shooting unit there, with the consent of India and Pakistan, to settle communal troubles, but merely to safeguard purely British interests.

Ismay replied to the C.-in-C.'s letter on behalf of the Viceroy in these words:

'The Viceroy has asked me to thank you for your paper COS (47) 29B in regard to the withdrawal of British forces from India. With reference to the recommendation in paragraph 8 (*b*) His Excellency does not feel that it would be possible to insist on British forces remaining until 1 January 1948. As he sees it, this would necessitate our safeguarding the position by an arrangement whereby the British forces in India would be directly under the C.-in-C., who would be responsible to H.M.G. through the Governor General or Governors General. This safeguard would be demanded by H.M.G. and the Chiefs of Staff but would be most unpalatable to the Governments of both India and Pakistan. It would defeat the object which is uppermost in the Viceroy's mind, namely that from the date of the transfer of power both the new Governments should be autonomous in every sense of the word without a vestige of the old restrictions.

'As for the argument that H.M.G. have a moral obligation to safeguard British lives until such time as those who have to leave have been able to make arrangements to do so, it looks as though the numbers are likely to be relatively small and that these could be got away in the next month or two. In any case, responsibility for the protection of all nationals including, of course, British nationals in the sub-Continent of India will from 15th August rest with the Governments of India and Pakistan; and unless both of them specifically ask for British forces to remain to help them carry out this duty, insistence on our part would be tantamount to an admission that we did not trust them to carry out their obligations with their own forces. Finally, if things really blew up, the handful of British troops that would remain in the country could do little to safeguard British lives as a whole.

'The Viceroy has asked me to add: (*a*) that at the meeting of the India-Burma Committee (I.B. 47, 28th meeting, Item 9) held on 28th May, 1947, he said that there would be every advantage in withdrawing the British forces from India as soon as possible after the enactment of the legislation providing for the transfer of power. The Committee decided to resume consideration of this question after the views of the Chiefs of Staff had been obtained; and (*b*) that at his Press conference he gave the impression without saying so in terms that the British troops would be withdrawn when Dominion status had been granted to the two new Dominions.

'In these circumstances, His Excellency has come to the conclusion that it is essential on political grounds that the withdrawal of British forces should be carried out as rapidly as possible. He further considers that a very early announcement of H.M.G.'s decision to do this would have a most excellent political effect. His Excellency therefore proposes subject to your concurrence (*a*) to submit the above conclusions to the Secretary of State for India and ask for their endorsement by H.M.G., and (*b*) to get authority from H.M.G. to inform the leaders of this policy before it is announced, *but to tell them that if both parties were to submit a formal request that British forces should remain in this country for say six months to tide over the initial period of transition he would be prepared to forward their request to H.M.G.*[1] He would of course explain that they could only be kept here with proper safeguards.

'The Viceroy would be grateful to have your comments as soon as possible. If it would be any help my coming round and having a talk, I am at your disposal. Yours ever, Ismay.'[2]

Ismay got a pained reply and the Viceroy a flea in his ear.

'My dear Ismay,' Auchinleck wrote on 20 June, 'Thank you for your letter of June 18 about the withdrawal of British forces from India.

'2. My Paper COS (44) 29B was submitted to the Viceroy in response to a request from him for my views on this subject. The Paper represents my opinion as the Viceroy's adviser on all military matters and was naturally written from the general military point of view. As Commander-in-Chief in India, one of my responsibilities is the maintenance of law and order when so required by the civil authorities.

'3. I adhere to the advice I gave in the Paper under reference

---

[1] My italics—L. M.
[2] Government of India Records.

but I realize of course that the Viceroy has every right to disregard it for over-riding political considerations. That is solely his responsibility and it is not my business to comment on his decision. It is my duty to accept it and I do accept it.

'4. I am afraid that I can not agree with your opinion that "the handful of British troops" that might remain in the country could do very little to safeguard British lives as a whole. My considered opinion, in which my advisers support me, is that even small forces of British troops at, say, Calcutta, Bombay, Delhi and Karachi, might make all the difference should the tide of feeling in the country take an anti-British or an anti-European turn. I agree that they could do little to protect individual Europeans in country districts, but the bulk of Europeans are concentrated in the larger seaports and towns. *I request that this opinion may be recorded and conveyed to H.M.G. in the representations that the Viceroy is going to make on the subject, as I feel that it would give H.M.G. a wrong impression if we were to say that they could do very little. It all depends on the circumstances prevailing at the time, of course, but the above is my opinion given as military adviser to the Viceroy.*

'6. I must in justice to myself and in pursuance of my duty as military adviser to the Viceroy point out that on the withdrawal of British troops, the only instrument which the civil authorities will be able to rely upon for the protection of British and European lives against mob violence will be the Indian Army. *That Army will soon be involved in reconstitution during which the majority of its units will not be capable of rendering armed assistance to the civil power even if the Indian officers and men composing them were willing to carry out these duties for the protection of Europeans, which I cannot in any way guarantee.*[1] In order to carry out the reconstitution of the Army in an orderly and logical way, the very large number of units now distributed in small detachments all over Northern India on internal security duties will have to be recalled to undergo reconstitution. Also, for the next six months and more, there will be a continual movement and cross-transfer of units between Pakistan and India which will virtually immobilise the units involved for the time being.

'7. *Moreover, I cannot state with any certainty that during this period of reconstitution the Army will retain its cohesion or remain a reliable instrument for the use of the civil power in the event of widespread*

[1] My italics—L. M.

disturbances.[1] I have dwelt on this aspect of the situation at some length as I wish to make it clear to the Viceroy and through him to H.M.G. that if I am to remain, as I understand is proposed, in central control of the Armed Forces during the process of their reconstitution, I can no longer be responsible in grave emergency for the protection of British lives and property should these be threatened, once the British forces have been withdrawn. I hope that no such need will arise, but it may, and should this happen it is essential that the position in respect of the Indian Armed Forces as it affects myself and my subordinate commanders should be clearly understood by H.M.G. I should very much like to discuss the whole question with you before the Viceroy returns to Delhi. Yours sincerely, Claude Auchinleck. P.S. We talked of this last night but should you wish to discuss the matter further I am at your disposal—as always.'[2]

One is forced to ask again whether Auchinleck really seriously believed that the British would be put to the sword the moment British troops disappeared from India. Or was this one more way of making his position clear—that he was against the division of the Indian Army, but if the Viceroy and the Indian politicians insisted that it should be done, only the retention of British troops could save the land from grave disturbances.

Whatever his motivations, he certainly could look for no support for them from the Viceroy. Mountbatten was too anxious to keep political peace with the Indian leaders (particularly Congress) to be prepared to risk disturbing it with an argument about the British Army. Both countries were insistent that they should have their own national armies by 15 August, and they did not care what chaos or confusion was caused in the process of getting them, nor whether the Indian Army as an instrument of war was ruined in the process. For them the Indian Army did not have the same mystique as it had for many British officers. They had always looked with a certain distaste upon it as a mercenary organization which had all too often been used against the Indian people to suppress their legitimate political aims. They (the politicians) would certainly not be sorry to see it disbanded and truly national armies (Muslim and Hindu) born in its place.

On the question of the retention of British troops, the Muslim

[1] My italics—L. M.
[2] Government of India Records.

League and Congress differed. Shortly after partition of India was accepted by both parties, Liaquat Ali Khan informally approached Lord Ismay on behalf of Mr Jinnah and asked whether British troops could remain in Pakistan after the transfer of power. He consulted the Viceroy, who said he felt strongly that a unilateral application from one government should be refused. He cabled the Secretary of State for India and formally requested permission, 'that I now be empowered formally to ask the representatives of both future Dominions whether they want the British forces to stay after August 15, (b) that unless both reply in the affirmative, the process of withdrawal should start on August 15 and be completed as quickly as possible, and (c) that if both reply in the affirmative, the provisional date for the withdrawal should be fixed for 1 April, 1948, and be reviewed on 1 January, 1948.'

In the same cable, he mentioned that if the representatives of both new Dominions failed to ask the British to stay, Auchinleck had recommended that HMG should insist that British forces should remain until 1 January 1948, 'to fulfil HMG's moral obligation to safeguard British lives'.

He added: 'I am unable to agree with Auchinleck's recommendation . . . for the following reasons: (a) Presumably, if British forces were retained against the wishes of the two new Governments, H.M.G. would demand safeguards. These would be most unpalatable to the two new Governments and would defeat our primary job of introducing complete autonomy from the date of transfer of power. *As I have always emphasised, it is by the introduction of this complete autonomy with no reservations that we are going to stand the best chance of India indefinitely retaining Dominion status* . . .'[1]

It was here that Mountbatten revealed one of his great ambitions, now that a settlement had been achieved with the Indian leaders. Having enticed Nehru and his comrades into the Commonwealth with the carrot of immediate independence (Jinnah did not need to be enticed; he came willingly) the Viceroy was determined to keep them there, and prepared to pay a high price in order to do so. Certainly, he was not going to allow Auchinleck to stand in his way.

The Secretary of State for India replied to his cable agreeing with his suggestions (and therefore repudiating Auchinleck) and

[1] Government of India Records.

also conveying permission for Mountbatten to make the requests to the representatives of the two new Dominions about the retention of British forces.

Liaquat Ali Khan answered that Pakistan would be favourably inclined. Nehru replied:

'I would sooner have every village in India put to the flames than keep the British Army here after August 15.'

Those words were to haunt him later in the year.

But, for the moment, though the pot was simmering it was not yet boiling over. There was rioting and massacre still in the Punjab and in Bihar and Bengal, but compared with what was to come these were mere bush fires, and could either be quenched or contained. Cables went back and forth between London and the Viceroy's House correcting and amending the Draft Bill. In London there was still a certain lack of understanding of the way the minds of the Congress leaders worked, to judge by some of the clauses in the Draft Bill. One clause specifically retained for Britain the right to maintain a military base in India after the transfer of power. V. P. Menon rushed in at once with a note to Miéville to say: 'I do not know what decision H.E. has reached on this. With this clause in the Bill, it will not stand circulation among the political leaders. As I mentioned to H.E., this clause will never pass through Congress.'

It was struck out.

A telegram arrived from the India Office saying:

'Problem arises how to describe new personages in the Royal Warrants when they take office. Usual practice is to put Esquire after names, but this hardly seems suitable in present circumstances. Assuming that Patel and Baldev Singh are described as Sardar, Zaheer as Syad, Prasad and Matthai as Doctor, and Nehru as Pandit, and Rajagopalachari as Sri, Bose and Asaf Ali are what?'

Abell replied: 'Prefixes for Patel, Baldev Singh, Prasad, Matthai and Nehru are correct. Bose and Asaf Ali should be Esquire. Rajagopalachari should be Shri not Sri.'

Jinnah heard that both Pakistan and India were referred to in the Draft Bill as 'the Indian Dominions' and sent a tart note of protest. They were thereafter referred to simply as 'the Dominions'.

Sir John Colville, Governor of Bombay, let it be known that

he would refuse to stay in his post as Governor after the transfer of power unless he were allowed to fly a Union Jack or some sort of flag with a Union Jack.[1]

In the case of the flags for the new Dominions, the Viceroy had not been inactive. Among his hobbies, along with the compilation of his family tree, was heraldry and design. He himself sketched and prepared the design for the flags of both Pakistan and India. One was based on the flag of Congress— with Gandhi's spinning wheel—and the other on the Muslim League's crescent. To each he added a small Union Jack, one ninth in area, sewn into the upper canton. He sent them to Jinnah and Nehru for their approval, as 'helpful suggestions'.

Jinnah coldly replied that in no circumstances could the design be accepted as it would be repugnant to the religious feelings of the Muslims to have a Christian Cross alongside the Crescent. Nehru rejected the design on the grounds that, although Gandhi and Sardar Patel and others had originally expressed their willingness to accept it, he had now come to the conclusion that the prevailing feeling among Congress extremists was that the leaders were pandering to the British. This had reached a point where it was inadvisable to press the design upon them. Nehru sent the Viceroy a design prepared by Congress which showed the Dominion flag as closely resembling the Congress flag, but with the wheel of the Sarnath Asoka replacing the spinning wheel. And, of course, no Union Jack.

It was the ubiquitous V. P. Menon who also noticed in the Draft Bill that 'the India Office appear to be assuming that His Excellency would be asked by both parties (Pakistan and India) to become Governor General of the two new Dominions. It appears that the India Office were expecting both Mr Jinnah and Pandit Nehru to write letters asking the Viceroy to accept this post, and that it would be possible to quote these letters in Parliament.'[2]

Menon gave it as his opinion that someone had better hurry and get the letter from Jinnah immediately, because he anticipated trouble.

He was quite right. The question of who was to be Governor General of Pakistan was to cause Mountbatten one of his worst

---

[1] Sir John did stay on after Independence and stoutly flew the Union Jack on all British occasions.

[2] Government of India Records.

embarrassments in the whole business of the transfer of power. It had all begun on 17 May 1947, the day before the Viceroy left for London with the new Menon-drafted Plan for the transfer of power. Nehru had, of course, seen this Plan and, in accepting it in principle, he wrote to Mountbatten:

'We [Congress] agree to the proposal that during this interim period [of Dominion status] the Governor General of the two Dominions should be common to both States . . . For our part we should be happy if you would continue in this office and help us with your advice and experience.'[1]

The idea appealed to Mountbatten tremendously. He got a good deal of pleasure out of contemplating the history books of the future in which he would be named, not only as the man who discovered how to give India independence, but also as the one who taught the two infant Dominions how to walk and talk. From a practical point of view, too, there were obvious advantages. The task, the awesomely complicated task, of dividing India's assets between the two countries had already begun, and so had the quarrels. Two Indians of great talent—one, a Muslim, Chaudri Mohammed Ali, the other a Hindu, H. M. Patel, but both close friends—were in charge of the operation and they worked together in harmony and with understanding of each other's problems. But they were under constant fire from the politicians—Mohammed Ali for not getting enough, H. M. Patel for giving away too much. A joint Governor General could obviously do much to smooth the operation by impartial judgement and arbitration.

Mountbatten indicated to Nehru and Patel that he would accept their offer with great happiness, but he pointed out that it would be difficult for him to remain as Governor General of one Dominion only. He hoped to receive a similar invitation from the Muslim League.

That same day, he called Jinnah and Liaquat Ali Khan in to see him. He told them that he was taking the Plan to London the following day, and that he intended to recommend that His Majesty's Government should grant both Pakistan and India their independence as soon as possible, preferably 1 October. (This was 17 May, remember. Mountbatten had not yet decided to rush independence forward even more quickly.) The question which would require clarification was whether Mr Jinnah would

[1] Government of India Records.

prefer Pakistan to have its own Governor General or share a common Governor General with India. He asked for Mr Jinnah's personal view.

The moment Jinnah considered that he was being rushed, he became immediately suspicious; his instinct was to retire to his cave and roll a stone in front of the opening. He reacted in such a fashion now. He said he could not possibly commit himself on this subject straight away. Jogged by the Viceroy, he then admitted that he had given the matter some thought and that he felt it would be better to have two Governors General. He also felt that there should be a Representative of the Crown who would be responsible for the division of the assets between the two States. Jinnah indicated that he was very keen that Mountbatten should fill this post, for, he went on, with a certain unction, 'I have complete faith in the impartiality of Your Excellency and all your awards would be binding. Moreover, I am extremely anxious that you should remain in India, for we have need of you.'

The Viceroy replied that he was honoured by Mr Jinnah's remarks. However, he had not considered taking on such a post nor could he think of anyone else who would wish to do so. In any case, he pointed out, it would be an untenable position if a so-called 'Arbitrator' was junior in rank to the Governors General, who would be the King's representatives.

Jinnah promised that he would send the Viceroy a letter by the following Monday (19 May) with a full description of his proposal for a Supreme Arbitrator and two Governors General. 'But let it be clear,' said the Viceroy, 'that I reserve my personal position until you, Mr Jinnah, clearly state in your letter that if your scheme is found by H.M.G. to be impracticable, you will accept as a less desirable alternative and as an interim measure the appointment of one Governor General between the two States.'[1]

Jinnah bridled immediately. He refused to suggest any such thing. But Mountbatten was determined that he should not go away without some concession having been extracted, and he kept the discussion going until Jinnah finally decided first to think it over and, second, to deliver his letter on 19 May to Sir Eric Mièville, who would cable it to Mountbatten in London.

During the next week, Mièville visited Jinnah and Liaquat Ali Khan repeatedly and asked for the letter. He never obtained it. The Muslim League leader would never say that he was *not*

[1] Government of India Records.

going to write it, but he never wrote it either. In the end, the Jinnah idea of a Supreme Arbitrator was put verbally to representatives of the India Office by Mountbatten for an opinion, and, of course, they agreed with him that such a post would be unconstitutional and unworkable.

He came back from London to Delhi more determined than ever to persuade the Muslim League leader that he (the Viceroy) should become joint Governor General. It should surely have been obvious to him by this time that Jinnah, selfish, proud, jealous, was going to allow no such thing, but Mountbatten persisted. It had become for him a matter of pride, too; and it was also rapidly becoming a matter of wills.

The Viceroy at one point thought of calling in Sir Walter (now Lord) Monckton, who was in India as legal adviser to the Nizam of Hyderabad, and having him concoct a convincing case for the Viceroy's assumption of the twin positions. Ismay hurriedly replied that there was no need to call in an outsider. In a memorandum he wrote (on 8 June):

'We have considered the advantages of Hindustan and Pakistan having the same man as Governor General. We suggest that they are broadly as follows: I. You personally have earned the confidence and trust of both parties. This is by far the most important factor. II. There will be an immediate number of standstill orders and although both Dominions will become autonomous it will be essential for certain matters to be run on a unified basis until they can be separated. A good example of this is the Army. In all these matters your personal assistance towards enabling an agreement to be reached would be of the utmost benefit. III. If there were separate Governors General, one for each Dominion, they and their Governments would look at all problems purely from their own point of view. There would be nobody whatsoever in India as a whole capable of taking a completely impartial viewpoint. Incidentally, two Governors General would be more expensive than one. IV. Pakistan would stand to gain even more from your continued presence than would Hindustan, because they are the weaker party and because Hindustan at present has nine points of the law . . .'[1]

He ended by suggesting that: 'a member of your Staff should see Mr Jinnah, that he should find out which way the wind was blowing, and that he should point out the immense advantages

[1] Government of India Records.

which Pakistan would gain from having the same man as Governor General.'

It was not, however, quite so easy to see Mr Jinnah. The old man was brooding in his cave. In desperation, Ismay and Sir Eric Mièville went to see Liaquat Ali Khan on 20 June.

'I told Mr Liaquat Ali Khan,' Ismay reported later, 'that we had already received certain propositions for the Draft Bill and that the Bill might reach us on Monday or Tuesday next. Meanwhile, H.M.G. had asked us to consult the Indian leaders on the following points: (a) Was there to be a common Governor General to start with, and (b) What was to be the procedure for appointing Governors? As regards (a) I reminded him of a conversation which I and Sir Eric Mièville had had with him some days ago. He said that he had not yet had the opportunity of talking it over with Mr Jinnah. I pressed upon him the urgency of this matter and emphasized how impossible it would be to get any sort of continuity or any sort of orderly partition if each Dominion had a separate Governor General. He said he would consult Mr Jinnah at the earliest possible moment.'[1]

But, of course, Liaquat Ali Khan knew that this was a subject upon which his chief preferred to keep his own counsel, and he was far too terrified of him to insist. Jinnah rarely took his subordinates into his confidence, and certainly did not allow them to influence his decisions.

The hours ticked away until 23 June. On that day, the Viceroy sent for Jinnah. Mountbatten said that he was not raising it on personal grounds, but he must really ask him to give his earnest and earliest consideration as to whom he would wish to be the first Governor General of Pakistan. The Viceroy pointed out that, while he did stress the advantages of having, during the partition period, a common Governor General for both Dominions, he must make it abundantly clear that he was not asking for the appointment for himself, and that it was an entirely free choice of the two Dominions concerned.

He also explained that an early decision was required because it affected a clause in the Bill which was shortly to be laid before Parliament. Jinnah saw a perfect opportunity to change the subject and remarked that he trusted he would be able to see the Bill and be allowed to comment upon it.

The Viceroy told him that he had had a great tussle with His

[1] Government of India Records.

Majesty's Government, who had taken the line that it was entirely contrary to Parliamentary procedure for anyone outside the Government to see a Bill before its presentation before the House of Commons. He had, however, fought hard and won, and Mr Jinnah would be allowed to see the Bill,[1] although he could not allow him to take a copy away. As Jinnah was about to comment, the Viceroy brought him smartly back to the point.

'Reverting to the question of the Governor General,' he began. Jinnah interrupted him and said:

'So far as the decision I shall reach is concerned, I hope it will not be interpreted as not wanting Your Excellency, in whom I have implicit trust and confidence. But it is a rule of my life that I must always consider the interests of my people. At various times in my life, I have had to pass over those nearest and dearest to me. But I have my duty to do.'

After this pious statement, he added: 'I hope to let Your Excellency have my decision in two or three days' time.'

Mountbatten waited and waited and waited, but still the reply did not come. It was not until 2 July, nine days after their interview, that Jinnah finally conveyed the information that he himself had decided to be the first Governor General of Pakistan. But even that did not convince the Viceroy that he had lost the battle. On the morning of 2 July a Staff meeting was solemnly called at Lord Ismay's house 'to consider the consequences of Mr Jinnah's declared wish to be Governor General of Pakistan'. The main purpose of the meeting was 'to devise a formula whereby His Excellency the Viceroy could remain Governor General of both Dominions *and, at the same time, satisfy Mr Jinnah's vanity*'.[2]

That evening, the Viceroy decided to fight one more round before conceding defeat. He sent for the Nawab of Bhopal, whom he knew to be a trusted friend of Jinnah, and asked him to see the Muslim League leader and ask him to reconsider his decision. Bhopal left his capital and came to Delhi at considerable inconvenience, and did as he was bid. But the old man was adamant.

On the morning of 5 July, Liaquat Ali Khan confirmed in a

---

[1] Shortly before the Bill came before Parliament, the Indian leaders met at the Viceroy's House and were given copies of the Bill. They were then shown into private rooms and, with their legal advisers, allowed to study it for two hours, after which they handed it back.

[2] Government of India Records.

letter to the Viceroy that Jinnah had made up his mind and asked His Excellency formally to recommend to the King the name of Mohammed Ali Jinnah as Governor General of Pakistan. In the same letter, he expressed the hope that Mountbatten would stay on as Governor General of India—and this hope was reinforced by a message from Nehru and Sardar Patel, both of whom expressed the wish that he would remain as Governor General of India.

But should he do so?

The Viceroy's Staff argued and debated the question for many a long hour. The general consensus of opinion was that Mountbatten should stay on, on the following grounds:

'1. It was felt that Field Marshal Auchinleck would resign if the Viceroy left, and British officers in the Armed Forces would refuse to stay on, which would mean that nationalization of the Indian Army would be taking place at the same time as its partition, with disastrous results. ["The one stable element in India, namely the Indian Army," said Ismay, "will disintegrate. Riot and appalling bloodshed would result."] If, on the other hand, His Excellency remained, British officers and officials as a whole would be more likely to volunteer to remain themselves. This would apply to both new Dominions. The result would be that partition of the Armed Forces would go through smoothly;

'2. Smooth partition and His Excellency's general information on other matters would, it was felt, mean that relations between India and Pakistan would stand a good chance of being friendly. One of the first objectives of Indian policy should be the maintenance of good relations with Pakistan, and vice versa. If the Viceroy were to go, one of the main reasons for a deterioration in the relations between the two Dominions would be that Congress would feel that it was because of Mr Jinnah's action that His Excellency had not stayed on and that he [Jinnah] had again sabotaged their plans.

'3. It was also thought that if the Viceroy stayed there would be a greater chance of stability within the Dominion of India itself. Although there was still communal tension, the situation had improved out of all measure in the past three months as a result of His Excellency's presence.

'4. It was also stressed that His Excellency would probably be the only independent agency capable of resolving the differences which were bound to arise between India and the Princely States, and that his advice to the Indian Government on how to deal with the States and their Rulers would be invaluable.

'5. It was further pointed out that though the reactions on the "Westminster front" were unpredictable, the (Tory) Opposition would be unlikely to oppose the passage of the Indian Independence Bill if they knew that the Viceroy was going to stay on. Ismay emphasised that if the Opposition turned sour at the prospect of two Governors General of Indian origin in the two new Dominions, they could so delay the passage of the Bill that it would not be possible to transfer power on 15 August.'[1]

The Viceroy's Staff, therefore, jointly agreed that Mountbatten should be advised to accept the invitation of Nehru and Patel and stay on as Governor General of India only.

Having convinced themselves, it was up to them to convince the Government and Opposition at home. On 7 July, Ismay flew to London. There he saw the Prime Minister, Mr Attlee, and the leaders of the Opposition. He went down to Chartwell to see Winston Churchill. He went to Buckingham Palace to see King George the Sixth. He argued long and eloquently along the lines which have been set out above.

As a result, all doubts crumpled. Even Churchill urged Mountbatten to stay on because, he said, his rôle would be valuable in mitigating 'the communal tension, preserving the interests of the Princes, and strengthening the ties of sentiment between India and the rest of the Commonwealth'.

On 4 July 1947 the Indian Independence Bill was introduced in the House of Commons, and passed into law a fortnight later. It included a clause confirming the appointment of Admiral Lord Mountbatten as the first Governor General of India. There was also a clause confirming the appointment of Mohammed Ali Jinnah as Governor General of Pakistan. Neither man had any doubt who had emerged the victor from the manœuvres and intrigues of the past few weeks.

[1] Based on a summary in India Government Records.

CHAPTER SEVEN

THE DOWNFALL OF THE PRINCES

SHORTLY BEFORE HE left for India to become the last of the Viceroys, Lord Mountbatten was summoned by the King to Buckingham Palace. During their talk, George the Sixth mentioned that he was particularly worried about the position of the Indian Princes in the coming negotiations, since they enjoyed direct treaty relations with Britain and these would inevitably be broken when independence came for British India. Unless they made preparations to establish some liaison with the new State or States which would emerge from the transfer of power, the Princes might find themselves in a dangerous vacuum. He urged Mountbatten 'as my cousin' to persuade them to accept the inevitable and come to some arrangement with the new régime or régimes beyond their frontiers.

Whether the King meant by this that he wanted the States to 'join up' or merely to establish federal relations with independent India is not clear. Certainly, Mountbatten interpreted his mission as one to get the Princes somehow or other into one Dominion or another. Unlike his cousin, he did not have much time or admiration for the Indian princes, whom he regarded as semi-enlightened autocrats at their best and squalid degenerates at their worst. He called them 'a bunch of nitwits' for not democratizing their administrations when they saw the power of Congress rising and for not joining the Indian Federation when they had the opportunity in 1935.

The bold front which some of the Princes, particularly the Nawab of Bhopal, had hoped to present to the politicians in British India was already in disarray by the time Congress and the Muslim League had agreed to accept the Plan for Indian independence, and the situation deteriorated rapidly thereafter. As Chancellor of the Chamber of Princes, Bhopal was given a prior look at the general outline of the Independence Bill (even before the Congress and Muslim Leaders saw it), for it was felt that his word not to divulge its contents was rather more likely to be kept than that of the politicians. His immediate reaction was to ask whether it was the intention of His Majesty's Government to grant Dominion status to individual Princely States in the same way as Pakistan and India. The Viceroy replied that this was not HMG's intention. Bhopal, thereupon, bitterly complained that the British were once more letting the Princely States down, and that he, as the Muslim prince of a Hindu state, would be put at the mercy of Congress.

Three days later, he resigned his position as Chancellor of the Chamber of Princes and announced that he would consider himself free and independent the moment the British departed from India to choose the destiny of his State for himself. He left Mountbatten in no doubt that he abhorred Congress and would have nothing to do with a Congress-dominated India. These were brave words, but they were not very realistic. The Viceroy, while agreeing that the Independence Bill contained the words: 'On the other hand, should any State not enter into a relationship with a Dominion, we should be forced to consider a separate relationship with it', flatly informed the Princes that he would consider any representations from the Princely States on this matter as 'purely hypothetical'. He was resolved to do nothing about it.

In any case, he realized that the scurry for shelter had already begun. The Maharajah of Bikaner had already gathered a considerable number of important Princes together into a group which had expressed its willingness to join the Indian Federation *before* independence, and would, therefore, become part of India after the transfer of power. They hoped in this way that they would safeguard their rights and privileges. Like Bhopal, who hoped by a show of independence to do the same, they were doomed to disappointment.

It was perhaps typical of Mountbatten's attitude towards them all that he warmly supported Sir Eric Mièville when he suggested that a good way to persuade the Princes to join either the Indian or the Pakistan Constituent Assemblies would be to point out that 'if they fail to join either, they will be outside the Commonwealth and therefore ineligible for future decorations from the King'. To sweeten them further, particularly the minor Princes, the King announced that he was extending the style of Highness to all rulers with a salute of nine guns, and to their lawful wives and widows. George Abell hastily recommended that this concession should not be mentioned to a meeting of the Princes which was due that day, for although it would please and make more amenable the minor Princes to whom the title was now extended, it would not please the more important Princes who already had this privilege.

At the same time, the King indicated that he would be prepared to grant the title of His Highness to the second son of the Nizam of Hyderabad. The Viceroy said he had asked for this because he realized that in future negotiations the Nizam was going to be difficult, and this grant might tip the scales in favour of the Nizam's co-operating.

In truth, the Indian Princes were on the verge of panic and practically on the run. The Political Adviser, Sir Conrad Corfield, had tried from the moment independence for British India became inevitable to persuade them (a) to liberalize their administrations, and (b) to form a solid block with which to resist the encroachment of the politicians of British India. He was a convinced royalist himself and he hoped that the presence of a 'cousin of the King' as Viceroy would give him the backing he needed to keep the Indian Princes out of the hands of the Indian politicians, particularly Congress politicians.

To his dismay, he found the Viceroy extremely unsympathetic. He did not seem to be worried about the future of the Princes. 'When the date (for the transfer of power) was fixed for August 15,' wrote Sir Conrad Corfield, in a note to the author, 'it became more important than ever that he should appreciate the difficult position of the Indian States. It proved impossible, however, to distract his attention from British Indian problems.'

For the Indian Princes had much to lose. Vast incomes, for instance, from customs and taxes and mineral wealth, which until now they alone had controlled. Almost godlike privileges, which their subjects might deny only at the risk of their livelihood or their freedom. The power to decide, with no one to gainsay them, whether their people should live in squalor or comfort, and whether they themselves should be profligate or sober and just. It is true that some of the rulers were wise, employed professional premiers who ran their administrations, and did not waste all their privy purse on dancing girls and wild living; but even these rulers were autocrats, often ruling by whim. It is true that Sir Conrad Corfield, as head of the Political Department, had the power to remove those Princes who indulged in 'excesses', but excesses never included political persecution, and no ruler was ever removed for imprisoning those who tried to bring democracy to his State.

Corfield has since confessed to the author that he regrets this. He feels that the history of the Indian Princely States might have been changed had the British intervened more freely in their affairs and insisted that they 'constitutionalize their authority, limit their private expenditure, and group themselves into viable units'. He admits that the Crown should have proffered more advice to secure these reforms. 'But how could the Crown do so,' he says, perhaps a little disingenuously, 'when the Rulers were the first to point out that pressure would be contrary to treaties and engagements governing their relationship?'

Corfield was determined, however, to do two things when independence came for British India. He set out to make sure that at least two or three Princely States, chief among them being Hyderabad, would be saved from engulfment by Congress. He also decided that he would make it as difficult as could be for the other States to be absorbed.

For this he used the instrument known as 'Paramountcy'. The Princely States had treaties with the British Crown. Otherwise, they were completely independent States, owing no sort of allegiance to British India. When the transfer of power took place, paramountcy would automatically lapse—and the Princely States would immediately get back those powers which had been taken over by the British. In other words, all of them, the largest and smallest of them, would become independent States. They would be within their rights in expelling from the territory troops of the Indian Army, which had been stationed there by agreement with the British. Indian railways, which ran through their States by agreements arranged by the British, would be stopped. Indian post and telegraph offices, which operated under a franchise from the British, could be closed. Passage through the States from one part of British India to another could be barred.

Pandit Nehru and his Congress colleagues argued that the Princely States could never really call themselves independent because 'they had not the power to declare war or conduct their own foreign affairs'. They must therefore, Nehru insisted, come to some interim arrangement to ensure a continuity of agreements with the rest of India, and absorb themselves into the new Indian Dominion without delay.

This was something Sir Conrad Corfield was determined to prevent.

Having failed to interest the Viceroy in his problems, he had for some time been carrying on a direct correspondence with the Secretary of State for India in London, Lord Listowel, who, for a Labour Minister, showed surprising sympathy for Sir Conrad's view that the paramountcy which Britain held over the Princely States should not, at any price, be handed over to the new Indian Dominion.

When Lord Ismay and Mr George Abell left for London in May 1947, with the first and disastrous (or Dickie Bird) Plan for Independence, Sir Conrad went with them. He told the Viceroy that he was going home to 'arrange about the lapse of paramountcy'. He said afterwards:

'I don't think he understood, and I did not explain, what the lapse of paramountcy would mean. My job was to look after the interests of the Princely States. It was no part of my job to make things easier for India.'[1]

In London, Corfield had several talks with Lord Listowel and secured from him a pledge to which both the Secretary of State for India and the Government afterwards stuck, despite repeated protests from Mountbatten and the Indian leaders. He agreed with Corfield to include a clause in the India Independence Bill which lapsed paramountcy only on the day when India became independent, so that India—unless it could make arrangements by agreement beforehand—would be confronted on 15 August by nearly six hundred Princely States containing a hundred million people, each State completely independent. As Pandit Nehru afterwards said, this would go a long way towards the process which he called 'the Balkanization of India'.

This plan of Corfield's might well have succeeded in creating chaos and confusion for India had it not been for an act of omission, no doubt inadvertent, which earned him the antagonism of the Viceroy. It will be remembered that when the first or 'Dickie Bird' Plan was abandoned in favour of the second or Menon Plan for independence, the Cabinet summoned Mountbatten to London and the Viceroy agreed, somewhat reluctantly, to go.

He cabled for his York aircraft (which had taken Ismay, Abell and Corfield to London with the first plan) to be sent back to

[1] In conversation with the author.

him. Corfield, having obtained all that he wanted from Lord Listowel, came back in it. And here he made an error—though, as has been said, it was no doubt inadvertent. He did not tell the Viceroy of his negotiations in London or even inform him of his return. Instead, the moment the Viceroy left for London in the York plane, Sir Conrad Corfield immediately went to work on the brief which he believed (rightly, as it turned out) he had received from Lord Listowel.

He ordered his Staff in the Political Department to begin cancelling all the arrangements, such as the stationing of troops, the operation of railways, the working of post offices, customs and such like, which had been made between the Paramount Power (Britain), acting on behalf of the Princely States, and British India. He also ordered his subordinates to extract from the files all the confidential reports and communications which had taken place between his Department and the Princes, including those murky and squalid occasions when Princes had had to be rebuked or disciplined or removed for their excesses. These files he ordered to be burned. The file on the 'Mr A. case' involving the Maharajah of Kashmir was consigned to the flames, as were those concerning the pyromaniac tendencies of the Maharajah of Alwar, the murder of the dancing girl Mumtaz Mahal, and other notorious scandals; also other predilections and peccadilloes of the Princes which had not, for one reason or another, ever been allowed to become public. Altogether, four tons of papers concerning the Princes were destroyed. Certain others were shipped by diplomatic bag to the Imperial archives in London, to be sifted there.

Mountbatten was annoyed by Corfield's neglect to get in touch with him and by the excess of zeal and speed with which he started to execute what he believed to be his ordained duty to the Princes.

It was only when his plane was flying between Delhi and Karachi on its way to London, that a member of the crew mentioned to the Viceroy that Sir Conrad Corfield had been a passenger on the journey the other way. He scribbled a message to V. P. Menon, who was a passenger with him, saying:

'D'you know what that son-of-a-bitch Corfield has done?'

'No, what?' scribbled back Menon.

'Sneaked back to India without telling me. I wonder what he's up to?'

From this moment, the position of Corfield and the Princes deteriorated rapidly. On 13 June, a meeting was held at the Viceroy's House over which Mountbatten presided, and Nehru, Jinnah and Conrad Corfield were among those present. It was obvious from the start that Nehru was in a boiling rage, and when he rose to speak he lashed out at Corfield.

'By what right have the Political Department,' he asked, 'gone ahead and taken action that will be highly injurious to the Government of India?'

He soon made it obvious that he was referring to the Political Department's action in relinquishing rights acquired by the British through paramountcy in the Princely States.

'I have been writing letters on this subject for four months,' said Nehru, 'and have got nowhere. I and my colleagues have not till now been shown the common courtesy of being brought into consultation. A completely unilateral action has been taken.' Then, turning to the Political Adviser, he said: 'I charge the Political Department and Sir Conrad Corfield particularly with misfeasance. I consider that a judicial enquiry on the highest level into their actions is necessary.'[1]

He sat down, obviously in the grip of violent emotion. Sir Conrad Corfield looked at Mountbatten to see whether he would rebuke Nehru for his extraordinary attack, but the Viceroy remained silent. Eventually, Jinnah drew back his chair and said frigidly:

'If Mr Nehru is to introduce emotion, bombast and unfounded allegations into the discussion, it does not seem worth while going on with the meeting.'

Corfield rose and said smoothly:

'I have nothing to hide. Everywhere I have acted under the instructions of the Crown Representative and with the approval of the Secretary of State. As to the relinquishing of rights, it has been accepted by the Secretary of State that if such rights were retained by the Paramount Power up to the very date of transfer, His Majesty's Government would be false to their promise that paramountcy would not be transferred to the new Dominions.'[1]

Both Nehru and Jinnah, the latter more mildly, then attacked Sir Conrad for his destruction of State documents. He replied

[1] Government of India Records.

that the process he was following was being carried out in consultation with the Imperial Record Department, which was a very skilled body. He was ready to give his guarantee that nothing of value would be destroyed. But he was obviously determined that nothing should get into the hands of the politicians which might give them a stick with which to beat the Princes. While the documents were being sorted, he said, there would be some which should not be handed over to the Government of India; but he agreed in future not to put them to the flames but to hand them over to the U.K. High Commissioner.

It was at this meeting that Nehru announced that the Congress Party had accepted a suggestion that a States Department be formed to deal with the Princes, and Jinnah thereupon said that the Muslim League would do the same. Corfield strenuously objected. He contended that though each Dominion could decide this question for itself after the transfer of power, it would not be in keeping with the spirit of British promises to the Princes if these Ministries were allowed to be established in advance of the transfer.

'It seems to me,' he said, 'that whatever the safeguards or precautions, these Ministries will, if established under the aegis of the Crown, be looked upon and will behave as though they have inherited the paramountcy which the Political Department has exercised hitherto.'[1]

He protested in vain. The meeting ended with baleful glances between Corfield and Nehru, and an icy politeness between Corfield and the Viceroy. Next day, the Viceroy tried to make amends for his failure to support his subordinate the day before. He wished to take this opportunity of telling Sir Conrad, he said, what he thought about the attack which had been made upon him at the last meeting with the Indian leaders by Pandit Nehru. He explained that it had always been his policy to refuse to enter into discussions with the Indian leaders concerning the behaviour of British officials. Nevertheless, he felt that on the occasion referred to he should perhaps have made it absolutely clear to Nehru (who was, however, not present on this occasion) that he, of course, completely dissociated himself from the latter's remarks and was unable to consider accepting the strictures which he had made. He added that he could not believe that Pandit Nehru would even have followed up his accusations if he had been asked

[1] Government of India Records.

to substantiate them, or had been told that they would be gone into carefully.

Sir Conrad accepted the gesture with a cool nod. Relations between the two men were henceforth extremely strained.

For Sir Conrad, however, there were two great consolations. He had, first, seen to it that documents likely to help the Indian Government in their relations with the Princes had been destroyed or whisked out of their reach; and, second, he had made sure that in no circumstances would paramountcy be passed on to either of the new Dominions. He bustled around among the more important Princes stressing that, when the transfer of power came, they had three choices and not two for their future. They could opt to join either Pakistan or India, but they could also decide not to accede at all and declare themselves independent. He stressed this interpretation of the Indian Independence Bill was not just his own, but also that of the Secretary of State.

The Maharajah of Travancore was sufficiently encouraged by this to announce that his would become an independent sovereign State after 15 August, and that he was appointing a trade agent with Pakistan. The next day, the Nizam of Hyderabad announced that his State would also remain independent.

It looked for a time as if Sir Conrad was winning his battle on behalf of the Princes. Congress was alarmed and alerted. A meeting was called in Delhi on 14 June by the All-India Congress Committee to protest against the 'Balkanization' of the country. A strongly worded resolution was passed declaring that Congress did not agree with the British Government's interpretation of paramountcy. It maintained that relations between India and the States could not be adversely affected by the lapse of paramountcy, and refused to admit the right of any State to declare its independence and live in isolation from the rest of India.

But Sir Conrad told his Princes to hold firm. The position was clear: On 15 August paramountcy ended; they were free. And many a Prince, whose private armies had been built up to great strength during the War, began to flex his muscles and smell the untrammelled independence ahead, when the British nanny would have been called away and there would be no one to say to him nay.

The best hope that Sir Conrad had of seeing an independent Princely State established was in Hyderabad, where the territory was vast, the coffers were full, the Nizam was fiercely anti-Congress, and his army was large and well-run. There was only one trouble here. The Indian Army had nearly a division of troops inside the State, and one of the reasons why Sir Conrad was so anxious to relinquish arrangements with the States in such a hurry was to get these troops out. But in this case, he had no luck. Repeated requests to Baldev Singh, the Defence Member, had been side-tracked.

In desperation, Sir Walter Monckton, the Nizam's legal adviser, wrote to Ismay on 22 June to ask him to persuade the Viceroy to intervene.

He wrote: 'I am by no means at the end of my troubles here [in Hyderabad]. The State has been pressing the Political Department for the removal of the Indian Army troops from our cantonments. There are 7 or 8,000 Indian Army fighting troops in the State including armoured formations. The Nizam thinks it quite intolerable that they should remain here after the 15th of August. They would in effect be an Army of Occupation. But such pressure as the Political Department has been able to exert has been quite ineffective. Whether the Defence Member is stalling or not, I don't know; but it does look as if those who will form the Government of the Indian Union would not be unwilling to find themselves with an Army of Occupation here. I spoke to the C.-in-C. [Auchinleck] about it and he said (privately) that we should have nothing to worry about while he was directing the Army. This is cold comfort.

'The Crown Representative is still the Crown Representative and he could direct the Government to take steps to move the troops out of State territory by the 15th August.

'The State is writing a further letter asking for information about the dates and stages of the programme by which the troops will be removed, in view of the acceleration of the departure of the British. The letter will ask for a reply within a specified time. If no reply is forthcoming, a question will be asked in the House giving the steps taken by the State and the result, and asking whether this Army of Occupation will be permitted to remain.'[1]

It was the first major move in the struggle for Hyderabad's future which was to intensify in the days to come. V. P. Menon wrote in his *The Story of the Integration of the Indian States* that any

[1] Government of India Records.

decision which allowed the States, comprising two-fifths of the land, to 'return to a state of complete political isolation was fraught with the gravest danger to the integrity of the country'.

He added: 'The prophets of gloom predicted that the ship of Indian freedom would founder on the rock of the States.'

Sir Conrad Corfield and other defenders of the Princes were, however, being a little too optimistic. At the very moment that they breathed the heady air of victory something came out of the blue and floored them.

The blow came from the clasped hands of those two able political operators, Sardar Patel and our old friend V. P. Menon. When the Congress Party had decided to form a States Ministry they picked Patel as the obvious man to head it. Their mood was belligerent. They despised the Princes and they resented the British for lapsing paramountcy. They hoped and expected that the strong man of the Party would roll up his dhoti and wade in with sound, fury, and effect.

Patel was far too wily a negotiator to do any such thing, particularly since he had the measure of Sir Conrad Corfield and admired him as a skilled and dangerous adversary. This was, he decided, no time for flailing fists and loud cries of screaming rage and fury. The blow must be subtle, unexpected, and must leave no unnecessary bruises.

Three days after his own appointment, he called in V. P. Menon and asked him to accept the job of Secretary of the States Department. 'I told Sardar,' Menon wrote later, 'that it was my intention to take all the leave I had earned and to retire from Government service after 15 August. Ever since 1917, I had been dealing with constitutional reforms. I have never expected that I would see freedom for India in my lifetime. Since that had materialised, my life's ambition was achieved . . . Sardar told me that because of the abnormal situation in the country, people like myself should not think in terms of rest or retirement. He added that I had taken a prominent part in the transfer of power and that I should consider it my bounden duty to work for the consolidation of freedom. I naturally agreed that the country's interests, and not my personal predilections, should be the guiding factor.'[1]

Menon agreed to take on the job. The combination of his agile brain and Patel's driving personality was to prove even more

[1] V. P. Menon, *The Story of the Integration of the Indian States.*

formidable on this occasion than it had been during the negotiations for the Independence Treaty.

Almost at once V. P. Menon demonstrated his skill as an adviser and tactician. Sir Conrad Corfield, he said, had tried to make things as difficult as possible for India by having paramountcy lapse immediately the British departed. Well, it was true that this might make things awkward for the new Indian Dominion if they had to start negotiating with the Princes over every little arrangement—army arrangements, postal arrangements, customs arrangements, currency arrangements, railway arrangements—which the British had now begun to cancel. But since there was less than eight weeks to go before independence, why bother about such details? Why not approach each Prince in turn and negotiate on a simple formula. Ask them simply to accede to the Indian Union under three subjects only: Defence, External Affairs, and Communications.

'But what if they refuse?' asked Patel.

'How can they refuse?' replied Menon. 'Until now, the British protected each Princely State from unrest. If there were political or communal agitations, the British saw to it that order was restored. But now the British are going. It is true that some of the bigger States can keep some sort of order through their own private armies. But if the people rise up and begin to demand their freedom, the right to be independent themselves, to join India—if popular agitation begins to threaten the rule and safety and even the lives of the Rulers, where can they look to for protection except to us?'

Sardar Patel said that he saw what Menon meant. He had for some time been head of the organization which controlled the Congress underground movements in the Princely States.

Patel still could not stomach the action of the British in allowing paramountcy to lapse. It was not a friendly action, he insisted; it would endanger Indian security. Menon immediately reassured him.

'The Political Department thinks that it will ruin us,' he said. 'But my view is that the lapse of paramountcy is a blessing in disguise. All those treaties which the British had with the Princes gave the Princes all sorts of privileges—non-interference in their affairs, for example, except in cases of flagrant misbehaviour. If paramountcy had been passed on to us, we should have inherited them. We would have had to go on treating the Princes as demigods in their own States. But not now. Paramountcy lapses. So do the privileges. We start with a clean slate. It is our turn now to say how the Princes will behave.'[1]

V. P. Menon had another brilliant idea. 'I proposed that the active co-operation of Lord Mountbatten should be secured,' he wrote afterwards. 'Apart from his position, his grace and his gifts, his relationship to the Royal Family was bound to influence the rulers. Sardar wholeheartedly agreed and asked me to approach him without delay. A day or two later, I met Lord Mountbatten and mentioned to him my talk with Sardar and our tentative plan. I asked for his help in getting the States to accede to India on three subjects (defence, external affairs and communications).'[2]

Menon adroitly argued his case, pointing out that the States would not be losing anything in the result, but that it needed great statesmanship to bring it about and who but the Viceroy was capable of it?

'I felt that he was extremely touched by my remark,' Menon went on, 'that the wounds of partition might to some extent be healed by the States entering into relationship with the Government of India and that he would be earning the gratitude of generations of Indians if he could assist in achieving the basic unity of the country. He told me that he would think the matter over . . . I confess that I was seized momentarily by the fear that Lord Mountbatten might be adversely influenced by some of his advisers. But to my relief and joy he accepted the plan . . . Nehru, with the approval of the Cabinet, readily entrusted Lord Mountbatten with the task of negotiating with the rulers on the question of accession and also with the task of dealing with Hyderabad.'[2]

It was done. The Viceroy had come in on the side of the new Indian Dominion—and against Sir Conrad Corfield and the Political Department. Sir Conrad fought bitterly for his view that the Princes had every right to choose independence if they wished, and need not accede. 'But Lord Mountbatten thought otherwise,' he wrote later, in a note to the author. 'He was persuaded that unless he used his influence to persuade the States to adhere to their neighbouring Dominion in advance of the lapse of paramountcy, there was grave risk to the economic and peaceful administration of the country after the transfer of power . . . It

[1] Remarks recalled in conversations with the author.
[2] Op. cit.

is interesting to note that Mr Jinnah had no desire to force adherence upon the States within Pakistan's sphere of influence. He was quite prepared to negotiate with each of these States on the basis of their legal independence and technical freedom of choice after Pakistan was established. Mr Nehru and Mr Patel, however, persuaded His Excellency that a similar course for India would be too dangerous.'

Sir Conrad was ordered to summon rulers and representatives of the States to a conference at which the Viceroy proposed to persuade them to choose adherence to India in advance of the lapse of paramountcy.

'Mountbatten is now in the thick of the States problem,' noted his Press adviser, Campbell-Johnson. 'As with his diplomacy prior to the June 3 plan, he took a calculated risk and is personally sponsoring the Instrument of Accession and undertaking to get all the Princes into this particular bag, while V. P. sold the project to Congress. He embarked with the assurance of Patel's decisive support.'[1]

The meeting with the Princes on 25 July 1947 was probably the most spectacular example of Mountbatten's skill, charm and tremendous arts of persuasion. He was by this time fully convinced that accession to India or Pakistan—with no alternative of independence—was the only possible course for the Princes to follow. His estrangement from the Political Department was well-nigh complete. He began to share Patel's resentment over the lapse of paramountcy after a visit from a distinguished Indian, Sir B. N. Rau, who pointed out that 327 Rulers of petty States, whose average area was about 20 square miles apiece, average population about 3,000 and average revenue about £1,000 per annum, would with the lapse of paramountcy gain the powers of life and death over their subjects. Rau appealed to Mountbatten to have a clause inserted in the Independence Bill which would restrict their powers and make it certain that the authority of the Crown Representative in respect of the small States should hereafter be exercised by the new Dominions. Mountbatten cabled to the Secretary of State saying: 'I did not myself realise that 327 owners of small estates would after lapse of paramountcy have power of life and death, where before they only had power to give three months' imprisonment,'[2] and gave full backing to

---

[1] Alan Campbell-Johnson, *Mission with Mountbatten*.
[2] Government of India Records.

Rau's suggestion. The Secretary of State for India replied that this would fundamentally alter the intention of the Bill towards the Princely States; that the lapse of paramountcy must stand, and that no alteration could be made. For the first time, the Viceroy began to understand what the lapse of paramountcy really meant, and what arrangements Sir Conrad Corfield had made while in London.

At the meeting on 25 July, therefore, to quote the words of Campbell-Johnson, 'he used every weapon in his armoury of persuasion, making it clear at the outset that in the proposed Instrument of Accession, which V. P. Menon had devised, [the Princes] were being provided with a political offer from Congress which was not likely to be repeated . . . He reminded them that after the 15th of August he would no longer be in a position to mediate on their behalf as Crown Representative, and warned those Princes who were hoping to build up their own store of arms that the weapons they would get would in any case be obsolete.'[1]

He then proceeded to use every blandishment in his repertoire to persuade the Princes to sign on the dotted line, not least of them being a promise that he would persuade Congress that, if they did so, the Princes would be allowed to go on receiving titles and honours. He was by turns bullying and bantering. As the Princes sweated in the heat of the Delhi summer—it was 108·4 in Delhi that day, and the fans in the Chamber of Princes merely whipped the princely perspiration into a froth—he picked them out like schoolchildren and asked them whether they would sign. The expression on the face of even the richest of them was the sad, lost look of men in defeat. They had come to the meeting convinced that the Viceroy was going to save them and their privileges from the encroachment of the Congress vandals. After all, he was one of them, wasn't he? At first, the very sight of him had bucked them up, for, despite the heat, he had come to the meeting in full Viceregal uniform, his chest flashing with a breastplate of orders, decorations and medals. He looked every inch a cousin of the King, symbol of their hopes, protector of their privileges.

It was typical of his magnetism that, even while forcing them to realize that they were doomed, he still kept them good-humoured and compliant. There were no angry outbursts, only

[1] Op. cit.

spurts of laughter at his sallies. Perhaps the most famous incident occurred when he questioned the Dewan (or Prime Minister) of one large State and asked him whether his maharajah would sign the Instrument of Accession. The Dewan replied that he had received no instructions from his master, who was abroad.

'Surely you must know your Ruler's mind,' said Mountbatten, 'and can take a decision on his behalf?'

'I do not know my Ruler's mind,' replied the Dewan, 'and I cannot get a reply by cable.'

The Viceroy picked up a glass paper-weight which was on his desk. 'I will look into my crystal ball,' he said, 'and give the answer.' Pause and heavy silence. 'His Highness,' said the Viceroy, dramatically, 'asks you to sign the Instrument of Accession.'

The Princes broke into spontaneous laughter and applause. At least, if they were signing their death-warrants, Mountbatten was making it possible for them to go to their doom with a smile on their lips.

The smile on the face of Sir Conrad Corfield, however, was wintry. And his private comment afterwards was bitter indeed.

'In order to make this proposal [the Instrument of Accession] less unpalatable,' he wrote in a note to the author, 'he [the Viceroy] had persuaded Mr Patel to agree that adherence would be limited to the sphere of Defence, External Affairs and Communications, with a definite promise that no financial liability would be involved and that in no other matters would the new Dominion encroach upon the internal autonomy or the sovereignty of the States.'

He (Corfield) added: 'As there was nothing to prevent the new Dominion, after the transfer of power, extending its sphere of influence through the States Department, these limitations and safeguards could obviously be made valueless in due course, and in fact quickly became so. For the Viceroy to use his influence, built upon the past exercise of paramountcy, in order to persuade trusting Rulers to accept such dubious propositions was, to say the least, un-British.'

But the Viceroy's soothing words had their effect, and one by one the Princes queued up to sign. Not all of them. Hyderabad still stood aloof. So did Travancore and Bhopal and Jodhpur and Indore, among others. With the exception of Hyderabad,

Mountbatten called the recalcitrant Princes in to see him, or their Dewans.

'A leading Dewan informed me after one such interview with His Excellency,' said Corfield, 'that he now knew what Dolfüss had felt like when he was sent for to see Hitler; he had not expected to be spoken to like that by a British officer; after a moment's pause, he withdrew the word "British".'

This was undoubtedly the Dewan of the Maharajah of Travancore, who came to see Mountbatten in private to tell him of his master's determination to proclaim his State's independence after 15 August. He sharply attacked Nehru as unstable and Patel as ruthless. The Viceroy told him not to be a fool nor too precipitate. He then turned him over to V. P. Menon, who reminded the Dewan that Travancore[1] was the strongest breeding ground of Communism in India. What if the Communists suddenly rose up in revolt against the Ruler after 15 August? If Travancore was independent, the Dominion of India would have to refuse to come to its aid. The Dewan departed, thoughtful and discomfited.

The States Department had by this time found its feet. Patel and Menon were increasingly confident that, with Mountbatten's influence in the background, they would have most of the Princes signed, sealed and delivered before 15 August. Menon, particularly, felt that the time had come at last to break the influence of Sir Conrad Corfield. His affection for the Political Department had been cool ever since the occasion, during the War, when it had vetoed his appointment as Dewan of a large Princely State because he was 'not sufficiently above his nationality'. He now went to the Viceroy with reports ('I naturally had my spies in the Political Department,' he said) that Sir Conrad was persuading Bhopal and a number of other Princes to make a last-ditch stand against accession, urging them to form themselves into a Third Force of independent States along the lines which Bhopal had been pursuing some months before. Menon protested that this was intolerable interference.

'The position is such,' he said to Mountbatten, 'that I am afraid that a choice must be made. Either Sir Conrad Corfield goes, or I go.'[2]

He knew, as the Viceroy knew, that there really was no choice. Mountbatten had gone so far with Menon and Patel now that,

[1] Which became part of Kerala after independence.
[2] Recollected during conversations with the author.

in the face of such an ultimatum, there was nothing to do but call in Sir Conrad and tell him to pack his bags.

The Political Adviser was more than willing to go. 'As soon as the new States Departments were established,' he wrote in a note to the author, 'I fixed July 25th as the date of the proposed conference and obtained permission to vacate the post of Political Adviser and return to England by air on July 23rd.'

His feelings as he left were bitter indeed. 'Even at this late stage,' he wrote, 'the Rulers found it difficult to realise that they were being deserted by the Crown and left to make their peace with the new Dominions in circumstances in which complete power was being transferred to their political opponents. Had they listened to the Crown's past advice to constitutionalise their authority, to limit their private expenditure and to group themselves into viable units, they could have negotiated from strength.

'It can be argued that the Crown should have proffered more than advice in order to secure these reforms; but how could the Crown do so when the Rulers were the first to point out that pressure would be contrary to the treaties and engagements governing their relationship? To denounce these treaties and engagements as out of date might have been politically disastrous. The new Dominions however were not so squeamish.'

He added: 'Meanwhile, the time was so short in which to make a decision that most of the Rulers accepted Lord Mountbatten's advice and signed their Instruments of Accession without demur.' And he ended, sadly:

'Indeed, so strongly had the tide begun to turn that when the Political Adviser left, three weeks before the lapse of paramountcy, only three Rulers came to bid him farewell. Six months earlier, in Bombay, no State was unrepresented when he was invited by the Conference of Rulers and their Ministers to proffer his advice. Up to that time the States had maintained a united front; but no advice would prevail against communal discord, and as soon as that common front disintegrated, the day of personal rule in India came to an end.'

But not quite as quickly as that.

It is true that a majority of the Princes accepted the inevitable and signed the Instrument of Accession at once. The first of them was the Maharajah of Bikaner, who had once been an old friend of the Viceroy. He put his name to the paper with a dramatic gesture.

The Maharajah of Baroda signed, then clasped his arms around Menon's neck, and wept like a child. One of the rajahs had a heart attack immediately after signing.

Still a number of important Princes were holding back, in spite of Mountbatten's persuasion. The Dewan of the Maharajah of Travancore, Sir C. P. Ramaswami Ayar, had returned to Cochin to tell his master of the Viceroy's advice that he should sign the Instrument and of Menon's hint that, in the event of trouble in the State, India would refuse to help unless he acceded. The Maharajah tried to temporize by telegraphing Mountbatten to say that he would 'agree' to the conditions but hoped that this would preclude him from signing them. The Viceroy telegraphed back that this was not enough. A signature was necessary. At the same time, the Working Committee of the States Congress Committee in Travancore, an underground organization, called for demonstrations against the Maharajah. There were clashes in the streets with the State police. Sir C. P. Ramaswami Ayar was stabbed and seriously wounded by an unknown assailant. The Maharajah telegraphed to the Viceroy that he was signing the Instrument. Sardar Patel ordered the local Congress Committee to cease their demonstrations at once.

It was a clear demonstration of Congress's power to incite disaffection in the Princely States and of the determination of Patel and Menon to act ruthlessly against those princely fish who refused to swim into the net. The lesson was salutary, and it was not lost upon the other Princes. They began to sign in increasing numbers.

But certain Princes still held out. Hyderabad, of course; Kashmir, Mysore, Bhopal and Jodhpur; and the Nawab of a small State on the Kathiawar coast of Western India called Junagadh.

Menon's Intelligence Service in the Political Department informed him that British members of the department were actively working to persuade the Maharajah Hanwant Singh of Jodhpur not to sign the Instrument of Accession to India but to choose Pakistan instead. This he had the perfectly legal right to do. The Viceroy had downed his thumb on princely independence, but he had emphasized that each State could choose to accede to the Dominion whose frontiers were contiguous with it. Jodhpur's frontiers, like those of two other Rajput Princes, were contiguous with both India and Pakistan.

Like the majority of the Princes, Jodhpur was antipathetic to Congress and suspected that there would be little future for him in the Indian Dominion. He was a free-swinging young man who loved polo, flying, and dancing girls. He was extravagant and reckless and gay. One of his grandfathers had once given a party for Lord and Lady Curzon at which a pie was served to each of the two hundred guests, and when the top was taken off, out flew a tiny coloured song-bird. 'One of them perched in my tiara,' Lady Curzon reported. The young Maharajah went in for rather different kinds of tarts, though no less expensive. He had little time for equality and ran his State on arrogantly authoritarian lines, and he was in no mood to change his ideas or his way of life.

He decided to make a secret visit to Mr Jinnah, who might be more amenable to his charms. He took with him the Maharajah of Jaisalmer, whose State also flanked Pakistan. Jinnah was overjoyed to see them. He knew that if these two big States acceded to Pakistan, many of the other Rajput States might well do so, too; their accession would more than compensate for the loss of half of the Punjab and Bengal by partition, and it would be a severe blow to Congress' plans for capturing all the most powerful Princes. He, therefore, took a blank sheet of paper from a drawer in his desk, slid it across to Jodhpur, and said:

'Write your terms on that, your Highness—and I will sign them.'

Jodhpur turned to Jaisalmer. 'Will you join me?' he asked.

'On one condition,' Jaisalmer answered. 'I must have it agreed in writing that, in the event of trouble between the Muslims and the Hindus, I and my State will be allowed to remain completely neutral.'

Jinnah assured him that there would be no trouble anyway, and that he must not worry about such trifles. But the conversation seems to have made Jodhpur realize for the first time that he, the Hindu Maharajah of a State with a Hindu majority, would be going over to a Muslim country. He said he would like time to think things over, and returned to his hotel in Delhi.

It was there that V. P. Menon, who had been apprised of what was afoot, arrived that evening to see him. Jodhpur at first refused to receive him. Menon sent a note to say that he had brought an urgent message from the Viceroy. When he was shown into the Maharajah's suite, he said:

'I have come from the Viceroy. He wishes to see you at once. You must come with me to the Viceroy's House.'

Mountbatten was, in fact, at this moment completely unaware of what was happening and had not asked to see Jodhpur at all. None the less, the Maharajah and Menon hurried across to the Viceroy's House where Menon left Jodhpur in the waiting-room. He himself sent an S O S to the Viceroy asking to speak with him at once and was shown up to his bedroom. He told the Viceroy of Jodhpur's meeting with Jinnah and of the Muslim League plot to capture the Rajput States for Pakistan. He asked Mountbatten to see Jodhpur and talk him out of his wish to accede to Pakistan. Then the two of them went down to the waiting-room to see Jodhpur, who was by this time impatient, surly and suspicious. It was the sort of prickly situation which Mountbatten cherished.

He was immediately his most charming and yet his steeliest self, a patient schoolmaster about to read a lesson to a promising but unruly pupil. He said at once that the Maharajah had every legal right to accede to Pakistan if he wished, but did he really realize what the consequences might be? As the Hindu ruler of a largely Hindu State, he was surely going against the principle that India was being divided into a Muslim and a non-Muslim Dominion. His decision to accede to Pakistan might cause considerable communal disturbance in Jodhpur, where there was a strong, if unofficial, Congress movement.

The Maharajah was quickly reduced to bluster. 'Mr Jinnah gave me a blank sheet of paper on which to write my own terms,' he said. 'What will you give me?'

Menon: 'I'll give you a blank sheet of paper too, if you like. But it will bring you nothing but false hopes, like the other.'

With Mountbatten urging compromise by both sides, it was eventually agreed that Menon should make certain minor concessions to Jodhpur, and that he should visit him in Jodhpur with these terms set out in a letter a few days later.

'Then that's settled,' said the Viceroy, slapping them both on the back. He was by this time in a high good humour. He was called away for a few moments at this point, and, as soon as he had gone through the door, the young Maharajah swung on Menon.

'You tricked me,' he said. 'You got me here on false pretences. I'm going to kill you!'

He had a revolver in his hand, and he was pointing it straight at V. P. Menon's head. 'I refuse to accept dictation from you,' he went on.

Menon is a portly man whose figure and face do not suggest heroics, but he faced the angry Prince with what dignity he could muster.

'If you think that by killing me you will get more concessions,' he said, 'you are mistaken. Stop these juvenile theatricals.'

At this point, Jodhpur burst into laughter and put the revolver away. When Mountbatten returned, Menon told him that he had been threatened with a revolver.

'This is no time for jokes,' the Viceroy said mildly. 'Now what about signing the Instrument?'

But it was not until three days later that the pugnacious and resentful Jodhpur was finally corralled. He had by this time returned to Jodhpur, and it was there that Menon took the Letter of Agreement containing the concessions which he had made. When his car reached the Maharajah's Palace, he found a vast and hostile crowd outside it, all of them shouting and gesticulating against Menon and Congress. It was with difficulty that he was rescued by the State police and taken into the palace. There a grinning Jodhpur was waiting for him.

'That was just to show you that I can call up demonstrators too,' he said.

It was the first incident in what, for Menon, was to prove a trying day.

The Instrument of Accession was signed. The terms of Agreement were accepted by both parties.

'And now,' said Jodhpur to Menon, 'you and I must have a drink. This is a day for drinking. I have been defeated. You have won a victory. Let's drink.'

He clapped his hands and summoned whisky and two glasses. He poured out two half-tumblerfuls and downed his own, while Menon sipped his. More and more whiskies disappeared down the Maharajah's throat, and he kept urging the abstemious Menon to drink, drink, drink.

Finally, Menon said he would drink no more with Jodhpur unless he first went away and bathed and changed. His own head was throbbing. Jodhpur was becoming good and drunk.

'All right,' said the Maharajah, 'but only if, when I come back, you and I drink champagne. Lots and lots and lots of champagne.'

Menon protested that he could not drink champagne. It gave him a headache. He preferred whisky.

'See what a dictator you are!' cried Jodhpur. 'Now that you are in the ascendant! Already you tell me what to drink.'

He was eventually persuaded to leave and change. When he came back, bottle after bottle of champagne came with him. Weakly, Menon called for whisky. He got another glass of champagne instead. Meanwhile, the Maharajah's A.D.C. had been summoned. He must call the band and organize a banquet for that evening.

At the banquet, there was meat and game and wines and more champagne. The band played indefatigably. Dancing girls flitted back and forth. The worthy Menon kept his eyes away from them and went on talking about Accession, until, at one point, Jodhpur angrily ordered the band away.

'I can't hear what you're saying for all this bloody noise,' he said. 'Why on earth didn't they get me an orchestra instead?' To his A.D.C.: 'Go on, bring me an orchestra.'

Menon mildly pointed out that the Maharajah himself had asked for a band.

'That just shows,' said Jodhpur solemnly. 'It's about time the Government of India took over. What a State—when an A.D.C. takes orders from a man who has drunk a bottle of whisky and three bottles of champagne!'

He took off his turban and threw it on the floor.

It was time, Menon thought, to take his train back to Delhi. But Jodhpur would have none of it. He bundled the Secretary to the States Department into his private plane and, still very drunk, took off for Delhi, diving, twisting, and doing every aerobatic in the book except a loop, on the way.[1]

It was a very sick Menon who landed in Delhi. But he had his Instrument of Accession, and he had saved the Rajput States from Pakistan.

A few days later, the Nawab of Bhopal gave in too. His plan for a Third Force was in ruins. Though a Muslim himself, his State was largely Hindu and he dare not take the risk of turning it over to Pakistan. His surrender was a handsome one. He wrote to Sardar Patel:

'I do not disguise the fact that while the struggle was on,

[1] The Maharajah of Jodhpur was killed while stunting his plane in 1952. His latest wife, a dancing girl from Bombay, died with him.

I used every means in my power to preserve the independence and neutrality of my State. Now that I have conceded defeat, I hope that you will find that I can be as staunch a friend as I have been an inveterate opponent. I harbour no ill feelings towards anyone, for throughout I have been treated with consideration and have received understanding and courtesy from your side. I now wish to tell you that so long as you maintain your firm stand against the disruptive forces in the country and continue to be a friend of the States as you have shown you are, you will find in me a loyal and faithful ally.'

Patel rose to the occasion.

'Quite candidly,' he wrote back, 'I do not look upon the accession of your State to the Indian Union as either a victory for us or a defeat for you. It is only right and propriety which have triumphed in the end, and, in that triumph, you and I have played our respective rôles. You deserve full credit for having recognized the soundness of the position and for the courage, the boldness and the honesty of having given up your earlier stand which according to us was entirely antagonistic to the interests as much of India as of your own State. I have noted with particular pleasure your assurance of support to the Dominion Government in combating disloyal elements irrespective of caste, creed or religion and your offer of loyal and faithful friendship. During the last few months it had been a matter of great disappointment and regret to me that your undoubted talents and abilities were not at the country's disposal during the critical times through which we were passing, and I therefore particularly value this assurance of co-operation and friendship.'

It was the end of the beginning, but only the beginning of the end. Large States, small States, maharajahs, rajahs, and jagadirs, they all queued up to sign. But as the day for independence approached, three still stood out—and two of them were the most important Princely States in India.

The one which was not, which was merely a pawn in the game, was a small but rich princedom among the Kathiawar States of Western India called Junagadh. It was the only Kathiawar State with a Muslim Prince, and the Nawab of Junagadh was something special. He was a Ruler in the same tradition, though not of the same religion as the pyromaniac Maharajah of Alwar. Not that he set fire to racehorses. But he had the same taste for the exotic, the bizarre and the brutal. Junagadh happens to be one of the most lovely and fascinating corners of India. Up above its walled, Moghul city rise two great hills, over 3,800 feet in height, which are centres of Hindu religious pilgrimage. To one come lepers hoping, by praying in the temple on the summit, to be cured. To the other, the mountain of Girnar, come members of the Hindu sect, the Jains.

The Jains are vegetarians who believe in Right Cognition, Right Conduct and Right Faith. Right Cognition means acceptance of the fact that every living person or thing in the world has a soul. Right Conduct means charity towards everything, including the minutest creatures of the earth. Nothing living must be killed. Jain priests wear gauze masks to prevent the inhalation of a fly which thus might be destroyed. Right Faith naturally includes non-violence towards all men and all living creatures. In a land not over-considerate towards its animals, Jains collect and care for birds and donkeys, dogs, cats, mules and camels which fall victim to age, disease or the savagery of man.

On the mountain of Girnar, the Jains have built a magnificent and, in the circumstances, fantastic monument to their ideals and beliefs. Up the mountainside, much of it of Alpine steepness, they laid a stone staircase whose route, in parts, has been hacked out of solid rock and which is only three feet wide, with a drop of a thousand or fifteen hundred feet over its edge.

Up the stairs the Jains carried blocks of marble with which, on the higher slopes right up to the summit, they have built a series of elaborate temples, filled with beautiful carvings, to which a Jain ascends to pray for his soul, or his marriage, or the birth of his children. Only a too fat, too weak, or too rich Jain (or an effete tourist) allows himself to be carried to the top by porters. The majority of pilgrims march up through the blazing heat, and then descend to join the naked sadhus and sacred monkeys at the bathing ghats below.

Junagadh had (and still has) one other claim to uniqueness. In its large forest of Gir live the only remaining lions in Asia.

It seems ironic that in this centre of dedicated non-violence, within sight of the temples of Girnar, should be a Nawab who was particularly devoted to the more sanguine pursuits. It was, to some extent, a family tradition. His father had a favourite habit of destroying his political opponents and those courtiers who earned his displeasure by making them perform a sort of 'walk the plank' ceremony from a castle orifice on to some particularly sharp rocks below. The Nawab himself had two hobbies: breeding dogs and hunting. He bred dogs and he loved dogs. Around his palace he had built a series of elaborate kennels (rooms would be a better description) in which he kept his favourite pets—about a hundred and fifty of them—each with its own bath, serving table, bed, attendant and telephone. There was a palace vet, an Englishman, to look after them. When dogs were brought in, they were placed on palanquins and carried by retainers into the Nawab's presence. When two of his dogs were mated, the Nawab invariably declared a public holiday in the State.

He also kept a pack of hounds with which he went hunting. The Indians say that his particular pleasure was to starve his hounds, deliberately shoot deer or lions to wound them, and then release the hounds for the pleasure of watching them tear their prey to pieces.

As a Muslim, the Nawab had four wives and several concubines. His attitude towards them proved to be as ambiguous as it was towards the Instrument of Accession.

After the Viceroy's meeting with the Princes, the Nawab of Junagadh indicated at once that he would sign the Instrument and accede to the union of India. Despite his attachment to Islam, this seemed logical in the circumstances. Junagadh's population was between 80 and 90 per cent Hindu. Its territory was surrounded on all sides except the sea by Princely territories, all of whose rulers were Hindu and had opted for India. Its nearest link with Pakistan was by sea, 240 miles away. India's largest, fattest and most amiable Prince, the Jam Sahib of Nawanagar, had been appointed spokesman for the rest of the Kathiawar rulers, and he reported to Delhi that there would be no trouble about accession from any of them. It seemed as if the future of this large and complicated jig-saw puzzle of States had been settled.

So far as Junagadh was concerned, however, it had not. While he spoke soothing words to Congress, the Nawab was, in fact, in touch with Pakistan. It is hard to believe that Mr Jinnah really wanted Junagadh within his new Dominion. Separated from Pakistan, surrounded by Indian territory, it would have proved an administrative nightmare at a time when Mr Jinnah had more vital problems than he could cope with. But as a pawn in the game which both the Muslim League and Congress were playing at this moment, Junagadh was invaluable.

There was a much larger and more important State to the north—the prosperous and lovely state of Kashmir—which had not yet signed the Instrument of Accession, and whose Ruler had not yet indicated to which Dominion he would accede. Both Dominions wanted the territory, and it had a common frontier with both of them. Which side would Kashmir choose? The situation here was the exact opposite of Junagadh in that the Maharajah was a Hindu and the population was almost overwhelmingly Muslim; but the problem of accession was so similar as to make Junagadh, at least for Mr Jinnah, the perfect testing ground of Congress strategy and sincerity in Kashmir.

A Muslim League politician, Abdul Kadir Mohammed Hussain, had been infiltrated into Junagadh early in 1947, and, shortly after both the League and Congress agreed to partition, this politician succeeded in ousting the old Dewan, Nabi Baksh, who was in favour of acceding to India. Hussain now went to work on the Nawab and soon convinced him that the Congress would kill off his beloved dogs, curb his passion for cruel sports, ration his concubines and nationalize his Gir lions. On the other hand, Pakistan would not only encourage him in the free life but would also send armed police to restore order should his people protest against his decision to consign them to Pakistan.

The Instrument of Accession had been sent to the Nawab to sign immediately after the Viceroy's meeting, but days passed and it was not returned. Repeated telegrams were sent to him by Menon and Patel, but they were ignored. The days of independence drew nearer, but so far as Congress was concerned the Nawab remained mum. There was, therefore, panic in the States Department when it was learned from the newspapers that Junagadh had decided to accede to Pakistan. No other notification was sent to the Indian Union, and it was in the Press that they read the Nawab's communiqué, which said:

'The Government of Junagadh has during the past few weeks been faced with the problem of making its choice between accession to the Dominion of India and accession to the Dominion of Pakistan. It has had to take into very careful consideration every aspect of this problem. Its main preoccupation has been to adopt a course that would, in the long run, make the largest contribution towards the permanent welfare and prosperity of the people of Junagadh and help to preserve the integrity of the State and to safeguard its independence and autonomy over the largest possible field. After anxious consideration and the careful balancing of all factors the Government of the State has decided to accede to Pakistan and hereby announces its decision to that effect. The State is confident that its decision will be welcomed by all loyal subjects of the State who have its real welfare and prosperity at heart.'

Now Jinnah and the Muslim League leaders knew that this statement was a farrago of nonsense, even if the Nawab of Junagadh did not. The State of Junagadh was not just one tract of territory. Several enclaves of Junagadh territory were inside other Kathiawar States, such as Baroda, Gondal and Bavhnagar, which had already acceded to India. Slap-bang in the middle of Junagadh itself were a number of Mangrol States, which had also acceded to India. They were now surrounded by Pakistan territory and could not trade with the rest of Kathiawar except by going through Junagadh customs. The situation was one of hopeless confusion, and only a dunderhead like the Nawab of Junagadh would have failed to see it.

The Indian Government immediately telegraphed to Liaquat Ali Khan to ask him whether Pakistan intended to accept the accession of Junagadh, but got no reply. The Muslim Leaders were obviously enjoying the chaos of the situation and the fury of the Congress, and had no intention of doing anything to help. Weeks passed before they finally issued a statement to the effect that Junagadh's accession had been accepted, and that the State was now considered by them as part of the Dominion of Pakistan. Except for dispatching a small force of police, however, they did nothing practical to incorporate the State within the Dominion. They knew only too well that the Hindu majority in the State was pro-Indian, that the underground Congress movement was exceedingly powerful, and that any overt move to exploit the State as part of Pakistan would lead to an explosion. Except for a few fanatics, anyway, the Muslim League had no wish to do anything. All they had to do was sit back and wait.

Soon the Indian Union was announcing that Hindu refugees were fleeing from Junagadh as a result of repressive measures by the Nawab. They received an appeal for help from the inhabitants of the Mangrol States inside Junagadh, who claimed they were besieged. The Nawab immediately sent in his troops and occupied Mangrol territory.

Inevitably, the Indian Army marched into those parts of Junagadh territory without the State proper as a reprisal. After that they hesitated, because Congress realized it was being led into a trap. But finally, they decided to act. They had for some weeks been blockading the State, which was getting short of food. Now, laden with supplies, they marched in to a rapturous welcome from the populace. The Nawab had already fled to Pakistan in his private plane. He crammed aboard as many of his dogs as he could, plus his four wives. One of them discovered, at the last moment, that she had left her child behind in the palace and asked the Nawab to wait while she fetched her. The moment she left the airfield, the Nawab loaded in two more dogs and took off without his wife. He had with him sufficient of the family jewels to ensure the future comfort of himself and his family, but otherwise he had left everything.

Though the Pakistan Government professed to be outraged by the events, it is almost certain that Jinnah and Liaquat Ali Khan were overjoyed. Junagadh had always been expendable. Its main use, so far as they were concerned, was to test Congress's good faith. And how had Congress reacted? When a Muslim Prince in a Hindu State opted for Pakistan, they refused to recognize it.

Surely here was a lesson—and they hoped the world was listening—for the future of Kashmir. If the Maharajah of Kashmir, a Hindu Prince in a Muslim State, opted for India, Pakistan had every right to say No, too.

As the last days of the British Raj ticked by, however, the Maharajah of Kashmir went on refusing to say anything at all. Sir Hari Singh was, in fact, receiving every encouragement to keep his mouth shut. Pandit Nehru had no reason to love the Maharajah, who stood for everything which the Indian leader hated; he was a bigot, a profligate and an autocrat with small concern for the people of his State; and he had shown his contempt for Congress by suppressing its members, jailing its leaders, and threatening arrest to Nehru, himself a Kashmiri Brahmin, if he dared set foot inside the State. Yet Nehru sent messages to the Maharajah of Kashmir advising him not to decide too precipitately what he should do. Gandhi emerged from his preoccupation in the South and sent a similar message. Nehru said he felt he ought to go to Srinagar and talk to the Maharajah about his future. Gandhi said he ought to go first, to prepare the way for Nehru, who might get himself arrested.

Mountbatten told them that he would, instead, go himself. After all, he was an old friend of Sir Hari Singh. They had both been A.D.C.s on the Staff of the Prince of Wales when he toured India in 1921. Who could better advise and guide him to the right decision?

He accordingly set off for Kashmir on 21 June 1947 and stayed with the Maharajah in Srinagar. He took George Abell with him and, in the next forty-eight hours, for a negotiator who could be a typhoon of energy when he wished, he accomplished extraordinarily little. To quote his Boswell, Campbell-Johnson:

'When he got there he found the Maharajah politically very elusive, and the only conversations which took place were during their various car drives together. Mountbatten on these occcasions urged him and his Prime Minister, Pandit Kak, not to make any declaration of independence, but to find out in one way or another the will of the people of Kashmir as soon as possible, and to announce by August 14 their intention to send representatives accordingly to one Constituent Assembly or the other. He told them that the newly created States Department was prepared to give an assurance that if Kashmir went to Pakistan this would not be regarded as an unfriendly act by the Government of India. He went on to stress the dangerous situation in which Kashmir would find itself if it lacked the support of one of the two Dominions by the date of the transfer of power.'[1]

He goes on to say that it was the Viceroy's intention 'to give this advice privately to the Maharajah alone . . . The Maharajah suggested that the meeting should take place on the last day of the visit, to which Mountbatten agreed, feeling that this would allow him the maximum chance to make up his mind, but when the time came the Maharajah sent a message that he was in bed with colic and would be unable to attend the meeting. *It seems that this is his usual illness when he wishes to avoid difficult discussions. Needless to say, Mountbatten is very disappointed at this turn of events.*'[2]

What is remarkable about this episode is Mountbatten's fatalistic acceptance of the Maharajah of Kashmir's evasions and subterfuges. One could understand if Nehru or Gandhi had

[1] Op. cit.
[2] My italics—L. M.

accepted his prevarication; they had everything to gain by it. Time was on their side. At any moment the Maharajah might be persuaded, or panicked, into releasing from jail Kashmir's most influential political leader, Sheikh Abdullah, who was pro-Congress in spite of being a Muslim and could, as a close friend of Nehru, be trusted to campaign for accession to the Union of India.[1]

But why did the Viceroy so meekly accept the Maharajah's excuses? Here was a State whose future was more likely than any other to cause friction between the two new Dominions if its destiny was not decided. It not only shared its frontiers with both of the new Dominions, Pakistan and India, but also with Tibet, China and Russia and Afghanistan. It was essential that, for the sake of world peace as well as local harmony, its fate should not be left hanging in the air. Aside from its importance to the Indian sub-Continent, Mountbatten as a soldier might have been expected to recognize its geopolitical significance. Here was an opportunity to do a service not only to the two new Dominions but also to stability in Asia. Any strategist could have told him (if he really needed to be told) that it was from this quarter of the world that all the threats to India's safety and security had hitherto come. He might have been forgiven for saying: 'All right, let India take it over. They will guard its frontiers better, even if its people are Muslim.' Or: 'Give it to Pakistan. It is Muslim territory. As a consolidated Muslim block, Kashmir will help to protect the Northern frontiers of India too against outside invasion.'

What is surprising is that he not only said neither, but that he also did not bounce into the Maharajah's bedroom and declare, with typical Mountbatten boldness:

'Look, I know you are trying to get out of a difficult decision. You want to be independent and you know you can't be. As a Hindu, your inclination, if you have to accede to someone, is to opt for India. But you know your people won't like it. You know they would rather favour Pakistan. It's a problem, I admit. But for God's sake, man, make up your mind. And if you don't make up your mind before I leave for Delhi in two hours' time, I shall make up your mind for you—and announce it to your people.'

It would have been no bolder a gesture than many others he had made during the negotiations for the transfer of power,

---

[1] His close friend did not, however, hesitate to send him back to jail when he opted later for Kashmiri independence.

against opponents much more powerful than the effete, ineffective and miserable Maharajah of Kashmir.

Why did he not do it? Why did his flair disappear on this all-important occasion?

Can it be that, exhausted by his constant round of talks, sickened by Jinnah's evasions over the problem of the Governor Generalship of Pakistan, allergic for the moment to the Muslims, he was suffering from a diplomatic colic too?

As Nicholas Mansergh says in his authoritative *Survey of British Commonwealth Affairs*:[1]

'Kashmir lay at the frontiers of both successor States, it was neighbour to both, and while its ruler was Hindu its people were predominantly Muslim. There was no State in the sub-Continent the future of which, if left unsettled when the independent imperial authority withdrew, was more likely to occasion dissent between the two Dominions. The failure to concentrate more closely upon the problem it presented was destined to prove an oversight fraught with grave consequences.'

For Pakistan, of course, it was a considerable defeat, and it rankled for more than one reason. Junagadh had proved that India was not prepared to stomach the accession of a Muslim Prince to Pakistan when the population of the State was Hindu. But when the opposite came about, when a Hindu Prince signed a Muslim State over to India, what happened? India rushed in troops to protect its booty, piously proclaimed its intention of remaining only long enough to restore law and order, and then held on.[2] The waters of Indo-Pakistan relations were embittered for years to come.

While Kashmir was going by what might justifiably be called the Viceroy's default, the question of Hyderabad was not going at all, in spite of his avid and repeated intervention.

[1] Oxford University Press, 1958.
[2] The Maharajah of Kashmir was encouraged to procrastinate long after both Pakistan and India became independent. In late October 1947, Pathan tribesmen invaded the State. The Maharajah appealed to India for help. V. P. Menon visited him and he signed the Instrument of Accession to the Indian Union. Immediately, Indian Army troops flew in, beat back the invaders, and took over the State. Lord Ismay has since said (in a conversation with the author) that he approved this intervention because 'there were Britons in Kashmir who might have been massacred if someone hadn't gone to their rescue. I therefore encouraged Indian intervention.' The Maharajah was pensioned off. An Indian promise for a plebiscite of the Kashmir people's wishes has not yet been carried out. And Sheikh Abdullah, once Nehru's friend, is in jail.

On 9 July 1947, the Nizam of Hyderabad had once more tried to persuade the Viceroy to come in on his side in his fight to retain Hyderabad's independence from either India or Pakistan. He wrote a letter to Mountbatten in which he said:

'My dear Lord Mountbatten—During the last few days I have seen Clause 7 of the Indian Independence Bill as reported in the Press. I regret that, as has so often happened in recent months, the Clause, though it was closely discussed with Indian leaders, was never disclosed to, much less discussed with, representatives of my State. I was distressed to see that the Clause not only contains a unilateral repudiation by the British Government of the treaties which have for so many years bound my State and my Dynasty to the British, but also appears to contemplate that unless I join one or other of the two new Dominions my State will no longer form part of the British Commonwealth. The Treaties by which the British Government many years ago guaranteed the protection of my State and Dynasty against external aggression and internal disorder have constantly been solemnly confirmed in recent years, notably by Sir Stafford Cripps in 1941. I thought that I could safely rely on British arms and the British word. Having been persuaded in consequence right up to the last moment to refrain from increasing my Army and adapting my State factories for the manufacture of arms and equipment, nevertheless repudiation of Clause 7 of the Bill has been made not only without my consent but without any consultation with me or my Government.

'Your Excellency knows that while you were in England I asked that my State should be accorded Dominion status when the British leave India. I had always hitherto felt that after more than a century of faithful alliance in which I reposed all my confidence in the British I should certainly be able to remain, without question, a member of the family of the British Commonwealth. Clause 7 appears to deny me even that. I still hope that no differences will be allowed to interfere between me and direct relations with His Majesty's Government. I was recently informed that Your Excellency had undertaken to have a declaration in Parliament that the establishment of such relations can be made.

'My hope is that once established these relations will lead to a closer union between my State and the British Crown, with which I have been for so many years in faithful alliance.

'I feel bound to make this protest against the way in which my State is being abandoned by its old ally the British Government.

'The ties which have bound me in loyal devotion to the King Emperor are being severed.

'I hope Your Excellency will place my letter before His Majesty's Government. I shall for the moment refrain from publishing it lest it should in any way embarrass my old friends and allies in the eyes of the world. I must nevertheless retain my right to publish it at a later stage if it should become necessary in the interests of my State.'

But neither the Viceroy nor the Labour Government at home was going to allow Hyderabad, no matter how great his wealth, his past associations, or the size of his State, to opt out of India. It was pointed out to him that His Majesty's Government would never accept a Dominion Government which was, as in Hyderabad's case, completely surrounded by territory which would, in the circumstances, be hostile. 'It would be like Poland all over again,' Mountbatten said. For him there was only one solution: for Hyderabad to sign up under the same three headings as had been accepted by the other Princely States, and then begin bargaining with Menon, Patel and Nehru for special concessions.

It was, as it turned out, good advice, but the Nizam's advisers both in Hyderabad and in the Political Department, where Sir Conrad Corfield's influence was still strong, persuaded him not to take it. He began to build up his army and his band of unofficial terrorists, the fanatic Muslim Razakhars, instead, and gave every evidence that he would fight for his independence, confident that in the end his Faithful Ally, Britain, would come to his rescue. And all Mountbatten's pleadings were in vain; not even his promise that he would secure considerable concessions from the Indian Union if the Nizam would only sign would move the stubborn old Ruler.

Hyderabad was still independent on the day that the British Raj ended. But the moment the British influence completely disappeared, the Indians moved in.[1]

[1] So long as Mountbatten remained Governor General of the Indian Union, V. P. Menon and Sardar Patel held their hand. He was allowed to continue his 'personal negotiations' with the Nizam. Two days after he left for England, the Nizam indicated that he would be prepared to accept the arrangement known as the 'Mountbatten Plan'. Replied Pátel: 'Tell him it is too late. The Mountbatten Plan has sailed for home.' Shortly afterwards, Indian Army troops moved into Hyderabad and occupied it. The Nizam was kept on as a figurehead.

So, with the exception of Junagadh, Kashmir and Hyderabad, all the proud Princes had signed on the dotted line. There would be negotiations in the days ahead to decide how much they would be allowed to keep of their wealth and how much the new Dominions would pay them in pensions.[1] For a time they would be allowed to play a small share in the Government of the new Dominions.

But as a Princely Order, their day was done and they knew it. They had been swallowed into the belly of India in a few short weeks after centuries of arrogant independence from the rest of the sub-Continent. The act of gobbling them up had been a remarkable achievement on the part of India's strategists— perhaps the most remarkable of all the events leading up to Indian independence. For its almost bloodless achievement, the Congress Party had two people to thank: Mountbatten for his blandishments and persuasiveness, and V. P. Menon for his shrewdness in inventing the tactics and recruiting the Viceroy himself to carry them out.

[1] The majority of them, thanks to V. P. Menon, were treated with great generosity. E.g., most 21- and 19-gun Princes kept their personal fortunes and got an average pension of 18 lakhs a year (£135,000).

CHAPTER EIGHT

DARKNESS AT NOON

IT IS ALL very well to decide, just like that—and *just like that* was how it *was* decided—to partition the Indian sub-Continent. But where do you draw the lines that separate one new Dominion from the other?

The lines of demarcation had, of course, to be made in those Provinces where there was a roughly equal number of Muslims and non-Muslims. These consisted of the Punjab, where there were something over 16,000,000 Muslims against 12,000,000 Sikhs and Hindus, and Bengal, where there were 33,000,000 Muslims against 27,000,000 Hindus, Untouchables and Christians. The other Provinces where there were sizeable but nowhere near equal minorities of Muslims or Hindus (such as the North West Frontier Province, Sind, Assam, Bihar and the Central Provinces) went automatically into the Dominion of the majority community, except for certain small tracts of territory.

The inhabitants of the Punjab and Bengal had themselves voted to cut themselves in two, just as the North West Frontier Province (the only Muslim area governed by a pro-Congress régime) had voted to accede to Pakistan. But there was the difference that the Punjab and Bengal decided their future by a vote of elected representatives, whereas the N.W.F.P. decided by a referendum.

The question was where to split the Punjab and Bengal in twain, and who was going to do it.

The proposition was originally made that the aid of the newly-born United Nations Organization should be enlisted for the job, but it was considered as too puling an infant by all parties for such an adult task. At the suggestion of the British Government, the name of Sir Cyril Radcliffe (now Lord Radcliffe) was put forward as likely to be the most admirable and practical chairman of a small Partition Committee, and it was pointed out to both Muslims and non-Muslims (particularly the Sikhs) that, though an expert on arbitration, Sir Cyril had a particular claim to be a most impartial adjudicator in this tricky situation: he had never been to India in his life, and did not know a Hindu from a Muslim, a Sikh from a Jain, or a tamarind from a peepul tree. Both the Congress and the Muslim League immediately telegraphed their spies in London to probe the background of Sir Cyril, but even the suspicious Mr Jinnah could not find anything to say about him except that 'he seems to be most successful in the legal profession'.

Sir Cyril Radcliffe had, in fact, first been approached by the British Government to go to India at the end of June 1947. He was asked if he would sit as the neutral head of a joint Indo-Pakistan Commission which would not only decide the future frontiers of the two countries but also assess their joint assets, and divide and assign them. He had barely accepted the task before advices from India persuaded Mr Attlee to change his mind. A separate committee to deal with assets was set up in India under the chairmanship of Sir Patrick Spens. Someone had reached the conclusion that the two jobs combined might prove too much even for the most dedicated committee. Sir Cyril Radcliffe was told that his only task would be to divide the country. 'Otherwise,' said an India Office official, 'you will have nothing to worry about.'

Nothing to worry about! It was a job to make a man boggle.

Sir Cyril arrived in Delhi on 8 July 1947. Independence day was 15 August. Of India's 350,000,000 people, he had the future homes, livelihood and nationality of 88,000,000 of them to decide. His only briefing for the job was, in his own words, 'a thirty-minute session over a large-scale map with the Permanent Under-Secretary at the India Office'. It is true that, according to the theory, he would only be the Chairman of the Partition Commission, and that two separate boards of four judges—two for Pakistan and two for India—would make the final decisions which would actually divide the Punjab and Bengal. They were all Indian High Court Judges, and they were all admirable men (with possibly two exceptions). Under Sir Cyril's guidance, Justices C. C. Biswam and B. K. Mukherki (for Congress) and Saleh Mahomed Akram and S. A. Rahman (for the Muslim League) would partition Bengal; and Justices Mehr Chand Mahajan and Tejah Singh (for Congress) and Din Mahomed and Muhammed Munir (for the Muslim League) would partition the Punjab.

That, at least, is what Sir Cyril was told before he left England.

He went on believing it for at least forty-eight hours after he arrived in Delhi. On the evening of his arrival, he was summoned by the Viceroy to meet the Indian leaders. Nehru and Patel were there for Congress and Jinnah and Liaquat Ali Khan were there for the Muslim League. Sir Cyril modestly pointed out that it was quite a considerable task which had been assigned to him and his two boards of judges. He spoke of the vastness of India, of the multitudinous population, of the difficulty of cutting through the great acres of territory on each side of the sub-Continent and so dividing it that communities of people would be cherished, districts saved from division, towns and villages left connected with their hinterland. Normally, he pointed out, this was a job which would take even the most careful arbitrators years to decide, but he realized that here was something urgent. He and his two commissions would do their utmost to help. How long had he got?

'Five weeks,' said Mountbatten.

Before Sir Cyril Radcliffe could express his astonishment and dismay, Nehru interrupted:

'If a decision could be reached in advance of five weeks, it would be better for the situation,' he said.

The others, Jinnah included, nodded agreement.

It was obviously impossible to explain to any of them that you could not possibly divide a country in such a time, that injustices would be bound to occur, that a little time and patience and research might save endless bickering in the future. It had to be a quick amputation—and that would mean blood.

Sir Cyril established his main office in Delhi, but had two sub-headquarters, one in Lahore for the Punjab and the other in Calcutta, for Bengal. Forty-eight hours after his interview with Mountbatten and the Indian leaders, he plunged into an experience which was to haunt him for the rest of his life.

From the moment he had his first meeting with the members of the two Boundary Commissions, he realized that his would have to be a unilateral decision. In Bengal, the four judges (two Hindu and two Muslim) were quite frank about the position.

'We did not volunteer for this task,' they said. 'We were drafted into it. You must realize that we cannot possibly be associated with any decisions you may make on the question of dividing the Provinces. It is not simply that our careers would be harmed. Our very lives would not be worth a scrap of paper if we were involved in decisions where the division of territory is disputed. We will help you all we can with advice. But they will be your decisions, and yours alone.'

In the Punjab, the judges not only refused to co-operate, but they also intrigued against him and against each other. His private discussions with them were 'leaked' into the Muslim Press in bowdlerized form. The Sikh judge could barely bring himself to remain in the same room as the Muslims, and while there he exuded an air of blazing anger. He had some reason. A few weeks before, his wife and two children had been murdered in a Muslim riot in Rawalpindi. Sir Evan Jenkins, the Punjab Governor, had suggested to the local Muslim League Committee that, in the circumstances, it might help if they called upon him and expressed their sorrow at what had occurred. They were not in that sort of mood, and refused.

The task of division in Bengal was difficult but not impossible. Both Sir Frederick Burrows, the Governor, and Mr Suhrarwardy, the Chief Minister, had lobbied assiduously to have Bengal recognized by Britain as an independent State or, failing that, Calcutta accepted as a Free City. But both the Viceroy and the Labour Government in Britain turned down the proposals on the grounds that Congress would never accept them.

'When you've carved up the Province,' Sir Frederick Burrows said to Sir Cyril Radcliffe, 'two things will happen. First, there will be absolute bloody murder. Second, East Bengal will become a rural slum.'

In the event, only the second part of his prophecy came true; and that for obvious reasons. East Bengal had always been the hinterland which grew food and jute for Calcutta. Henceforth, it would be deprived of its markets and its port. But Calcutta, with or without East Bengal, would always be Calcutta.

Radcliffe cut cleanly and swiftly, and the fact that outside Calcutta itself most of the Muslims worked in the East while the Hindus concentrated to the West made his task that much easier. This is not to suggest that everyone, or even anyone, was satisfied with his decisions; but the idea of a partitioned Bengal seemed so obviously impossible to most Bengalis that no one could really believe it would be permanent.

The situation in the Punjab was something else again. The moment he arrived in Lahore and studied the facts, Radcliffe was appalled. The sheer impossibility of the task before him was enough to daunt any man. The tempers of the Muslims, Hindus and Sikhs alike were frayed to breaking point. It was as if the Sikhs had only now begun to realize just what they had done in accepting partition; only now begun to see that their most cherished shrines, their richest lands, their most prosperous communities, were in West Punjab and, therefore, could well, under the Boundary Commission Award, go to Pakistan. They descended upon Sir Cyril Radcliffe with petitions, maps, arguments, threats and bribes. The Muslims in turn began to harry him. And in the background, the trouble-makers of each side began to build up the campaign of violence and intimidation.

The monsoon was late in India that year, and in the Punjab it was oven-hot. To those who have not experienced Indian summer heat, particularly when the rains are late, the first bout of it is an ordeal to remember. By nine in the morning, the body is wet with sweat, clothes are soaked, and the mind is sapped by the fear that it may grow even hotter. It does. In the Punjab, there is the extraordinarily hellish experience to be gone through of finding it so unbearably hot and so blindingly dazzling that it seems as if night—an awful, fire-breathing night—has descended.

'The heat it so appalling,' Sir Cyril recalled later,[1] 'that at noon it looks like the blackest night and feels like the mouth of hell. After a few days of it, I seriously began to wonder whether I would come out of it alive. I have thought ever since that the greatest achievement which I made as Chairman of the Boundary Commission was a physical one, in surviving.'

He had, by this time, realized that so far as this assignment was concerned he was on his own, completely and utterly. He knew now that he could trust no one. Not even the British. He would be invited to dinner or to have a drink, and then his host would start hinting. In the end, he decided to cut himself off from everyone. He had a young Indian A.D.C. who was leaving India after the transfer of power, anyway, but who had strict instructions not to mention politics. He was also given an enormous Punjabi bodyguard who followed him everywhere. He wore only a nightshirt and a bandolier around his waist with two pistols, and when he stationed himself outside Radcliffe's bathroom or hovered near his bed, the judge often used to pray— particularly in the hot, dark watches of the night—that he was on his side.

[1] In a conversation with the author.

The brief which he had been given for the partition of the Punjab was simply that 'the Boundary Commission is instructed to demarcate the boundaries of the two parts of the Punjab on the basis of ascertaining the contiguous majority areas of Muslims and non-Muslims. In doing so it will take into account other factors.'

But how was he to interpret those 'other factors'? To the meeting each day came Muslim, Sikh and Hindu delegations with suggestions. Sir Cyril never did actually see the land which he was in process of dividing. The delegations arrived armed with their maps, and it was from these that he must make his decisions. The only trouble was that the maps of each side were different. They had 'doctored' them according to their arguments and petitions. One of his principal worries was to obtain a big enough ordnance map upon which he could work and use as a master map—because the two sides were always up to their tricks. It seems extraordinary that when you have to decide the fate of 28,000,000 people you are not even given the right map to do it with.

And always he was confronted by hostile faces, angry arguments and exaggerated claims. One of the memories which remains particularly vivid in Radcliffe's mind is of the day in Lahore when a Hindu came up to him and said: 'Well, I suppose there *may* be one or two instances where the India Union asked too much.' It was the only occasion when one side indicated that the other side might have a case. And the remark was, anyway, said in a whisper behind the Hindu's hand.

Distressed as he was by the appalling task which faced him, it seemed to Sir Cyril Radcliffe that there was only one thing which could make it both bearable and workable. The biggest problem in the Punjab, as he saw it, was not the disposition of its races, the future of isolated communities, or the division of assets, but a decision as to the control of its irrigation system. This had been built, with a good deal of British inspiration, largely by Sikh money, design and sweat to take the waters of the Province's five rivers through a system of elaborate canals to the arid wastes of Western and Central Punjab. It was this irrigation system which had turned a desert into the granary of India. Thanks to the canals, the Punjab was a great wheatfield for India, supplying the whole sub-Continent with food. It is true that in 1947, with a late monsoon, the canals were getting dry and the crops would be meagre, but even so they would feed India's millions.

But this great watering system was, as Sir Cyril saw at once, vitally threatened by partition. The rivers which supplied the water were all in the East, which would inevitably come under India, and the lands which they supplied were all in the West, which would be part of Pakistan. Radcliffe immediately contacted the Viceroy and told him that he would like to submit a proposition to Jinnah and Nehru. Whatever he decided as to the lines of demarcation, he said, would it not be a good idea if both the leaders agreed at once, before the announcement of his Award, that the Punjab Water System should be a joint venture run by both countries. It would thus safeguard the interests of both peoples and form a basis of co-operation which might prove fruitful in the years to come.

He was rewarded for his suggestion by a joint Muslim-Hindu rebuke. Jinnah told him to get on with his job and inferred that he would rather have Pakistan deserts than fertile fields watered by courtesy of Hindus. Nehru curtly informed him that what India did with India's rivers was India's affair.[1] Both leaders were obviously furious with him and hinted that he was playing politics. It was his one and only attempt to try to make a constructive suggestion.

With the slings and arrows of importunate Muslims, Hindus and Sikhs whistling about his ears, he took up the largest contour map he could find and began to draw. Despite the pleas from the Sikhs, who asked for their beloved Lahore, and the Muslims, who pleaded for their communities in Eastern Punjab, there was little he could do. He was not there to decide the fate of religious shrines. He was not there to partition according to the ownership of irrigation canals or factories or farmlands. He was there to slice a province in two parts so that each one could reasonably be joined to the State of which the majority of its people would be ethnically and communally a part.

Sir Cyril Radcliffe had been asked to divide India in five weeks. For such a task, needing as it did years rather than weeks, it did not really matter whether he produced his Award in four weeks, five weeks, or six. In the circumstances, he was bound to cut a town

[1] It must in fairness be admitted that he modified this attitude later, and subsequently became one of the prime movers in the agreement on River Waters which was signed between India and Pakistan—in 1960.

off from its river, a village from its fields, a factory from its storage yard, a railway from its goods-yard. But having been urged to move with speed, he moved with desperate urgency.

This account will have conveyed the fact that he hated his job. The experiences he had with the people of India were hardly calculated to make him love the country. Rarely can one honest, well-meaning man have seen so many of the nastier sides of human nature in so short a time.

He had his Award ready and written well before the deadline which he had been given. He had listened to all the advice. He had studied all the maps, real and fake. He had worked through the heat of midday and the fears of midnight, a lonely and miserable man. When he put his signature to his Award he was too physically worn and too mentally exhausted to wonder what the reaction to it would be from the two communities. He had done the best he could. He had only one desire left: to get out of India. On 9 August 1947 his Award for the division of Bengal was ready. Two days later so was that of the Punjab. Only some minor work needed to be done on the district of Sylhet, a part of Assam which would, as predominantly Muslim, be assigned to East Pakistan.

The task was done. Sir Cyril Radcliffe flew back to Britain on 15 August, Independence Day, having loathed every moment of his time in the territory of the two new Dominions. 'Amazing people,' he said, later.[1] 'They had absolutely no conception. They asked me to come in and do this sticky job for them, and when I had done it they hated it. But what could they expect in the circumstances? Surely, they must have realized what was coming to them once they had decided on partition. But they had made absolutely no plans for coping with the situation. Strange chaps. Just didn't do their homework.'

He added: 'People sometimes ask me whether I would like to go back and see India as it really is. God forbid. Not even if they asked me. I suspect they'd shoot me out of hand—both sides.'

In every part of India now there were signs to be seen of the upheaval that was coming. Mountbatten had plastered his offices with large tear-off calendars on the sheets of which, in diminishing numbers, was written 'X Days Left to Prepare for the Transfer of Power'. In turbulent groups all over the sub-Continent, Hindus and Muslims were meeting to argue over the division of

[1] In a conversation with the author.

assets. (*Twelve typewriters for you and four for me. And what do we do with this odd one? You take the ribbon and give me the rest.*)[1] The Delhi newspapers had begun to publish advertisements saying: 'Are you leaving for Pakistan? If so, do not forget to surrender your ration cards (Food and Clothing) to the Rationing Officer, Delhi Station.'

The railways themselves were in a ferment, and not simply because theft and murder on trains was becoming increasingly prevalent. Muslim engine drivers who had been driving out of Delhi or Calcutta for years, and Hindus who had been driving from Karachi or Dacca would soon be taking trains to new destinations, over tracks which they had never travelled before.

On top of an announcement that 'the railway programme to run special trains from New Delhi to Karachi with Pakistan Staff and records begins on 3 August' came an editorial in the *Statesman*: 'During the next few weeks the railways will renew their wartime appeals to reduce travel. Everybody should be reminded to ask himself whether his journey is really necessary. We suggest that this is not primarily because of crimes in trains or on the tracks, although there have been some horrid examples recently of those involved in communal grievances considering trains a legitimate target, but because of officials moving from one part of India to another. Indeed, their moves have already begun. Families, wives, children, impedimenta and so forth, as well as the melancholy division of the Armed Forces, will make very heavy demands on railways. Drivers will be travelling over tracks unknown, past signal boxes manned by strangers or from which signalmen have departed. The trains will have to travel cautiously. It will be best if the public keeps off until the sorting is completed. The others may be expected to travel hopefully in order to arrive.'

Could they have guessed what was going to happen, the editors of the *Statesman* might have been moved to advise absolutely everyone to stay off the trains. 'Fearfully' rather than 'hopefully' was the mood in which most Indians would soon be travelling.

In Lucknow, capital of the United Province, the Nationalist-minded among the population were beginning to cock their eyes at the relics of the Indian Mutiny which their British rulers had cherished for so long. The Metropolitan of India sent an urgent message to the Viceroy asking about the Residence at Lucknow, suggesting that it should be destroyed; otherwise 'an element

---

[1] The basis of division was three to one in favour of India.

among the population might perhaps enter and defile it'. He suggested that the Well at Cawnpore should be turned into a cemetery and the Cross on Massacre Ghat be removed and buried.

'And what,' asked Lord Ismay, 'do we do about the Union Jack at Lucknow? It has flown from the Residency and never been hauled down since the days of the Mutiny.'

The United Provinces Government meanwhile issued a note to the populace saying: 'In order to uplift the cultural life of the people, certain changes will be made in the spelling of certain places in the State. A large number of names of rivers and towns have been transliterated as a result of the way in which they are mispronounced by foreigners. Reformed spelling will now be used in all official correspondence and records. Examples; Benares will now be known as Banaras, Cawnpore will be Konnanpur, Ganges will become Ganga, Jumna will be the Yamuna.'

There were other more sinister things happening, too, and not all of them communal. While the Sikhs, Hindus and Muslims jabbered at each other in the Punjab, the sun was burning up the crops around them. The cracking and splitting of the baked land was almost audible, and still no rain came. It looked as if this year—this vital year for India—there would be no monsoon to fill the Five Rivers and give them the water to feed the crops that would in turn be needed to feed India. 'There are other problems bothering us here in addition to Independence,' wrote a British official from Madras. 'This city has food for only fifteen days. The whole of South India may be said to be living from ship to mouth.'

In Delhi, they were already beginning to put up the ornate gilded arches and plan the procession and festivities with which Independence Day would be celebrated, and there were committees sitting to decide which public parks and open spaces should be allotted to singing and dancing. To the annoyance of the Delhi City Council, certain open spaces were already filled, and filled, moreover, by those who were aliens in the city and alien to the celebrations. In Urdu Park, opposite a Muslim mosque, were encamped 4,000 refugees, and in the fields between the Great Mosque and the Red Fort were several thousand others. The newspapers were being circumspect. No one was saying why they were here, except that they were Meos, a Muslim sect from Alwar, who had suddenly fled the State. It seemed that what was going on in Alwar now was not the burning of racehorses but the

firing of villages. Sir Evan Jenkins, the Punjab Governor, part
of whose territory abutted on Alwar and also contained communities of Meos, had been in contact with his Intelligence
agents in Alwar State to try to find out what was happening; but
for the moment his sources had dried up. No one was saying
anything. Villages were put to flames and their populations
butchered; but then the bodies were carefully taken out into the
fields and buried, or stuffed down wells. It was impossible to
discover who was behind the massacres, or how to pin the killers
down. The Maharajah and his Dewan, a fiery little character of
belligerent pro-Hindu persuasion named Dr Khare, strenuously
denied any responsibility for the killings. But they were certainly
having one effect for which Dr Khare, a member of the extremist
Mahasabha Party, had campaigned: the Muslims were leaving
Alwar, and in their panic, leaving their lands and their belongings
behind them.[1] They had begun pouring into Delhi at the rate of
several hundreds a day, and the City Council's principal worry
was how to feed them, and what to do with them on Independence Day.

It was this daily infiltration into the city of the victims of communal excess which gradually planted in the minds of both
Viceroy and politicians the realization that, by the time the
transfer of power took place, they would have a grave problem on
their hands. To some extent, Mountbatten and his Staff still
believed that the main troubles, if any, would come in Bengal,
which had been the scene of such horrible atrocities the year
before. It was only the presence of distress around them, plus the
continual nagging of Sir Evan Jenkins from his uncomfortable
perch over the furnace in the Punjab, which gradually brought
them face to face with the possiblity that perhaps it was here that
the holocaust might come.

Sir Evan Jenkins was the epitome of all that is best in a servant
of the British Crown in foreign places. He had been in India since
just after the first World War, when he was appointed a district
officer in the Punjab. He learned from that moment on to love
the Punjabis, though not blindly. From forty years of experience
among what obviously, after a time, became his people, he arro-
gated to himself no superiority other than that given to his

[1] The Maharajah of Alwar was removed from his State by the Indian States
Department (on the advice of V. P. Menon) after Independence. Dr Khare also
lost his Dewan-ship.

position. 'All civil officials were quite accustomed to serving under Indians,' he pointed out.[1] 'I joined the ICS in 1920 and my immediate superiors were frequently Indians, both officials and politicians. In fact, the feeling within the ICS was excellent. The idea that any one of us would object if our boss was an Indian was ridiculous, or that we would refuse to obey one of his orders.'

Jenkins was, in these last days of the British Raj, one of its most important and knowledgeable servants. He was a great friend of India. Yet the remarkable thing is that the Punjab was all that he knew of the country. He was a supreme example of the India Office practice of putting a man into an area and giving him a lifetime's chance to learn about the people among whom he would have to live, advise and rule. He never really moved out of it, except to go on leave to Britain.

He knew the Punjabis for their vices as well as their virtues, and in the summer of 1947 it was their vice with which he was most concerned. Sir Evan Jenkins had never made any secret of the fact that he did not believe in (a) the partition of India, and particularly (b) the partition of the Punjab. He repeatedly pointed out to the politicians of the Province, Muslim, Hindu and Sikh alike, that a division of their land would end its importance for India. He stressed the fact that it was not only the most prosperous State in the sub-Continent but also the most viable. The Punjab, possibly alone among all the other Indian States, was self-sufficient, could supply its own food, run its own industries, finance its own building, export its products, educate its own people. He emphasized this not as an argument (as Sir Fred Burrows and Suhrarwardy were doing in Bengal) for independence, for breaking off from the two new Dominions, but as a plea to keep the Punjab intact, somehow, for the benefit not only of its own people but for Independent India as a whole.

He was attacked and vilified in the vernacular Press, as a result, as a conspirator to preserve British rule. It was manifestly not true, but there it was. Meanwhile, his main obsession was with Delhi. How could he keep the Viceroy and the Indian politicians aware of the situation into which they had got themselves by their precipitate decision to split an unsplittable Province? There was danger ahead, and only ruthlessly clear minds would avert catastrophe.

[1] In a note to the author.

On 10 July, he asked if Lord Ismay would meet him to discuss 'the serious situation' and convey its purport to the Viceroy. Abell went to meet him instead in Simla and produced the following report:

'I had a long talk with the Governor of the Punjab, Jenkins, last night (July 10). There is no doubt that the Sikhs are in a very dangerous mood . . . The Muslims and the Hindus are in touch about everything except law and order. The problem of law and order related primarily to Lahore and Amritsar. These, and especially Lahore, are disquieted cities. The Sikhs and the Hindus are reluctant to set up any Government at all until August 15 except in Lahore. They consider that a move from Lahore would prejudice their claim to the city . . . Your Excellency should talk to Nehru and Patel and pray them to get the Congress and the Sikhs to drop their claim to stay in Lahore and hold up all the partitioning proceedings until the Boundary Commission reports.'[1]

But this was not strong enough for Jenkins. He began to write his own reports. He had a State on his hands which had taken years to build up into its present prosperity, and would soon crash into ruin. How could he save it? Obviously, the decisions of Sir Cyril Radcliffe and his Boundary Commission could not help; for if realistic lines were drawn through the Punjab, assigning the West to Pakistan and the East to India, the great Sikh communities in the Western Punjab would be left stranded, puddles of anti-Muslim life in a Muslim country. He wrote to the Viceroy on 10 July:

'Dear Lord Mountbatten,—I think your Excellency may be interested in the record of a conversation which I have just had with Gianni Khartar Singh [spokesman for the Sikhs]. The Gianni was extremely frank about the intentions of the Sikhs. What he said confirms my view that they mean to make trouble if the decision based on the Boundary Commission is not to their liking, or if the new Governments of Pakistan and India are set up before the decision is given . . . '

To this he attached a confidential report which read, in part:

'Gianni Khartar Singh came to see me today . . . He said he had come to see me about the Indian Independence Bill and the Boundary Commission . . . He said that in the Punjab there would have to be an exchange of populations on a large scale. Were the British ready to enforce this? He doubted if they were, and if no

[1] Government of India Records.

regard was paid to Sikh solidarity a fight was inevitable. The British had said for years that they intended to protect the minorities and what had happened? The present situation was a clear breach of faith by the British.

'I replied that I realized that the Sikhs were dissatisfied, but when independence came to any country some classes, who had formerly regarded themselves as protected, inevitably suffered. At the same time, I thought that the Sikhs had only themselves to blame for their present position. The Gianni himself had insisted on partition and Baldev Singh had accepted the Plan . . .

'Gianni then said neither had viewed partition as being based on population alone. The Sikhs were entitled to their own land just as much as the Hindus or the Muslims. They must have their shrine at Nankana Sahib, at least one canal system, and finally arrangements must be made so as to bring at least three-quarters of the Sikh population from West to East Punjab. Property must be taken into account as well as population in the exchange, as the Sikhs on the whole were better off than the Muslims. Gianni said that unless it was recognised by His Majesty's Government, the Viceroy and the Party leaders that the fate of the Sikhs was a vital issue, there would be trouble . . . they would be obliged to fight . . . that the Sikhs realised that they would be in a bad position, but would have to fight on revolutionary lines by murdering officials, cutting railway lines, destroying canal headworks and so on.

'I reiterated that this would be a very foolish policy, to which Gianni replied that if Britain were invaded, no doubt my feelings would be much the same as his . . . The Muslims were now putting out some conciliatory propaganda about their attitude towards the Sikhs in their midst, but their intention was that of a sportsman who is careful not to disturb the birds he means to shoot He believed the Muslims would try to make the Sikhs of West Punjab feel secure and then set about them in earnest.'

Sir Evan Jenkins ended his dispatch:

'Finally, the Gianni appealed to me to do all I could to help the Sikhs during a period of great trial. He said I surely could not wish to abandon the Punjab to tears and bloodshed. There would be tears and bloodshed here if the boundary problem was not suitably solved. The Gianni was matter of fact and quiet throughout our conversation but wept when he made his final appeal.

This is the nearest thing to an ultimatum yet given by the Sikhs. They are undoubtedly puzzled and unhappy. I see no reason to suppose that they have lost the nuisance value they have in the past possessed over a century.'[1]

On 13 July Jenkins wrote yet another letter to Mountbatten, reinforcing his warning of the dangers of the situation. 'The communal feeling is now unbelievably bad,' he said. 'The Sikhs believe that they will be expropriated and massacred in West Punjab and smothered by the Hindus and Congress generally in East Punjab. They threaten a violent rising immediately . . .'

He asked the Viceroy at all costs to get hold of Sir Cyril Radcliffe's report and announce it *before* 15 August, to stop panic and the mad hurrying to and fro of populations from one Dominion to the other. He suggested that a force be moved into the area along the likely line of the new border to preserve peace. And he ended:

'I believe that if the representatives of the future Dominions can make it clear now that there is no question of a chaotic changeover, that they mean business, and that they are sending an imposing organisation here to protect the people, with appropriate publicity, it will do much to steady the Punjab. For it is the Dominion Boundary that is in question and not a Provincial Boundary only.'[1]

At long last the Viceroy began to take the danger in the Punjab seriously. On the morning of 15 July, he called a meeting of his Staff to discuss the Punjab situation. On 20 July he visited Lahore and talked to Jenkins and to members of the Punjab Partition Committee, which was dividing the assets of the Province. He appears to have gained the impression from the Committee that 'things were going very well', in marked contrast to Jenkins's impression that 'hatred and suspicion are entirely undisguised. Partition goes very slowly indeed. Meetings of the Partition Committee resemble a peace conference with a new war in sight.' But once more the Viceroy was urged, by the members of the Committee this time, to get hold of the Boundary Award and announce it *before* 15 August.

He returned to Delhi with his fingers sufficiently scorched by the fires of communal hatred to persuade him that a fire brigade was necessary. He held immediate consultations with Sir Claude Auchinleck, now the Supreme Commander of the emerging

[1] Government of India Records.

Pakistan and Indian armies. From this meeting came the decision to form the Punjab Boundary Force which would have the job of ensuring peace in the Province both before and after the announcement of Sir Cyril Radcliffe's Award. On 22 July, the Viceroy presided over a meeting at which Sardar Patel and the Honourable Rajendra Prasad were present for the future Government of India, Mr Jinnah and Liaquat Ali Khan for the future Government of Pakistan and Baldev Singh for the Sikhs. They issued a statement afterwards which was supposed to make everything all right from now on.

'Now that the decision to set up two independent Dominions from August 15 has finally been taken,' it said, 'the members of the Partition Council, on behalf of the future Governments, declare that they are determined to establish peaceful conditions in which the processes of partition may be completed and the many urgent tasks of administration and economic reconstruction may be taken in hand.

'Both the Congress and the Muslim League have undertaken to give fair and equitable treatment to the minorities after the transfer of power. The two future Governments reaffirm these assurances. It is their intention to safeguard the legitimate interests of all citizens irrespective of religion, caste or sex. In the exercise of their normal civic rights all citizens will be regarded as equal and both the Governments will assure to all people within their territories the exercise of liberties such as freedom of speech, the right to form associations, the right to worship in their own way and the protection of their language and culture.

'Both the Governments further undertake that there shall be no discrimination against those who before August 15 may have been political opponents.

'The guarantee of protection which both Governments give to the citizens of their respective countries implies that in no circumstances will violence be tolerated in any form in either territory. The two Governments wish to emphasise that they are united in this determination.

'To safeguard the peace in the Punjab during the period of the change over to the new conditions, both Governments have agreed on the setting up of a special Military Command from August 1, covering the civil districts of Sialket, Gujranwala, Sheikhapura, Lyallpur, Montgomery, Lahore, Amritsar, Gurdaspur, Hoshiapur, Jullundur, Ferozepur and Ludhiana. With their concurrence, Major-General Rees has been nominated as Military Commander for this purpose and Brigadier Digambhar Singh (India) and Colonel Ayub Khan[1] (Pakistan) have been attached to him in an advisory capacity. After August 15, Major-General Rees will control operationally the forces of both the new States in this area and will be responsible through the Supreme Commander and the Joint Defence Council, to the two Governments. The two Governments will not hesitate to set up a similar organisation in Bengal should they consider it necessary.

'Both Governments have pledged themselves to accept the awards of the Boundary Commission, whatever these may be. The Boundary Commissions are already in session; if they are to discharge their duties satisfactorily, it is essential that they should not be hampered by public speeches or writing, threatening boycott or direct action, or otherwise interfering with their work. Both Governments will take appropriate steps to secure this end; and, as soon as the awards are announced, both Governments will enforce them impartially and at once.'

It was an admirable document. Indeed, Mountbatten's Boswell, Campbell-Johnson,[2] described the Viceroy as regarding it as a 'Charter of Liberties for all communities', though he also added the comment that 'he is greatly excited over this coup, but frankly does not believe that either Party really knew what it was signing'. V. P. Menon[3] went even further and commented:

'This statement was the first joint declaration of policy by the spokesmen of the two Governments on a matter of fundamental importance. It had a reassuring effect throughout the Punjab and Bengal for the time being, and was regarded as a charter of rights by the minorities in both Dominions. The Boundary Force, set up on August 1, consisted of about 50,000 officers and men, a high proportion of the officers being British. *This was possibly the greatest military force ever assembled for the express purpose of maintaining civil peace and it gave everyone a feeling of confidence.*[4]

If ever there was confidence misplaced, this was the occasion. Rarely had a military force of such strength worked so hard or fought so bravely to achieve so little.

[1] Now President of Pakistan.
[2] Op. cit.
[3] In *The Transfer of Power in India*.
[4] My italics—L. M.

The nucleus of the Punjab Boundary Force was provided by the 4th Indian Division, a fighting machine which all who saw it in action during the War—in Eritrea, in the Western Desert and in Italy—will acknowledge as one of the most intrepid and efficient of all. It far surpassed any British or American division in its willingness to take risks and ensure casualties. Against the bitter escarpment which blocked its path into Italian East Africa at Keren, in the minefields beyond Alamein, and on the slopes of Monte Cassino, the 4th Indian always achieved the tasks—no matter how bloody—which were assigned to it. In Major-General 'Pete' Rees they had a cocky and belligerent little commander who had no doubt of his capacity for success.

But this time there was only failure and disaster ahead of them; and though they would be the instrument of failure, the responsibility would not lie with them, for rarely has a pacifying and protective force been sent into action with such a misreading of the situation as that which would confront them.

From this moment on, the history of the transfer of power to India is one of over-confidence, half-thought-out enthusiasms, blunders, stupidities, carelessness and mistake after mistake.·

To the Viceroy, the situation was now in hand. He told one of his Staff conferences that the announcement of the Boundaries Award would bring the whole thing into the open. At the moment the communal disorders were sporadic and disorganized, and, therefore, difficult to cope with. But the Award was bound to bring matters to the boil. A general outburst of fury and violence would inevitably result, possibly from the Muslims, almost certainly from the Sikhs. This the Punjab Boundary Force would swiftly put down.

He had assured Maulana Abul Kalam Azad several weeks before that 'I shall see to it that there is no bloodshed and riot. I am a soldier not a civilian. Once partition is accepted in principle, I shall issue orders to see that there are no communal disturbances in the country . . . I will order the Army and the Air Force to act and I will use tanks and aeroplanes to suppress anybody who wants to create trouble.'

Well, with the Punjab Boundary Force, he had kept his promise.

On 30 July, he flew to Bengal to look over the situation there. Suhrarwardy took him by the lapel and made a last effort to persuade him to accept an independent Bengal. Suhrarwardy knew by this time that he himself had no future in Pakistan, for

Jinnah had already indicated that another Muslim, Nazimmudin, would become leader in East Pakistan. Suhrarwardy planned to remain in India, in his beloved Calcutta, anyway; it would be nice if he could stay on as boss of his own independent domain. The Viceroy, as he guessed, brushed him off.

Mountbatten then approached Lieutenant-General Tuker, the British Commander, and asked him whether he, too, would like an equivalent of the Punjab Boundary Force. Tuker replied with a brisk thank you, no; he would handle his situation with the troops he had got, though they were much less than 50,000; and he would personally guarantee that this time, since he would be in command, there would be no repetition of the atrocities of a year ago.

There was a chance to avert the catastrophe in the Punjab as late as the beginning of August, with as little as a fortnight to go before the two new Dominions were on their own. Here was a last opportunity for the Viceroy to exercise what Gandhi called 'your magic' upon both Congress and Muslim League leaders. He had now been warned repeatedly by Sir Evan Jenkins of the dreadful dangers ahead; already the skirmishings were increasing in what would soon become an outright war of succession.

V. P. Menon made the suggestion that Jinnah should be approached and persuaded to declare Nankana Sahib, the great Sikh shrine in Western Punjab, 'a sort of Vatican'. It was a gesture which might have had a calming effect upon the highly emotional Sikhs, and one which it would have cost Jinnah little to concede. The Viceroy and his Staff were well aware of what Nankana Sahib meant to the Sikhs. On 27 July, they had received a report which said:

'Information from a reliable source has been received that if Nankana Sahib, about twelve miles north of Lahore, is not included in the Boundary Award to East Punjab, the Sikhs intend to start trouble on a big scale. It is reported that the Sikhs intend to act on or about 7 August, and during the ten days before this, large meetings will be held to work up agitation. It is already known that the Sikhs have collected large quantities of arms. It is also reported that the Muslims are fully aware of the preparations and are, in fact, making counter-preparations. Both sides have attempted to subvert troops in the area and several of these attempts are said to have been not wholly unsuccessful. Promises of assistance from some troops have been received.'

Menon's suggestion was noted but there is no indication that it was ever acted upon.

Sir Evan Jenkins urged the Viceroy to go even further. He asked him to contact the political leaders immediately and ask them to make concessions at once, without waiting for the Boundary Award. Nehru and Patel could, for instance, be persuaded to say publicly that they were waiving their claim to Lahore. It would be by no means an expensive gesture, for it was almost certain that Lahore would be awarded to Pakistan; but to concede it beforehand would create the maximum goodwill. He asked Mountbatten to approach Jinnah for an important concession too.

'I believe there is quite a lot in the claims of the Sikhs, and, for that matter, of the other residents of the East Punjab for a share in the canal colonies of the West,' he wrote, 'and the Gianni's idea that the Montgomery district should be allotted to the East is by no means as ridiculous as it sounds. The district if so allotted to the East could be recolonised so as to concentrate the non-Muslims there, and transfer Muslims to Lyallpur.'[1]

But this, he emphasized, could not be decided by the Boundary Commission. Though Montgomery and district, for instance, contained nearly a million Sikhs to only a quarter of a million Muslims, it was geographically indubitably in West Punjab. Its fate should be settled, like all the other problems, by negotiations 'out of court'. And he asked the Viceroy to bring the parties together at once.

It was a mission which, two months earlier, Mountbatten would have relished as a supreme challenge to his powers as a persuader. To reconcile the two brothers at the moment of parting by cajoling them into a final act of mutual goodwill would have filled his beaker of achievement to the brim. Why then did he not attempt it?

There is evidence that, in the case of Nehru and Patel, he did make an approach, though without much conviction. The Congress leaders were certainly in no mood to make even empty concessions to Jinnah. Having given him Pakistan, their mood was to say: 'Enough! Begone! And do not dare to ask for more!'

Jinnah was in a mood too, but there is evidence that, at this particular moment, it was a serene rather than an intractable one. Having achieved what he had always secretly regarded as impossible, and seen the birth of Pakistan by his own hand in his own

---

[1] Government of India Records.

lifetime, he might well have been susceptible to a last appeal to his magnanimity.

That he was not asked may have been due to the Viceroy's fatigue. He had been working a 16-hour day since March and even air-conditioned offices could not protect him entirely from Delhi's scorching heat. (It averaged 105 degrees in the shade throughout July.) There was also the psychological factor. Mountbatten was not the kind of character who takes kindly to a snub, and he positively loathed failure. He had been snubbed and he had failed over the question of the joint Governor Generalship. His temperament at the time may well have persuaded him that it was better not to attempt another battle with the old man, rather than fail again.

So no concessions were asked or given. The gestures that might have calmed or mollified the Sikhs did not come. The storing of arms, the sharpening of kirpans, and the plans for battle went on.

The incidents in the Punjab until this moment had followed no set pattern. There had been the ruthless massacre of the Sikhs in Rawalpindi in March, when the Muslims turned upon them and, in a welter of ferocity, murdered 2,000 of them. But since that time the killings had been only sporadic, and most demonstrations of inter-communal fury had been confined to pyromania. It was easy, both sides discovered, to set fire to an Indian city, town or village. In the narrow alleyways of the bazaar section of Lahore or in the tortuous streets of Amritsar, all a fire-raiser needed to do was to climb upon a roof, set it ablaze with a torch, and then decamp swiftly down an alleyway; leaving a fire that would often destroy a whole district. In Lahore alone in seven days the fire brigades were called out to 167 fires. From an airplane at night, one could pick out the villages by the flames of the burning huts.

But in the last fifteen days of the British Raj and on into Independence, the character of the conflict changed.

Master Tara Singh came into the picture. This counsellor, elder statesman, father of the Sikhs, had from start to finish been against the partition of the Punjab, against the acceptance of Muslim hegemony in all but a small part of the province, and for a Sikh State which would be carved out of both Dominions. Tara Singh looked and acted like a mixture of an Old Testament Prophet and a witch doctor from a romance by Rider Haggard; and, in the Golden Temple at Amritsar, he talked to his people in language which sounded like a satire on a village soothsayer out of Rudyard Kipling.

'Oh Sikhs,' he cried, 'know ye that our brethren are threatened in the West by those who call us infidels. Our lands are about to be overrun, our women dishonoured, our children forced to take alien vows. It is time for our warriors to arise and once more destroy the Moghul invader. Remember Rawalpindi! Revenge our people! Spare no one who stands in the way of Sikh rights in our land.'

It was language which the Sikhs took seriously, and Master Tara Singh was well aware of it. The Golden Temple at Amritsar was not only a Sikh shrine but also a great communal centre at which the Sikhs gathered to talk and plan as well as pray. A Sikh gurdwara, of which the Golden Temple is a particularly blessed and hallowed example, is more of a community centre than a simple temple of worship. In it the passing stranger can always find food and lodging for the night. In it the locals gather for their political meetings. And in it, the Sikh leaders conspired in the last days of July and the first days of August 1947, in a belated attempt to wreck the plan for the partition of the Punjab.

It was no idle conspiracy. On the afternoon of 5 August, after a meeting of the Partition Council in the Viceroy's offices in Delhi, Mountbatten asked Nehru and Patel, and Jinnah and Liaquat Ali Khan to stay behind. He produced for them a Criminal Investigation Officer from Lahore who had been sent to him by Sir Evan Jenkins—in what was Jenkins's final effort to make the Viceroy and the politicians in Delhi nip the blossoming revolution in the bud.

The C.I.D officer brought considerable documentation with him. Trouble-makers had been arrested in Lahore, Amritsar and several other centres in the Punjab. They had been closely questioned. As a result, the C.I.D were convinced that not only were several Sikh plots afoot to sabotage the plans for partition, but that several of the Sikh leaders were implicated.

He produced letters from a number of Sikh personalities, and copies of leaflets and instructions issued to Sikh gurdwaras. One plan was to blow up the canal system in West Punjab; another was to attack trains proceeding to Pakistan; a third to force Muslim villagers to leave their homes in East Punjab, and then ambush and kill them on the way; and finally, there was a plot to assassinate Mr Jinnah as he rode to power in Karachi in the celebrations of 14 August 1947—the day before Pakistan Independence Day.

The documentation was sufficiently authentic to convince everyone present of its seriousness. Jinnah and Liaquat Ali Khan at once demanded the arrest of Master Tara Singh and other Sikh leaders mentioned in the plot. It seemed at least reasonable that, in the face of such proof—backed as it was by repeated warnings of trouble from Jenkins—the Sikh troublemakers should be put out of the way until the Independence arrangements were completed. For once Jinnah appeared to have right on his side in asking for action to be taken at once.

Yet once more Mountbatten hesitated. On this occasion, Lord Ismay urged him to take action. There was no doubt of the dangerous possibilities in the situation. Master Tara Singh made no secret of his belligerent intentions, and there was ample evidence of the elaborate preparations which had been made for action. Surely, here was an occasion when a heavy hand should have descended upon the trouble-makers and put them out of harm's way.

The Mountbatten of a few weeks ago would not have hesitated. He would have called in Master Tara Singh and his cohorts, secured guarantees from them, and if they were not forthcoming would have put them under restraint. It was still in his power to do it. He was still Viceroy. He was quite aware of the devastation which might come about if trouble-makers were allowed to remain free over Independence Day. Yet he refused to take a decision. It is true that Sardar Patel advised against the arrest of Master Tara Singh, on the grounds that it would cause trouble among the Sikhs; but a few words from Mountbatten and Nehru[1] would have talked him round. In fact, Nehru was not consulted. The Viceroy announced instead that he would confer with Sir Evan Jenkins and the two Governors-designate of East and West Punjab (Sir Chandulal Trivedi and Sir Francis Mudie) and ask them what they would advise.

They agreed in counselling the Viceroy to leave Master Tara Singh and his colleagues free. Sir Evan Jenkins's reason was specious. 'What would have been the good of arresting the old rascal at the beginning of August,' he said, 'if in mid-August, when Independence came, he was set free.'

But would he in fact have been set free? Nehru was as anxious as the Viceroy to see the transfer of power come about peacefully.

[1] Who was to fling the fiery old Sikh into jail five times in the next ten years.

He would (as he subsequently showed) have been more than willing to offend the Sikhs if, by sequestering their leaders, he averted a massacre.

Step by step, Delhi had been advised of the increasing gravity of the situation in the Punjab. The warnings were there. The Viceroy had at least three chances to avert a massacre, and each time—from weariness, from lack of foresight, or from aversion to another clash with Jinnah—he looked the other way. The result was disastrous.

On 6 August 1947 there was a party at the Red Fort in Delhi which brought the curtain at least part of the way down on the drama which was now being played out. That night, officers of the future Indian Army gave what the local newspapers called a 'Farewell Comrades' party to Pakistan officers who were leaving shortly for service, after 15 August, with their own Dominion Army. Pandit Nehru, Sardar Baldev Singh, the new Indian Commander-in-Chief, General Cariappa, and a few British senior officers were present.

It was a sentimental occasion, for many of the officers belonged to the same regiment but would henceforth be serving in different armies; but it would be untrue to say that it was a melancholy one for any save the British officers present. For them the splitting of the Indian Army was a tragedy, and this party was the symbol of it. On the other hand, it celebrated for the politicians the end of a hated instrument of British domination, and for the Indian soldiers the beginning of vast new opportunities for promotion. In the light of what was to happen in a few months' time, the occasion had its ironic moments.

'We are here to say au revoir,' said General Cariappa. 'I say au revoir deliberately as we shall meet each other in future as the best of friends and in the spirit of good comradeship. We have worked together for so long as members of the same team. We will continue to do so, in the same spirit, for the defence of our two Dominions against external aggression. We now serve in two different armed forces but we fervently hope that nothing anyone says or does will mar our present spirit of friendship.'

To which Brigadier Raza, on behalf of the Muslim officers, said a fervent 'Amen'. And then they all linked hands, and, some with tears in their eyes, sang: 'For they are jolly good fellows.' Three days later, four Muslim officers who attended the party were hacked to death by Sikhs aboard the train taking them to Pakistan. One hundred and fifty Pakistan officials, with their wives and children, were murdered on the same train.

On 7 August 1947, Mr Jinnah flew to Karachi to await the arrival of Independence Day. The Viceroy lent him his official Dakota for the journey, and gave him a farewell present of his Rolls-Royce and his Muslim A.D.C. Lieutenant Ahsan, and he went to the airfield to see him off.

With his departure disappeared the last chance of securing from him some concession in the Punjab. He left Delhi after delivering a conciliatory message in which he appealed to both Hindus and Muslims to 'bury the past' and wished India success and prosperity. He got a bucket of water in his face in return from Sardar Patel who said in Delhi the following day: 'The poison has been removed from the body of India. We are now one and indivisible. You cannot divide the sea or the waters of the river. As for the Muslims, they have their roots, their sacred places and their centres here. I do not know what they can possibly do in Pakistan. It will not be long before they return to us.'

Jinnah, who had been showing signs of an unusual magnanimity, froze from that moment into his normal attitude of cold hatred and contempt for Congress. Nor was his temper improved when he read a statement from Mr Kripalani, the Congress President, which he interpreted as inciting Hindus and Sikhs in Pakistan to practise non-co-operation with the new Dominion. It was one of those monumental misunderstandings which all too often bedevil Indian politics. Kripalani, was in fact, answering a query from a number of Congress Committees in Pakistan, which had asked whether they should fly the new Indian flag over their head-quarters on Independence Day. He had told them to fly no flags and organize no demonstrations. 'This had nothing to do with the celebrations organized by the Pakistan Government,' he explained.

Jinnah and his followers, however, chose to believe otherwise. 'Let me tell Mr Kripalani and other Hindu leaders that they are playing with fire,' declared Liaquat Ali Khan, in a tone as near to thunderous as that amiable roly-poly could get. 'If Hindu leaders like Kripalani succeed in inciting people, it would be foolish to expect that there will be no repercussions. No Government in the world can prevent such repercussions, no matter how undesirable they may be. Unless the Congress President and the Hindu leaders give up these dangerous preachings and join with us in restoring goodwill, and if they fail to stop acts of violence by their people, then God help both Pakistan and Hindustan.'

It was already a situation in the Punjab which seemed beyond the help of anyone but God, and even the efforts of Gandhi were useless. The panic had now set in, and from both sides of the province—Muslims from the East, Sikhs and Hindus from the West—the people were leaving their homes and fleeing to what they hoped would be safety. Gandhi pleaded with them to remain where they were, but in language scarcely calculated to quiet their fears.

'When something they love is dying, people do not run away but die with it,' he cried to an audience of Hindus in Lahore. 'When you suffer from fear, you die before death comes to you. That is not glorious.'

To the Sikhs he said: 'My conception of the Sikh has always been of a brave person who does not fear death or do any harm to an innocent person. If the present painful quarrel between Hindus and Muslims and Sikhs continues, it is an invitation to any foreign power to come and invade India. I therefore make an earnest appeal to the people to end the present quarrel, which does no credit to either community.'

But he only passed through the Punjab himself. More's the pity. He went on to Calcutta, and there his achievements were remarkable. But it was in the Punjab that he was really needed. Everyone was needed there in those first days of August—Gandhi, Nehru, Patel, Jinnah and the Viceroy himself. Anyone with the power and influence to halt the forces of darkness, which were now mobilizing in every part of the land. They were all well aware of the perils of the situation. Did they really believe that it could be kept in hand by military action alone—from a force which was, in any case, beginning to be riven by communal suspicion?

It was Gandhi who showed them what they might have done in the Punjab. Only, unfortunately, he could not be in two places at once, and his example was in Bengal.

CHAPTER NINE

'ONE-MAN BOUNDARY FORCE'

IN ALL THE brutishness, bestiality and bloodshed amid
which the two new Dominions of Pakistan and India were
baptized in August 1947, one city, containing a large Hindu-
Muslim population, alone remained free from communal killings
on a large scale. That city was Calcutta, where 6,000 Muslims and
Hindus had hacked each other to death exactly a year before.
This was the place, teeming with goondas, gangsters and trouble-
makers, in which the Viceroy and most Indian politicians had
for long believed the worst scenes of violence would occur;
which was why during his visit on 30 July, Mountbatten had asked
Lieutenant-General Tuker if he, too, needed a Boundary Force
like the one assigned to the Punjab.

Tuker refused the offer on the grounds that he was quite
capable of handling any likely outbreak with his own forces, and
there is no doubt that this tough, shrewd and unswerving soldier
intended to keep his Command area out of the communal battle
without help from any outside forces. He felt differently, however,
about one reinforcement. It came in the shape of Mohandas
Gandhi, and he was to prove a One-Man Boundary Force of far
greater efficiency than the 50,000 soldiers, with their guns and
armoured cars, who failed so abjectly in the Punjab.

It had been Gandhi's original intention to be in Noakhali, a
centre where Hindus had been cruelly persecuted, in the days
leading up to the transfer of power. He had not changed his mind
about the evils of partition. He was still convinced that Nehru
and Patel had chosen wrongly in accepting the plan for a divided
India; and he had no intention of being in Delhi or Karachi for
the 'celebrations'. For him Independence Day would be a day of
mourning, and Noakhali, where people were suffering, seemed
an appropriate location. But on his way there, he was visited by
Sir Frederick Burrows, the Governor of Bengal, and a delegation
of Muslims. Sir Frederick was determined that his last days in
India (for he would be going home after 15 August) should not
be disfigured by the murder and mayhem of the year before and

219

he was prepared to use every weapon at hand, moral as well as military, to prevent it. So were the Muslims with him. They pointed out that the situation in Calcutta was hourly growing more grave for members of their community. Most Muslim officials had left the city to go to East Pakistan. The police force (which had been predominantly Muslim) was now both small and Hindu. Communal frenzy was simmering and would obviously soon boil over.

'The Hindus feel that this is their opportunity to get even with the Muslims for last year,' said the bluff Sir Frederick, 'and they are bloody well going to take it. It'll be real carnage this time, if it starts—and buggerall we'll be able to do about it.'

Both he and the Muslim delegates pleaded with Gandhi to stay in Calcutta for a time and 'throw a pot of water on the fire'. He promised to think it over.

Next day an even larger delegation of Muslims arrived to see him and renewed their pleas for him to stay. The shrewd old man told them that he would stay, but on one condition. They must guarantee peace in Noakhali.

'If things go wrong there, my life will be forfeit,' he said. 'You will have to face a fast to the death on my part.'

The Muslims went into a hurried conference, and then came back and said they would send emissaries at once to the Muslim League leaders in Noakhali, including Mian Ghulam Sarwar, the chief trouble-maker, to ensure that the Hindus would be protected. Gandhi then agreed to stay. It was the sort of horse-trading at which he was an adept. He was to demonstrate more of it in the days to come.

It so happened that Mr Shaheed Suhrarwardy, the redoubtable Muslim who had for so long bossed Calcutta, was in Karachi when Gandhi arrived. He was for the moment in eclipse and had been to Karachi to see what was to be done about it. He would, of course, no longer have any power in Calcutta once Congress took over. Nor would he be able to dominate East Pakistan, for Mr Jinnah, who did not admire him, had appointed his rival, Nazimmudin, as Governor-designate of that province. Suhrarwardy had flown to Karachi to find out where he could fit into the new State of Pakistan. He quickly discovered that, at least while Jinnah was alive, he could not. He was out.

The ebullient Mr Suhrarwardy was by no means as cast down by this turn in his fortunes as other men might have been. He was a resilient character. Calcutta he had always considered to be his town; there he could find the night-clubs he loved, the blondes he loved even more; and there was something about the smell, squalor, poverty and even the wickedness of the city which appealed to his temperament. If he was to be in eclipse, where could it better be endured than in Calcutta, whose alleyways were dark anyway?

Fresh from a session in Karachi with Liaquat Ali Khan, he read in the Muslim League newspaper, *Dawn*, that Gandhi was going to Noakhali. He left immediately for Calcutta and rushed to see Gandhi and added his pleas to those of the local Muslim leaders, asking Gandhi to stay and help to quell the fires, which might soon be burning in the city.

The old man was only too well aware of Suhrarwardy's reputation as a ruthless political boss, a hedonist, and one whose hands were not entirely clean of the blood shed in the riots of the year before. But to achieve his goal, he was prepared to trade horses with anyone. He told Suhrarwardy that he would certainly stay—if Suhrarwardy would consent to stay at his side and work with him.

'But of course,' said Suhrarwardy.

Gandhi: 'Perhaps you do not completely understand what I mean. When I say at my side, I mean literally at my side. We will go into those parts of the city where the danger is greatest, and there we will set up our abode. We will live together under the same roof. We will have neither the police nor the military to protect us. And we will together preach that now that partition has come, Muslim and Hindu have no longer any need to hate each other or kill each other.'

Suhrarwardy was about to speak, but Gandhi interrupted him and told him to go home and think it over.

The Muslim leader arrived next day to tell Gandhi that he accepted the offer. At his prayer meeting that evening, Gandhi announced that he had elected to stay for a time in Calcutta and that he and Mr Shaheed Suhrarwardy would work together and do their utmost to restore communal peace. There were murmurs from his congregation that Suhrarwardy was a dangerous person, not to be relied upon.

'The same has been said about me,' Gandhi drily replied.

He had chosen for the site of his mission the Calcutta slum of Beliaghata, a Muslim district surrounded by Hindu slums equally noisome. It was (and still is) an area of appalling poverty, filth, degradation and crime; hovels, brothels and drinking dens, a breeding ground for every kind of disease and mischief, a sore rubbed red by communal killings and maimings. In its midst, like a crumbling stately Southern home out of a Tennessee Williams play, stood Hydari Mansion, once the property of a rich Muslim merchant who had fled when the scum of the slums began to wash against his door. Here Gandhi decided to set up his headquarters. Two of his girl disciples set to work to scrub the floors clear of excrement and drive out the rats and snakes, but it was rather like baling out a sinking boat with a teaspoon. The rains had come to Calcutta now, and there was mud and slime and stench everywhere.

'So you have got yourself detained in Calcutta,' wrote Sardar Patel to him on 13 August, 'and that too in a quarter which is a veritable shambles and a notorious den of gangsters and hooligans. And in what choice company, too! It is a terrible risk. But more than that, will your health stand the strain? I'm afraid it must be terribly filthy there. Keep me posted about yourself.'

Gandhi had arranged that he and Suhrarwardy should journey to Hydari Mansion together and made a rendezvous with the Muslim leader for 2.30 in the afternoon. Suhrarwardy has never been on time for an appointment in his life (at least not a day-time one) and this was no exception. Gandhi (who was late for an appointment only once in his life)[1] decided that he had funked it at the last moment and set out in the car on his own. By the time Suhrarwardy arrived at Hydari Mansion, half an hour late, a great crowd of Hindus had gathered around the festering house, many of them to greet the Mahatma and ask for *darshan* or blessing, but others to make trouble. They were young members of the militant Mahasabha Party, the violently reactionary Hindu organization, reinforced by *goondas* from the district hoping for some bloodshed.

'Why do you come here to protect the Muslims?' they cried. 'Why don't you go to Noakhali and save the Hindus?'

In the midst of all the noise and shouting, Suhrarwardy arrived. For a time he was trapped inside his car while the crowd gibbered around it crying: 'Muslim pig!' and 'Murderer!' and

---

[1] And that, curiously enough, on the last day of his life. He was late for prayers on the evening of his assassination.

'Thief!' Someone raised a cry which could only have been heard in India: 'Let us hang the cow-killing degenerate!' He sat through it all with, in the circumstances, admirable sang-froid; but he did not attempt to get out of his car until Gandhi sent out disciples to argue with the angry Hindus. It was finally agreed that if they would allow Suhrarwardy to leave his car, Gandhi would receive a delegation. The Muslim leader descended and walked into the house through the sullen, glowering mob. It was now seen that he had come on his mission dressed in an open shirt and a pair of tartan shorts.

Rarely have two men of such different quality, temperament, habits and ways of life come together on such a mission. It is typical of Gandhi that though he was a passionate devotee of cleanliness and fastidious in his habits, he did not appear to be disturbed by the noisome nature of his surroundings. It had begun to rain outside, and scores of the demonstrators swarmed into the house. They used the single latrine which the mansion possessed, and they spat phlegm and betel nut juice on the floor. Soon the corridors were awash with excrement, urine and spittle. The stench of it mingled with the disinfectant and bug powder, which the acolytes had sprinkled freely around the house, and produced a stench that turned Suhrarwardy green.

Gandhi: 'You should not think about it, my friend. Drive all thought of it out of your mind.'

Suhrarwardy: 'How can I drive it out of my mind, when it keeps coming in through my nostrils?'[1]

Yet though the bugs and the filth worried him, the menacing crowd seemed hardly to do so at all. While Gandhi talked to the delegation, the mob began to chuck bricks at the windows; Gandhi went to expostulate with them and ask them to show circumspection, but they shouted:

'Why doesn't Suhrarwardy show himself?'

Suhrarwardy moved to the window, but was told by the Mahatma to remain out of sight for the moment. The next night, however, when demonstrators shouted his name again, he came to the window. Gandhi stood beside him, his hand on his shoulder, while the Muslim cried to the mob:

'It is Bengal's great good fortune that Mahatmaji is in our midst

---

[1] It was typical of Gandhi that he persuaded the crowd to cease defiling his abode, not by requesting them to do so, but by taking off his sandals and walking about in the slime barefooted. They became slightly more circumspect, out of shame.

at this hour. Will Bengal realize its high privilege and stop the fratricide?'

A Hindu cried: 'You were responsible for the great Calcutta killing, were you not?'

Replied Suhrarwardy: 'Yes, we all were.'

The crowd: 'Answer the question!'

Suhrarwardy: 'Yes, it was *my* responsibility.'

He remained facing them, almost daring them to throw their bricks at him, but there was something in the attitude of this arrogant politician which impressed them; but this time it was humility. When next the extremist Hindus came in to argue with Gandhi, there were less outbursts and more questions. From that moment on, Gandhi and Suhrarwardy went together to his prayer meetings, and on several occasions addressed crowds of anything from ten to a hundred thousand people.

The amazing, the miraculous thing was that the magic of Gandhi's personality, plus the shrewdness of his tactics, worked. Twenty-four hours after his arrival, 5,000 Muslims and Hindus were walking in joint procession through the slums of Beliaghata, crying slogans no one had ever thought to hear any more:

Hindu Muslim ek ho! and *Hindu Muslim bhai bhai!* ('Hindus and Muslims Unite!' and 'Hindus and Muslims are Brothers!')

The killings ceased. Lieutenant-General Tuker had his British and Gurkha 'fire squadrons' ready for instant action, but they were not needed. The British population of Calcutta, which had looked on in disgust and despair at the communal slaughter of a year before, now saw Hindus and Muslims embracing each other. And the magic was spreading. In Bihar and in Noakhali the outbreaks of savagery were dying down.

'Here in the compound,' wrote Gandhi, 'numberless Hindus continue to stream in shouting the favourite slogans. One might almost say that the joy of fraternization is leaping up from hour to hour. Is this to be called a miracle or an accident? By whatever name it may be described, it is quite clear that the credit that is being given to me from all sides is quite undeserved; nor can it be said to be deserved by Suhrarwardy. It is not the work of one or two men. We are toys in the house of God. He makes us dance to His tune. The utmost, therefore, that man can do is to refrain from interfering with the dance and that he should tender full obedience to his Maker's will. Thus considered, it can be said that in this miracle He has used us two as His instruments and as for myself I ask only whether the dream of my youth is to be realised in the evening of my life.'[1]

It would not be realized, of course. His dream had always been of a free India but also one that was united, irrespective of the religions of its peoples. He could bring Hindus and Muslims together, but he could not rejoin the bleeding India which the politicians had torn in two.

Mountbatten wrote to him:

'In the Punjab we have 50,000 soldiers and large scale rioting on our hands. In Bengal our forces consist of one man, and there is no rioting. As a serving officer, as well as an administrator, may I be allowed to pay my tribute to the One-Man Boundary Force, not forgetting his Second-in-Command, Mr Suhrarwardy?'

There was little enough to be happy about in the Indian communal scene during the bloodthirsty days of August 1947, but Calcutta and the rest of Bengal produced events to make men rejoice and hope in a moment when there was so much to arouse feelings of despair.

The inspiration for it came from two men who, as they padded through the mud and filth of Calcutta on their mission of peace, looked like characters from an Oriental version of an old-time Laurel and Hardy film: Mahatma Gandhi, calm, serene, smiling, in his loin-cloth; and Shaheed Suhrarwardy, sweating profusely from the unaccustomed exercise, waddling along beside him, in his open shirt and tartan-patterned shorts.

While partition committees squabbled and bickered, Princes bargained for their pensions and politicians began practising before their mirrors for the great day, the Viceroy's office worried over the ceremonies which would be gone through on 15 August. There was no blueprint for the occasions and no precedent either. The British had never given away a slice of their Empire before. They were doing it in haste, but with goodwill. But how and with what ceremonial?

Lord Ismay wrote a note to the Viceroy under the heading, 'Ceremonies on the Day of Transfer of Power' in which he said:

'We suggest that this constitutes a major political issue. The following points arise:—

 a. There should be ceremonies in the capitals of both Dominions

[1] *Harijan*, Gandhi's newspaper.

... It would be perfectly possible for you to attend a ceremony in Delhi in the morning and in the Pakistan capital, having flown thither, in the afternoon.

b. We feel that, in connection with the Delhi ceremony, we should go out with the flag flying high. Pandit Nehru may not want too much ostentation and might prefer a simple ceremony. The form of the ceremonies would have to be a question of discussion between you and the two Prime Ministers and we are sure that they would fall in with your wishes.

c. The Durbar Hall would presumably be the venue of the Delhi ceremony. At both it is to be hoped that you would be able to read out a message from His Majesty the King.

d. It is hoped that Dominion representatives will be there.

e. The question of troops to take part in the ceremony arises. It is hoped that each Dominion would, by the date of the transfer of power, have at least one unit composed purely of its own nationals. British troops would take part and units would be available in both capitals.

f. We suggest that a letter should be sent to the India Office seeking guidance.'[1]

But this note was written at the time when it was still believed that Jinnah would allow Mountbatten to be the first Governor-General of Pakistan, and at the time, moreover, when Ismay presumed that Independence Day would be a ceremonial occasion at which Britain—as the hander-on of power—should be and would be the principal participant.

Neither Jinnah nor Nehru had, however, fought for power this long to be willing to share it with the British Raj (though Nehru did show every willingness to share it with Mountbatten). The Muslim League leader let it be known that he would like Pakistan's Independence Day to be purely his, and suggested that Mountbatten should fly in to Karachi on 14 August for a preliminary ceremony, leaving 15 August to him. This, in fact, suited Mountbatten admirably, for there was no doubt where he wanted to be on 15 August—in Delhi.

The Labour Government at home did not share Ismay's confidence that the Indian masses would appreciate a message from King-Emperor George the Sixth.

'The question of a message from the King seems to me a delicate matter,' cabled Lord Listowel, the Secretary of State for India. 'I

[1] Government of India Records.

should have thought that we did not want to lay too great a stress on the position of the King in relation to the two new Dominions. On the other hand, the message could hardly be a farewell message. Unless we can devise some context for it which is merely formal, and which is not likely to give offence in any quarter, British or Indian, it might be better to have no message . . . There will, of course, anyhow, have to be the formal Proclamation abandoning the style of Emperor of India.'[1]

And what about the playing of 'God Save the King', the British National Anthem? A month before everyone had been in favour of hearing it at the ceremony, but as the last days were torn off the calendar, the Viceroy began to have qualms.

It would be foolish, he indicated, to do anything which might be provocative. In his view, the playing of 'God Save the King' should be avoided as far as possible. He suggested that Campbell-Johnson should make discreet inquiries about the Delhi ceremony, and if the British National Anthem was not expected, it might be that a pipe band should take the place of a brass band. He ordered a note to be sent to Provincial Governors in which he said:

'My general policy about playing the National Anthem after the transfer of power is that playing it in public should be avoided. As far as possible, it should be confined to Governors' houses. At the ceremony of transfer, Governors are entitled to the Royal Salute and the first part of the National Anthem.' He added: 'But there is no need to insist on the latter, and there is no intention of insisting here.'[1]

Nothing, absolutely nothing, must be allowed to mar the ceremonials. On that Mountbatten was determined. He had moved too fast and taken too many risks to allow a blunder or a mistake, or any kind of bad news, to wreck the goodwill which he had built up between the new Dominions and Britain. At all costs 15 August must be a day of rejoicing for the people of India and Pakistan, and as the architect of their happiness Mountbatten was prepared to take a final risk to ensure it.

He had bad news in his pocket, but he refused to have it on his conscience as well. Since 9 August, he had been in possession of Sir Cyril Radcliffe's Boundary Awards. They would alter the lives of millions of people. They would cause shock, despair and

[1] Government of India Records.

insensate fury. In the East of India, Sir Cyril had awarded the Chittagong Hill Tracts to East Pakistan, and that would be bitterly resented by Congress. In the West, he had cut a line boldly down two of the Punjab's five rivers in such a way that most of the great canal systems, which the Sikhs had financed and built, most of the great wheatlands, which they owned, most of the Sikh shrines plus the city of Lahore went to Pakistan. All the places which, in fact, the Sikhs hoped out of hope to get in the end had been awarded to the Muslims.

But there was one award which was obviously bound to anger the Muslims too. The district of Gurdaspur, a No-Man's-Land between the two Dominions, *though one with a Muslim majority population*,[1] was given to India. Gurdaspur provided the only road and rail link between Kashmir and India, which otherwise would have had none. In the light of subsequent happenings, it seemed to some people, particularly friends of Pakistan, a suspicious decision to have given.

Here were the answers to the desperately anxious questions of millions of Indians, particularly in the Punjab. For the Sikhs and Hindus in Western Punjab and the non-Muslim inhabitants of Lahore, it was, of course, vital information; having hopes that the 'other factors' mentioned in Sir Cyril Radcliffe's brief would include the ownership of land or homes, they had stayed on. This Award would be the signal to them to collect up whatever belongings they had and go East. In the mounting glare of communal tension, the sooner they knew their fate the better.

Why then did not Mountbatten release the news of the Awards?

This is where trouble begins.

To anyone who has studied Mountbatten's character, the reason for holding it back was obvious. Campbell-Johnson puts his master's state of mind quite clearly when he writes:

'Various points of view about publication were put forward. On administrative grounds it was argued that earliest possible announcement would be of help to Jenkins and would enable last-minute troop movements to be made into the affected areas in advance of the transfer of power. Alternatively, it was suggested that insofar as the Award would in any case be bound to touch off trouble, the best date to release it would be 14th August. *Mountbatten said that if he could exercise some discretion in the matter*

[1] My italics—L. M.

he would prefer to postpone its appearance until after the Independence Day celebrations, feeling that the problem of its timing was one of psychology, and that the controversy and grief it was bound to arouse on both sides should not be allowed to mar Independence Day itself.'[1]

As a man of success, he was, of course, bound to be against anything which would cloud the clear skies of Independence Day. In the light of subsequent events, he was obviously wrong to suppress the report for so many days, and he was obviously even more wrong in failing to take the Indian and Pakistan leaders into his confidence. A prior report would have given millions of Hindus, Sikhs and Muslims a chance to pack their bags and leave; a confidential report to Nehru, Jinnah and to the Punjab Boundary Force commander, General Rees, would have made it possible for dispositions and arrangements to be made to allow them to leave in some semblance of order. But Mountbatten took no one into his confidence. He hugged the Awards to himself and suppressed them until after Independence Day. Independence Day was happy. But millions of people died or lost everything as a result.

This is a matter for Mountbatten's conscience. It obviously did not trouble him—or possibly did not even occur to him—for Campbell-Johnson writes of his mood in the last minutes of the British Raj:

'As midnight struck, Mountbatten was sitting quietly at his desk. I have known him in most moods; tonight there was an air about him of serenity, almost detachment. The scale of his personal achievement was too great for elation; rather his sense of history and the fitness of things at this dramatic moment, when the old and the new order were reconciled in himself, called forth composure.'

For a man sitting on a revelation which would, in the next few weeks, cause the death of nearly a million people and provoke the greatest and most miserable trek in history, it was a remarkable mood to be in. *And yet*, as Mountbatten was himself subsequently to say,[2] *what really did anything matter to the Indians except Independence?*

What is certain about the suppression of the Boundary Awards is that there was no ulterior motive behind it, as Mr Jinnah and certain Pakistanis were to believe in the days to come. Nor would

[1] Op. cit; my italics—L. M.
[2] To the author.

even they ever have come to believe it but for a succession of coincidences and mischief-making which, at the time, they were in no position to check.

It so happened that on 8 August, the evening before Mountbatten received the Radcliffe Awards, Sir Evan Jenkins came through from Simla on the telephone to George Abell, in a state of considerable agitation, to ask if the Award for the Punjab was ready. When told it was not, he pleaded with Abell to find out something about it in order that he could disperse his troops and police to meet the inevitable disturbances.

Abell got into touch with Sir Cyril Radcliffe's office and asked for information. What happened next is a mystery. Certainly Sir Cyril told him nothing. Whether any members of his Secretariat did is another matter, though it seems unlikely. George Abell, however, then sent a 'rough sketch map' which had, he said, been 'taken down over the telephone' to Sir Evan Jenkins. The sketch-map showed the towns of Ferozepur and Zira on the Pakistan side of the boundary.

When the award was subsequently published, both these towns were awarded to India.

The sketch was, of course, quite unofficial. In any case, to 'take down a map over the telephone' is obviously a chancy business. And the matter might have rested there, had it not happened that Sir Evan Jenkins left the sketch-map in his safe when he departed for England on 15 August. The Governor of West Punjab, who took over Jenkins's office in Lahore, was an Englishman, Sir John Mudie. He found the map. Instead of sending it on to Sir Evan Jenkins or to the India Office Records Department, he passed it on to Mr Jinnah. Mr Jinnah turned it over to his experts. They accepted it immediately as an official map. Noting its date as 8 August, they at once presumed that *this* was the reason why Mountbatten had held back the Awards until after Independence Day. He wanted Sir Cyril Radcliffe to make alterations which would be more in keeping with Nehru and India's wishes; and they charged that in the intervening days, he had not only persuaded Sir Cyril to transfer Ferozepur and Zira from Pakistan to India but also Gurdaspur as well, thus giving India a link with Kashmir which she would not otherwise have had, and without which she could hardly claim connexion with the State.

Mountbatten has never denied the Pakistan charges against

him in connexion with the 'sketch-map story', preferring to let the facts speak for themselves. The author has no doubt, after considerable investigation, that he may have been wrong in holding back the Awards, but that conspiracy is out of the question. To suggest, as many Pakistanis did, that he 'fiddled' the Awards in order to revenge himself on Jinnah for his snub over the Governor-Generalship is to misjudge Mountbatten's character profoundly.

His innocence of conspiracy is manifest. His innocence of considerable lack of judgement in suppressing the Awards is not so clear.

CHAPTER TEN

'TWO CHEERS FOR BRITAIN'

'To ALL BRITISH units in Eastern Command,' wrote Lieutenant-General Tuker on 14 August 1947. 'Today is the last day on which you perform your duties in India, as British Regiments of all arms have performed them for the last two hundred years. The British Army has been for all these years the firm structure on which our nation has succeeded in building for the first time in all history an India which was one single geographic and administrative whole . . .

'Your famous Regiments now leave India for good.

'Today, therefore, I am thanking you on behalf of every officer and man for all that you have done for us in these past two difficult years . . . In these last few days of waiting, do well as you have done so far, and leave India with your fame at the peak of its honour. Take with you to Britain the willing spirit of co-operation that you have shown out here in the cause of India, and so strive for your country . . .'

On that same day, Sir Claude Auchinleck issued his own order:
SPECIAL INDIAN ARMY ORDER
by
His Excellency Field Marshal Sir Claude J. E. Auchinleck, G.C.B., G.C.I.E., C.S.I., D.S.O., O.B.E. Commander-in-Chief in India. New Delhi, 14 August, 1947. S/A. O. 79/S/47. Discontinuance of India Army Orders. This is the last India Army Order.

Auchinleck, who was now Supreme Commander of both the new Pakistan and India Armies, was in no mood for valedictories. On 14 August his plane halted at Lahore on its way to Delhi from Karachi. In another twenty-four hours, Indian and Pakistan would be free. But what was freedom going to mean in the Punjab?

'As he looked down on the great plain of the Punjab,' wrote John Connell,[1] 'he saw smoke rising from every village, to the limits of that vast horizon, and along the dusty roads the endless streams of refugees trudging east and west.'

[1] *Auchinleck.*

The greatest treks had not yet, in fact, begun. Millions of non-Muslims in West Punjab and millions of Muslims in East Punjab were staying on, hoping against hope that the Boundary Awards would incorporate their villages, homes and land in the new Dominion of their choice. Their leaders—not knowing what only Radcliffe and Mountbatten knew—urged them to stay on, and many did so, in spite of constant and savage intimidation. In Amritsar, whole areas containing Muslim shops were aflame. Auchinleck, General Rees (the Punjab Boundary Force Commander) and Sir Evan Jenkins held an emergency conference at Lahore airport. Even as they talked, Muslims were turning on a crowd of Sikhs queueing for a train at Lahore Station and stabbed dozens of them, while police stood by and watched. Jenkins explained to Auchinleck that his police force had turned into a communal instrument and could no longer be trusted. Ten per cent of the houses in the city had been destroyed. There were not enough officials to maintain martial law, even if it were declared. The Governor was plainly at the end of his rope. In less than twenty-four hours, he would be on a plane flying back to England; but for the moment, as Governor of his beloved Punjab, he carried the whole weight of the crisis on his shoulders and his anguish was plain to see.

So also was the despair of General Rees. His Punjab Boundary Force—upon which Mountbatten and the politicians in Delhi had relied entirely for the peaceful transfer of power—had been in the field for only three weeks, but Rees knew that it was a complete and utter failure. How could it have been otherwise? The 4th Indian Division, which was the nucleus of the Force, was a splendid body of men, but it was now subjected to strains and stresses of a kind which it had never known in war.

As its Muslim members in the Sikh areas saw their fellow-religionists being killed and maimed, they became less and less inclined to succour and protect non-Muslims. The Sikh and Hindu troops were constantly subjected to propaganda from renegade soldiers—most of them ex-members of the pro-Japanese Indian National Army—and urged to desert with their arms or look the other way when an illegal raid was in progress. Each soldier, of no matter what community, worried about the safety of his family, for many a Muslim had his wife and children in Bombay and many a Hindu's regiment was based on Rawalpindi or Peshawar.

Not only that, but they knew that their British officers had lost heart and influence. This was not unexpected in view of the fact that tomorrow or the next day they would be on their way back to England. Their prestige and power had been pierced by the end of the British Raj and the division of the Army. They could no longer expect to be obeyed with unswerving and unquestioning loyalty. It was natural, in the circumstances, that when they were confronted by a situation which a sharp burst of machine-gun fire, or a mortar bomb, or a bombardment could have solved, they hesitated. Would their troops obey them? And if they obeyed, and scores of Indians were killed, what would the politicians say? Would they be made the scapegoats and condemned as murderers rather than praised as impartial custodians of the peace?

'Every day,' said Jenkins, 'the local leaders would come in and ask the Force to open fire on looters and raiders, but it was always the other side's looters and raiders, and they became furious when one suggested a few shots at their own.'[1]

It so happened that there were two Indian officers attached to the Punjab Boundary Force who were subsequently to rise to high rank in their own countries. One was Brigadier Ayub Khan, later to become Field Marshal Ayub Khan, President of Pakistan, and the other was Brigadier K. S. Thimayya, later to become General Thimayya, Commander-in-Chief of the Indian Armed Forces. One was, of course, a Muslim and the other a Hindu. Both, in conversations with the author, shared the opinion that the British officers were in an impossible position and that the Force should never have been sent out into the field. Both agreed that whatever forces were used should have been commanded by Indian officers rather than British; Indian officers who would not have hesitated to order their troops to fire, and would have been implicitly obeyed.

According to the official history of the 4th Indian Division, General Rees at the Lahore Airfield conference 'further voiced the opinion that the use of troops, even in prohibitive numbers, would fail to mend the situation. With communities, millions strong, completely out of hand, only the intervention of national and parochial leaders would halt the campaign of extermination.'[2]

But the national leaders were too busy preparing for the celebrations of Independence Day.

---

[1] In a conversation with the author.
[2] G. R. Stevens, O.B.E., *Fourth Indian Division*.

Rees reported his position roughly as follows: The Sikhs, as they had threatened (and as Delhi had been warned) had opened their campaign of violence in the second week of August. It was as if in realizing at last that they would be the scapegoats of partition, no matter where the new Boundary ran, they could think of only one anodyne for the pain that consumed them, and that was to kill, kill, kill. The killing was both planned and at the same time blind and insensate. The Sikh leaders sat at the feet of their leader, Master Tara Singh, in the Golden Temple at Amritsar and listened to his inflammatory encouragement to violence, and then slipped away to pass the word to the gurdwaras throughout the province. It is ironic that inside the compound of the Golden Temple *gurus* at one side were reading aloud the words of the Granth Sahib, the Sikh Holy Book, counselling their people to gentleness and goodwill to all men, while a hundred yards away, within the same sacred precincts, men were being exhorted to murder. They had already formed themselves into murder gangs known as *Jathas*.

'Jathas were of various kinds,' reported Rees, 'in strength from twenty to thirty men up to five or six hundred or more. When an expedition was of limited scope the Jathas did not usually increase beyond the numbers which had originally set out; but if the projected operation was to attack a village, a convoy or a train, the local villagers would join and swell the assailants to several thousands. They had recognized leaders, headquarters which constantly shifted about, and messengers who travelled on foot, on horseback and even by motor transport. The usual method of attack, apart from assaults on villages, was from ambush. Information as to the movement of convoys or trains was relatively easy to obtain. As the crops were high, it was simple to ambush marching columns of refugees. The attackers would remain concealed until the last moment and then would pour in a stampeding volley, usually in the North West Frontier fashion, from the opposite side from where the shock assailants lay in wait. In spite of the best efforts of the escorts to hold them together, the refugees would scatter in panic; whereupon the ambush parties would dash in with sword and spear. With attackers and attacked inextricably mixed, the escort usually was unable to protect its charges.'[1]

The Sikhs were the aggressors and they were better armed and

[1] Stevens, op. cit.

prepared than the Muslims. 'The *kirpan*—the token sword which is one of the five characteristic Sikh possessions—had metamorphosed,' it was reported,[1] 'for the purpose of vengeance into a formidable cutlass or *dah*. It was supplemented by home-made spears, hatchets and battle-axes, by crude bombards and mortars and also by shields and armour . . . The Jathas possessed hard cores of skilled fighters armed with rifles, grenades, tommy-guns and machine-guns. Although the Punjab Mussulmans also possessed firearms and trained men, and a nuclear military organization in the Muslim League National Guards, they lacked the cohesiveness of the Sikhs.'

Certainly, the Muslims were nowhere as near ready to strike as the Sikhs. They often met Sikh raids armed only with flails or scythes.

But they learned. In the last days and hours of the Raj, the casualties were mostly Muslim. The Jatha gangs had it all their own way. But though the killing and raping was planned and was successful enough to give even the bloodthirstiest a surfeit of flesh and an engorgement of revenge, it was obviously neither going to be successful in itself nor would it, in the end, do anything but harm to the Sikh people themselves. For the majority of the Sikhs were in West Punjab. Each killing of a Muslim in the East would inevitably menace the life of Sikhs in the West, for the Muslims were at least equally as thirsty for blood and even more ruthless when stimulated by the encouragement of revenge.

This was not a Hindu-Muslim war but a Sikh-Muslim war, and it is all the more difficult to understand why Nehru for Congress and Jinnah for the Muslim League did not intervene. A call to both of them from Mountbatten could surely not have failed to produce some result. As an official report, hitherto suppressed, said of the last few days before Independence Day:

'The influential Hindu community, although suffering heavily at times, played a relatively minor rôle in this war of vengeance. Extremists of the RSSS (the Hindu extremist storm-troopers, the Rashtarya Swayam Sevak Sangh)[2] confined their activities to back-alley strangling of Muslims and window smashing in the principal towns . . . but, like point and counter-point of a devilish harmony, the dark alleys and squalid warrens began to re-echo each other, as knives took toll of Sikhs in Lahore and grenades

---

[1] Stevens, op. cit.
[2] One of whose members later assassinated Gandhi.

blasted Mussulmans in Amritsar. In the key Sikh area of the Manja, the fruitful triangle of countryside between the junction of the Sutlej and Beas rivers, the first Jathas appeared in the fields and began to exterminate the Muslim population of the villages. Day by day killings mounted to peak ferocity. At Gujranwala, to the north of Lahore, the Mussulmans struck back and hundreds of Sikhs were hunted to death. From all parts of Central Punjab there flowed fearful tales of destruction.[1]

The killings were 'pre-mediaeval' (to use General Rees's word) in their ferocity. Lieutenant-Colonel P. S. Mitchison, D.S.O., who took over the 4th Indian Division as G.S.O., described a characteristic scene in this way:

'Motoring from Beas to Lahore, at a time when 100,000 Mussulmans on foot were making their way westwards through Amritsar, in the course of fifty miles I saw between 400 to 600 dead. One attack on the refugees went in from thick crops while I was nearby. In a few minutes fifty men, women and children were slashed to pieces while thirty others came running back towards us with wounds streaming.

'We got up a tank of 18th Cavalry which killed six Sikh attackers and took three prisoners. The latter proved most useful as under interrogation they gave the names of the villages responsible for the ambush. These villages were immediately searched and fined.'[2]

But everyone emphasized that there was one way, and one way only, to bring peace to the Punjab. That was to persuade Nehru for Congress and Jinnah for the Muslim League of its desperate nature. They must be brought personally to the Punjab to see what was going on. They must not only give orders to the ring-leaders to cease their incitement to murder and rape and massacre. They must show themselves as the real rulers of their new Dominions by exercising discipline and control. Jinnah must call off his Muslim raiders. Nehru must clamp down on the blind, berserk and blood-drunk Sikhs, even if it meant imprisoning their leaders.

Here was a last-minute task for the Viceroy which might have given a golden tint to his crown in the last hours of his reign. He had been so unorthodox in the past, that surely here was the moment to make his final envoi as a Viceroy in a blaze of mission-

[1] Government of India Records.
[2] 4th Indian Division Intelligence Report.

ary glory. He was hardly ignorant of what was happening in the Punjab. He must have known that the Punjab Boundary Force was a failure. He must have realized that his promise to Maulana Abul Kalam Azad to protect the hair and head of every Hindu, Sikh and Muslim was now a hollow mockery.

The Viceroy flew to Karachi on 13 August to convey his greeting and that of the King to the new Dominion of Pakistan, his last official duty as Viceroy, and he was perhaps even more charmingly cool and self-contained than ever. When told that the plot to assassinate Mr Jinnah had now been confirmed and that it was believed a bomb would be thrown at his car during the ceremonial ride on 14 August, Mountbatten at once offered to ride with the Muslim leader. He was unshaken when Jinnah, at a formal banquet in the evening, rose and began to read a long, prepared speech—after Campbell-Johnson had told him there would be no formal speeches. He replied with a ten minute discourse which, though extemporaneous, sounded as if it had been mugged up for weeks.

'The birth of Pakistan,' he said, in an address before the Assembly on 14 August, 'is an event in history. We, who are part of history, and are helping to make it, are not well-placed, even if we wished, to moralize on the event, to look back and survey the sequence of the past that led to it. History seems sometimes to move with the infinite slowness of a glacier and sometimes to rush forward in a torrent. Just now, in this part of the world our united efforts have melted the ice and moved some impediments in the stream,and we are carried onwards in the full flood. There is no time to look back. There is time only to look forward.'

He drove with Jinnah through streets crowded with politely rather than wildly enthusiastic crowds. Jinnah was tense and nervous. The Viceroy had never looked so relaxed. But no one booed and no bomb was thrown, and Mountbatten took it like a gentleman when, at the end of the ride, Jinnah put his hand on his knee and said:

'Thank God I was able to bring you back alive!'

Mountbatten was glad to be able to leave that afternoon and fly back to Delhi. For him Karachi and Pakistan were sideshows, and Delhi was where he wanted to be. He knew, in any case, that Jinnah was determined not to have him around on Independence Day to steal his thunder. He had told his A.D.C., the day he arrived in Karachi:

'I never thought it would happen. I never expected to see Pakistan in my lifetime.'

But it had come to pass. He would see its birth on the morrow, fully aware that it had been a one-man job, supremely conscious that without Jinnah there would certainly never have been a Pakistan. He did not want Mountbatten around in that glorious moment when he could face his people and say:

'*Pakistan Zindabad!*' or in other words, '*L'Etat, c'est moi!*'

The Union Jack, which had flown night and day since 1847 from the Residency at Lucknow, was unobtrusively hauled down on the evening of 13 August 1947, and sent to Field Marshal Auchinleck. He took it back to King George the Sixth to put with other historic British flags in the museum at Windsor Castle. When an Indian procession arrived next day to hoist an Indian Union flag in its place, they discovered that the pole had been severed at the base and removed.

Mountbatten had been cherishing a secret to himself, but now he confided it to his Staff. On Independence Day, he would be created an Earl for his services as Viceroy.

George Abell had already been knighted for his services in a ceremony conducted by Mountbatten, and the Viceroy had sent his own list of recommendations to London for the consideration of the King. On whom would the accolades fall? Sir Claude Auchinleck, having heard that he had been recommended for a barony, at once wrote a letter of refusal. Lord Ismay called for the list to see that his own subordinates had been rewarded for their work, and, to his astonishment, saw his own name at the head of the list. He had been recommended for a K.G.S.I. (Knight Grand Cross of the Star of India, the highest award in the Indian Empire). It was a decoration for which he had yearned as the summit of achievement when he was a young subaltern in India thirty-five years earlier. But as a true-blue Briton of the old school, he did not consider that the giving away of India was work worthy of being rewarded by his King.

He put a line through his name and went to tell the Viceroy that he could not accept the honour. Mountbatten tartly retorted that it was too late in the day: the recommendation had gone through. Ismay replied that if the Viceroy didn't cancel it, and at once, by cable, he would do so himself. The cable was sent off at once. The King was furious, but he took Ismay's name out of the list.

Ismay retired to bed with a bout of dysentery which lasted until the Independence Day festivities were over.

In Delhi now the air throbbed with excitement as well as heat as the last hours of 14 August ticked away. The ceremonial arches were all up now. Flags flew everywhere. Bullock carts packed with peasants crawled into the city, ready for the celebrations. It was doubtful if anyone would sleep in India that night, and, in Delhi, Bombay and Calcutta, at least, it would be because the mood was one of intense joy and jubilation.

In *dhotis* newly laundered and proud Gandhi caps, the members of the Legislative Assembly gathered in the evening for a solemn ceremony of welcome to the new Dominion. They would stay there until midnight in an ecstatic vigil of the kind that Indians had never known before and would never know again. Freedom at last. The freedom for which they had given up so much of their lives, for which so many of them had gone to jail. They were nearly all there: Nehru, his saffron face drawn with weariness, rings under his eyes, in a state of sublime exhaustion; Patel, more like a Roman Emperor than ever, wearing his *dhoti* like a toga and his triumph like a flag; a grinning Rajagopalachari, as near to a state of intoxication as that dedicated old teetotaller will ever be; Prasad, near to tears; Rajkumari Amrit Kaur, actually in tears; and only the sad, sad face of Maulana Abul Kalam Azad, to whom this occasion was something of a tragedy, sticking out from the sea of happy faces like a gaunt and ravaged rock.

The happy Congressmen ignored him. The only presence which might have disturbed them at this moment was that of the man who had done more than all of them put together to win India her freedom, but for whom, in the last months, the achievement had turned sour. For him, too, this was no occasion for rejoicing. It was true that the country was free. But more important, it was also torn asunder and bleeding. For Mahatma Gandhi, there was only one place to be at this moment—in a noisome slum where he could bring a little peace and comfort, where he could fast for his people's sins, and where he could mourn the India, united as well as free, for which he had worked and prayed and schemed and dreamed.

It was an occasion to challenge a leader to match his words with the mood and the hour, but Jawaharlal Nehru could always be relied upon to rise to the occasion. When he rose to call upon

the Assembly to take the pledge of dedication to the new Dominion of India, he said:

'Long years ago we made a tryst with destiny, and now the
time comes when we shall redeem our pledge, not wholly or in
full measure, but very substantially. At the stroke of the midnight
hour, when the world sleeps, India will awake to life and freedom.
A moment comes, which comes but rarely in history, when we
step out from the old to the new, when an age ends, and when
the soul of a nation, long suppressed, finds utterance. It is fitting
that at this solemn moment we take the pledge of dedication to
the service of India and her people and to the still larger cause of
humanity.'

Midnight came. It was over. With neither a roar nor a whimper,
but with a hardly audible sigh, 182 years of British rule in India
came to an end. The British Raj which had ruled the country,
unified the country, brought it justice, medicine, good government—and had also exploited its wealth and patronized its people
—was no more.

And perhaps the manner of its departure and the arrival of the
new order could not be better described than in a naïve poem
which Mr Chia Luen Lo, the Chinese Ambassador to India, wrote
to salute the occasion:

> 'India be free
>   Won't that be
> A Himalayan dream?
>   How fantastic
> How absurd an idea
>   That never occurred to me . . .
>
> Suddenly and incredibly triumphed
>   Wisdom
> Where the East and West met on a
>   common ground.
>   What a miracle
> That independence can be
>   Without a war! History will tell you
> It has never happened before.
>   Be Brave, forward
> Riders on the chariot of time!
>   While approaching the mountain peak

Redouble your efforts to climb!
    Unfailingly you will arrive at your ideal
Lofty and beautiful
    Noble and sublime.'

There were many similar sentiments voiced in India on the morning of 15 August. And around the world, in hailing the new Dominions, the statesmen and commentators praised the wisdom of
Britain for having given them their freedom. Everyone was happy.

The crowds celebrated in a delirium of delight in Delhi and
cried indiscriminately: *Jai Hind* and *Mountbatten ki Jai* and *Nehru
Mountbatten ek ho* whenever they caught a glimpse of their
heroes. The bands marching the streets of Bombay felt that they
could hardly play 'God Save the King' any more, so they played
'God Bless the Prince of Wales' instead. And far from wreaking
any vengeance on the ousted Britons, their hated masters, the
Indians rushed to embrace them. 'After you,' they cried, in front
of doors or lifts. 'You are our guests now.' K. M. Munshi, an old
Congress fighter, wrote:

'No power in history but Great Britain would have conceded
independence with such grace, and no power but India would have
so gracefully acknowledged the debt.'

It was a fairy tale play in which even the villain was reformed
and reconciled by the end. Or so it seemed.

But not all India celebrated with such harmless ecstacy on
Independence Day. That morning, in the bazaar quarter of Amritsar, the Sikhs rounded up a large group of Muslim girls
and women, stripped them of their clothes, and then forced them
to parade in a circle before the jeering crowd. Then a number of
the choicest and youngest were dragged off and raped repeatedly.
The others were chopped down by *kirpans*, and out of thirty of
them only half a dozen reached the sanctuary of the Golden
Temple alive.

In Lahore that evening, a Muslim mob attacked the chief Sikh
gurdwara in the city. Scores of Sikhs had taken refuge there. The
Muslim authorities in the city had pledged General Rees to
protect them. But their police stood by and did not interfere
when the gurdwara was put to the flames and the desperate
screams of its trapped inmates began to be heard.

India was free, and in Delhi and Karachi it felt wonderful.

But in the Punjab, independence was something else again.

EPILOGUE

IN THE NINE months between August 1947 and the spring of the following year, between fourteen and sixteen million Hindus, Sikhs and Muslims were forced to leave their homes and flee to safety from blood-crazed mobs. In that same period over 600,000 of them were killed. But no, not just killed. If they were children, they were picked up by the feet and their heads smashed against the wall. If they were female children, they were raped. If they were girls, they were raped and then their breasts were chopped off. And if they were pregnant, they were disembowelled.

It was a period in India's history when India's women in the Punjab and the United Provinces and Bihar were reminded of a useful hint handed down through harems and women's quarters from the time of the Moghuls—that the way to avoid pregnancy as a result of being raped is to struggle, always to struggle.

It was a time when trains were arriving in Lahore Station packed with passengers, all of them dead, with messages scribbled on the sides of the carriages reading: 'A present from India.' So, of course, the Muslims sent back trainloads of butchered Sikhs and Hindus with the message: 'A present from Pakistan.' In a land, which, under Gandhi, had adopted as a national religion the cult of *ahimsa* and non-violence there took place murder, looting, burning and raping such as the world has not seen since the days of Jenghis Khan. 'Freedom must not stink!' cried an Indian journalist in a famous pamphlet issued at the time.[1] But all India stank—with the stench of countless thousands of dead bodies, with the stench of evil deeds, with the stench of fires.

India in 1947 was a bumper year for vultures. They had no need to look for rotting flesh for it was all around them, animal and human. One convoy of Sikhs and Hindus from West Punjab was 74 miles long, and the raiders who attacked it constantly en route did not need to watch for it: they could smell its coming, for it was riddled with cholera and other foul diseases. And such was

[1] D. F. Karaka, *Freedom Must Not Stink*, Bombay—the account of a visit to the Punjab.

its mood that, upon sighting a long Muslim convoy of refugees coming the other way, the able-bodied members of the Indian convoy set off to do some killing of their own.

If the Sikhs were sullen and vicious before independence, they became mad with rage after the announcement of the Boundary Awards on 17 August. It was worse even than they had feared. Their lands, their canals, their homes in the rich and fertile West would all be within the boundaries of the hated Pakistan. They reacted in a monstrous reflex action, an ejaculation of berserk fury in which they cut down every Muslim in sight and vowed to kill them, but not too quickly. Sikh leaders and Sikh princes joined in exhorting their unhappy followers to ever more extravagant excesses.

Both sides had signed, on 20 July, at Mountbatten's behest, a declaration that they would respect the rights of minorities. But Mountbatten was right in suspecting that they did not know what they were signing. The Sikh policy was to exterminate the Muslims in their midst. The Muslims, with their eyes on the rich Sikh farmlands, were content to drive the Sikhs out and only massacre those who insisted on remaining. It is sad to have to admit that in their deliberate disobedience of their signed pledge they were encouraged by the British Governor of West Punjab, Sir Francis Mudie, who wrote to Mr Jinnah on 5 September 1947:

'I am telling everyone that I don't care how the Sikhs get across the border; the great thing is to get rid of them as soon as possible.'

600,000 dead. 14,000,000 driven from their homes. 100,000 young girls kidnapped by both sides, forcibly converted or sold on the auction block.[1]

In the light of what was achieved in giving India its freedom, the sacrifice was not so much, after all.

That, at least, is what supporters of Earl Mountbatten would say. They make the point that while Mountbatten was Supreme Commander in South East Asia during the War he tried, while continuing to fight the Japanese, to do something for the victims of the great Bengal Famine. He assigned ten per cent of the holds of his ships, bringing supplies to the Fourteenth Army, to food

---

[1] A combined Pakistan-Indian Commission to trace these young women was formed but its efforts petered out; principally, according to the Pakistanis, because the Hindus refused to have their wives and daughters back—they had been defiled.

for the Bengalis. Some members of the Government at home were furious when they heard about it.

'If Mountbatten can afford to assign ten per cent of his space to food for the natives,' they said, 'he can afford to do with less ships,' and they sent out an order to cut the 14th Army's convoys by ten per cent. In the event, even though Mountbatten got the cut restored, between three and four million people died in Bengal.

'If the Government could contemplate that number of dead with complacency,' say Mountbatten's advocates, 'why should they grumble about 600,000 dead to secure the establishment of a free and friendly India?'

These arguments will have been, it is hoped, completely answered by the facts which have been brought out in this book. No reasonable man will deny that Britain's decision to give India its freedom was a good one — taken not only because the Indian people could not be much longer kept under British control, *but because the British people were no longer willing to keep them under their control.* The decision of Prime Minister Clement Attlee to divest Britain of all control over India by June 1948 was a genuine expression of the British people's will even though some Tories, including Churchill, warned that it was too precipitate. There is no evidence that the Indians themselves—Hindus, Sikhs or Muslims—disbelieved Attlee's declaration. They accepted it as a genuine date limit for freedom.

Then why, after Mountbatten's arrival, did it have to be so drastically shortened to a date ten months earlier?

It had to be, Mountbatten will say, *because the situation was becoming beyond control. Conditions almost similar to civil war were brewing. To leave the situation any longer as it was would have produced bloodshed and riot on a large scale.*

The advisers of the Labour Government in Britain believed at the time, moreover, *that if freedom did not come very quickly indeed, the Congress Party would break up and the Communists would take their place.* In the light of the information they possess today, they know this to be a complete travesty of the facts. The stability and solidity of the Congress Party was never in danger. The Communists were never within a continent's distance of attaining power.

Which brings me to the point which seems to me important. 600,000 Indians died for Independence and 14,000,000 lost their homes. Men became brutes. The air over the Indo-Pakistan frontiers was soured for at least a generation. Unnecessarily.

It need not have happened. It would not have happened had independence not been rushed through at such a desperate rate. Never has such a grave moment in the lives of 350,000,000 people been decided with such efficiency, such skill and charm, and without any real consideration of its profound consequences.

This is not to deny the magnitude of Mountbatten's achievement. As Noel Coward said: 'When the job's hopeless, they call in Dickie.' The Labour Government picked him for the job because they were, in the American phrase, stuck. He was sent in to do a fast job of salesmanship and painless surgery. It would be wrong to blame him for doing a distasteful job as fast as possible —especially as he believed (wrongly) that speed would save lives.

But when one considers how much goodwill there was behind Britain's wish to give India her freedom, what a stinking bog of unpreparedness, blunders, and appalling lack of planning separated the wish from the achievement.

Mistake after mistake.

Wavell, whose plan would at least have kept India intact and unpartitioned, dismissed out of hand.

Jinnah's claim for separate rights for the Muslims accepted— but no attempt made to prepare for the consequences. No consideration of where Pakistan would be. No plans for dividing up the Army.

Agreement on partition secured—by a shuffling of the cards at Simla. But no realization of the significance of the decision.

If the Labour Government was prepared to give a *united* India its freedom by June 1948, how was it possible to promise a *divided* India freedom ten months earlier? The new date was admittedly an announcement with which to impress a Press conference—at which Mountbatten made it—but did he really expect it to create anything but chaos and the uttermost confusion— even if he could not have envisaged the killing and suffering which would stem from it?

Mistake after mistake, indeed.

Partition of India announced in May 1947, and no plans for dividing its Army until June, with only six weeks to go to the deadline.

Partition announced in May, but the Commission to decide the boundaries along which the two new States would be divided, not appointed until the end of June.

Partition in May, and Independence in August, but a people desperate to know deliberately kept in ignorance of which country they belonged to until two days *after* Independence.

These were surely avoidable blunders, and they cost hundreds of thousands of lives.

By those Britons who were the architects of Indian freedom, these criticisms will be swept aside. Mountbatten is convinced that his achievement will go down in history—as it will indeed, though not, perhaps, in quite the way he envisages it. He is backed in his profound conviction that it was not only done for the best but achieved in the best possible way by his Chief of Staff, Lord Ismay. Ismay hated every moment of his Indian assignment. His instinct was to do the job quickly—and damn the consequences. It hardly surprised him when the Indians, released from the benevolent control of the British, reverted to type and began to kill each other. He was too sick at heart at the end of the Indian Empire to have any desire to stop it.

But not all Indians will agree that it had to happen.

There are many who believe—and not only Gandhi's disciples—that they were the victims of a salesman's trick which won them freedom but cost them the unity of the country. A little patience and all the troubles might have been avoided. Pakistan was the one-man achievement of Mohammed Ali Jinnah, and Jinnah was dead within a year of Pakistan's foundation. A little patience. A refusal to be rushed. It was Gandhi's counsel and, of course, from the Indian point of view, it was right.

But for Nehru and Patel and all the Congressmen yearning for the fruits of power, the carrot Mountbatten dangled in front of their noses was too delectable to be refused. They gobbled it down. To Michael Brecher, his biographer, Nehru confessed afterwards (in 1956):

'Well, I suppose it was the compulsion of events and the feeling that we couldn't get out of that deadlock or morass by pursuing the way we had done; it became worse and worse. Further a feeling that even if we got freedom for India with that background, it would be a very weak India, that is a federal India with far too much power in the federating units. A larger India would have constant troubles, constant disintegrating pulls. And also the fact that we saw no other way of getting our freedom—in the near future, I mean. And so we accepted it and said, let us build up a strong India. And if others do not want to be in it, well how can we and why should we force them to be in it?'

But perhaps Pandit Nehru came nearer the truth in a conversation with the author in 1960 when he said:

'The truth is that we were tired men, and we were getting on in years too. Few of us could stand the prospect of going to prison again—and if we had stood out for a united India as we wished it, prison obviously awaited us. We saw the fires burning in the Punjab and heard every day of the killings. The plan for partition offered a way out and we took it.'

He added: 'But if Gandhi had told us not to, we would have gone on fighting, and waiting. But we accepted. We expected that partition would be temporary, that Pakistan was bound to come back to us. None of us guessed how much the killings and the crisis in Kashmir would embitter relations.'

There is little doubt of what events shaped Nehru's opinion. Once, in the summer of 1947, he had said: 'I would rather see every village in India put to the flames than have to call in British troops to protect us.'

But on 17 August 1947, two days after he became premier of Independent India, he flew to Amritsar and toured the Punjab. What he saw there drove him almost to the point of madness. For the first time he saw what the helter-skelter dash to freedom meant in terms of human lives; and he rushed among the butchering Sikhs and murderous Muslims and beat them with his fists in an outbreak of despairing fury.

On that day, he knew that Indian Independence had come just a little too fast. Another few weeks, another few months, a year, perhaps might have made all the difference, and saved so many lives. There is no reason to believe that Pandit Jawaharlal Nehru is particularly proud of Independence Day, 15 August 1947.

When the liquor's out, however, why clink the cannikin? India was free. The amputation had been performed and the patient bled; but he would live.

And in the years to come, only those who had lived and worked in India and loved her would regret that the final days of the British Raj were smeared with so much unnecessary blood.

The sub-Continent split into two nations which were soon

reduced to bickering, snarling and, at one point, over Kashmir, to the point of war. Pakistan turned into a Balkan State riddled with corruption and intrigue. The Congress crusade for an idealistic India diminished into a squalid fight for political supremacy.

But things would improve. They could hardly get worse.

Meantime, the British who had played their parts in all the events departed one by one for home. Some civil servants and soldiers stayed on in Pakistan, but most of them left India. As Philip Woodruff, himself ex-I.C.S., wrote in *The Guardian*: 'For most men, perhaps, the prevailing thought was simply that we had done our part and that the time had come to go. To stay could only blur responsibility . . . The cord must be cut. A few Englishmen stayed on in Pakistan, to become as a rule as ardent as any Pakistani; in India most Englishmen felt that it would be in no one's interest to remain . . . It was over. The long years of partnership and strife were ended and divorce pronounced.'

George Abell and Evan Jenkins departed on Independence Day. So did Sir Cyril Radcliffe, which, in view of the way his Boundary Awards were received by both States forty-eight hours later, was just as well.

Sir Claude Auchinleck remained until the end of August 1947, when Congress charges of pro-Pakistani bias by himself and the officers of the Punjab Boundary Force brought about his resignation and that of General Rees, and the dispersal of the Force. Auchinleck departed for Britain in a mood of bitter disillusion.

Lord Ismay was the next to go, and he was not much happier. He still could not stomach the idea of an India outside the British Raj. Some time after his return to London, he met the official at the British Court whose task it is to look after recommendations for awards and decorations.

'You know,' he said to Ismay, 'the King was absolutely furious at your last-minute refusal of the G.C.S.I. Thought it a very bad thing. That's why he didn't ask you to come and see him at the Palace when you first got back. But it's all right now. He's forgiven you. He's going to give you the Garter.'

Then he took one look at Ismay's face and hastily added:

'But not for India, *not* for India!'

Admiral of the Fleet Earl Mountbatten of Burma stayed on as

Governor-General of India for ten months after the transfer of power. He arrived in England in May and immediately reported to the Admiralty. He was back in the Navy by June 1948, just as he had always insisted he must be.

BIBLIOGRAPHY

John Connell, *Auchinleck,* Cassell, 1959. A detailed study of the career of Field Marshal Sir Claude Auchinleck, former Commander-in-Chief, India.

Richard Symonds, *The Making of Pakistan,* Transatlantic, 1950. A sympathetic study of the creation and consolidation of the independent Muslim State of Pakistan.

Pyarelal, *Mahatma Gandhi: The Last Phase,* Vols. I and II, Navajivan Publishing House, Ahmedabad. A detailed study of the great Indian leader's sayings, doings and feelings during the vital days of India's struggle for independence.

Michael Brecher, *Nehru,* Oxford, 1959. A critical and authoritative biography of India's prime minister and architect of independence.

The Memoirs of General Lord Ismay, Viking, 1960. A rich collection of life in peace and war by the man who stood at Churchill's side through the last War, and beside Mountbatten in India through the last days of the British Raj.

Marquis of Zetland, *Essayez,* Transatlantic, 1957. The enlightened recollections of a former Secretary of State for India, member of the Indian Civil Service, and biographer of Lord Curzon.

Lieutenant-General Sir Francis Tuker, *While Memory Serves,* Cassell, 1950. A fervent study of the last days of British rule in India seen from the point of view of a British officer who served gallantly on many fronts but shaped his career on Indian soil.

Duff Cooper, *Old Men Forget,* Dutton, 1954. The memoirs of a former Cabinet Minister.

Philip Woodruff, *The Men Who Ruled India,* St. Martin's, 1954. The sensitive and sympathetic recollections of a former member of the Indian Civil Service.

Louis Fischer, *Life of Mahatma Gandhi,* Harper, 1950. A biography of the Mahatma by an American journalist who became one of his most convinced disciples.

K. Datta, *India's March to Freedom,* Orient Longmans, Calcutta, 1949. An Indian view of the struggle for independence.

Qayyum A. Malick, *H.R.H. Prince Aga Khan,* Ismailia Association,

Karachi, 1954. The part played by the leader of the Ismaili sect in India to secure independence for the Muslims.

Collected Works of Mahatma Gandhi, Publications Division, Ministry of Information, New Delhi.

Sadath Ali Khan, *Brief Thanksgiving,* Asia Publishing House, 1959. The engaging memories of a young Hyderabad Muslim who served at Nehru's side during the independence struggle.

K. M. Munshi, *The End of an Era,* Bharatiya Vidya Bhavan, Bombay. The story of the conflict between India and Hyderabad, written by India's delegate to the Nizam.

N. B. Khare, *My Political Memoirs, or Autobiography,* V. R. Joshi, Nagpur. A passionate Hindu's version of the independence struggle.

Jawaharlal Nehru's Speeches, 1945–49, Ministry of Information, New Delhi.

G. V. Subba Rao, *The Partition of India,* Goshti Book Trust, India. The diehard Hindu version of the independence struggle.

I. H. Qureshi, *The Pakistani Way of Life,* Praeger, 1956. A study of the efforts and achievements of independent Pakistan.

Aziz Beg, *Captive Kashmir,* Allied Business Corp., Lahore, 1957. The Pakistani view of the Kashmir controversy.

Crescent and Green, Philosophical Library, 1956. A miscellany of writings about Pakistan.

Horace Alexander, *India Since Cripps,* Penguin, 1944. A sage wartime look at India's problems.

R. Coupland, *The Cripps Mission,* Oxford, 1942. Another wartime study.

Maulana Abul Kalam Azad, *India Wins Freedom,* Longmans, 1959. A moving account of the fight for independence from the point of view of a devout Muslim who was also a member of the Indian Congress.

Humphrey Evans, *Thimayya of India,* Harcourt, Brace & World, 1960. An American friend of the Indian Army's Chief of Staff tells the story of his life as an officer in the British-controlled Indian Army, with some fascinating and controversial chapters on his views about independence and the bloodshed which followed it.

Kushawant Singh, *Train to Pakistan,* Chatto and Windus, 1956. A Sikh's account of the atmosphere and events in the Punjab during the last days of the British Raj and the first days of freedom, with fictional characters moving before a factual canvas.

Madeleine Masson, *Edwina,* Robert Hale, 1958. The life story of Lady Mountbatten, with a detailed account of her gallant activities in the troublesome days before and after independence.

Vincent Sheean, *Nehru: The Years of Power,* Random House, 1960. A frankly hero-worshipping view of the Indian prime minister.

Gopal Das Khosla, *Stern Reckoning,* Bhawnani and Sons, New Delhi, 1950. An Indian judge's report on the massacres in the Punjab before and after independence.

Wilfred Russell, *Indian Summer,* Thacker, Bombay. A British business-man's account of the events of 1947.

A. Campbell-Johnson, *Mission with Mountbatten,* Robert Hale, 1951. The eventful and exciting day-by-day diary of Mountbatten's Press spokesman in the vital months of the struggle and achievement of Indian independence.

V. P. Menon, *The Transfer of Power in India,* Princeton University Press, 1957. A remarkably calm and impartial review of the events lead-ing to independence by a distinguished Hindu who was formerly a member of the I.C.S.

V. P. Menon, *The Story of the Integration of the Indian States,* Macmillan, 1956. The colourful tragi-comic story of the end of the princely system in India told by the man who, as Secretary to the States Ministry, was mainly responsible for bringing the princely order into the Indian Government.

R. P. Masani, *The British in India,* Oxford, 1961. A lucid and sym-pathetic account by an Indian of Britain's mission in the sub-Continent.

Foreign Relations of the United States. The British Commonwealth and the Far East, 1942. U.S. Government Printing Office.

Nirad C. Chaudhuri, *The Autobiography of an Unknown Indian,* Macmil-lan, 1951. A beautifully written evocation of life in India by a wise and gentle Bengali.

Hector Bolitho, *Jinnah, Creator of Pakistan,* Macmillan, 1955. A sympathetic account of the life of Pakistan's first president.

Letters from a Father to His Daughter (1929); *Recent Essays and Writings on the Future of India* (1934); *Glimpses of World History* (1934); *India and the World* (1936); *Toward Freedom: The Autobiography of J. Nehru* (1941); *The Discovery of India* (1946); *Nehru on Gandhi* (1948); *Independence and After* (1949); *A Bunch of Old Letters* (1958). Pamphlets and collected speeches. All by Jawaharlal Nehru; a panoramic tour of the great Indian leader's mind and opinions.

G. R. Stevens, O.B.E., *Fourth Indian Division,* McLaren, 1945. The official history of a division which fought from Eritrea through the Western Desert, with great gallantry and dash, and was in the Punjab through the riots and disturbances of the period during the transfer of power.

MAPS

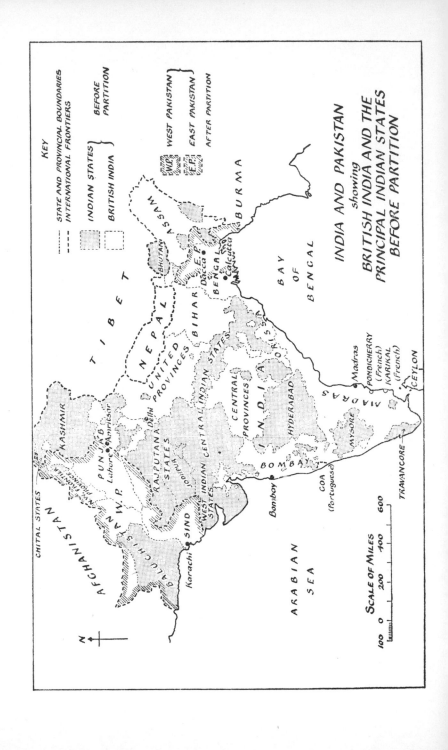

KEY

STATE AND PROVINCIAL BOUNDARIES
INTERNATIONAL FRONTIERS

} BEFORE PARTITION

INDIAN STATES

BRITISH INDIA

WEST PAKISTAN

EAST PAKISTAN

} AFTER PARTITION

INDIA AND PAKISTAN
showing
BRITISH INDIA AND THE
PRINCIPAL INDIAN STATES
BEFORE PARTITION

SCALE OF MILES
100 0 200 400 600

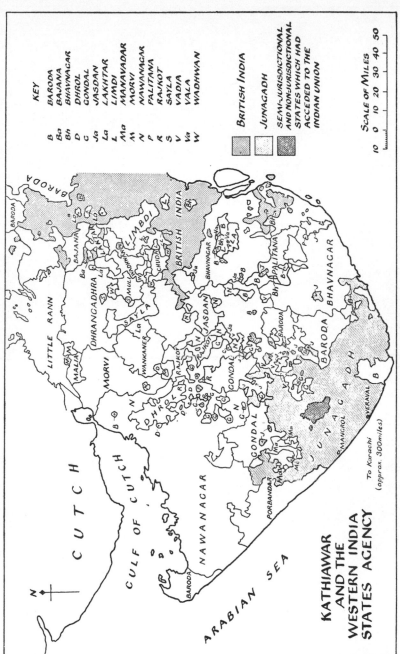

KEY

B	BARODA
Ba	BAJANA
Bn	BHAVNAGAR
D	DHROL
C	GONDAL
Ja	JASDAN
La	LAKHTAR
L	LIMDI
Ma	MANAVADAR
M	MORVI
N	NAWANAGAR
P	PALITANA
R	RAJKOT
S	SAYLA
V	VADIA
Va	VALA
W	WADHWAN

BRITISH INDIA

JUNAGADH

SEMI-JURISDICTIONAL
AND NONJURISDICTIONAL
STATES WHICH HAD
ACCEDED TO THE
INDIAN UNION

SCALE OF MILES
10   0   10   20   30   40   50

KATHIAWAR
AND THE
WESTERN INDIA
STATES AGENCY

Reproduced from V. P. Menon *The Integration of the Indian States* by permission of Longmans Green

INDEX